RELIGION AND EVERYDAY LIFE

Religion and Everyday Life explores the historical and contemporary relevance of religion to social life, through an examination of practice and belief. In this introductory text, Stephen Hunt reconsiders how theories and concepts are lived at the level of selfhood and cultural identity.

Religion and Everyday Life considers contemporary religiosity in all its forms, ranging from mainline Christianity, sectarianism and fundamentalism to new religious movements, ethnic religions and the New Age. Stephen Hunt uses up-to-date theory and research evidence to explore the vitality or otherwise of religion at the individual and everyday level. At the same time the book looks at contemporary changes in religious life and how these are impacted by socialization, institutional belonging, belief and practice through the life course, and the significance of class, gender, age and ethnicity.

This book provides an accessible and captivating introduction to the sociology of religion and will be of interest to undergraduate students of sociology and religion.

Stephen Hunt is a Reader in Sociology and lecturer at the University of the West of England. He has written extensively on the topics of contemporary Christianity and New Religious Movements. His publications include *The Alpha Initiative: Evangelism in the Post-Christian Era* (Ashgate, 2004), *Alternative Religion: A Sociological Introduction* (Ashgate, 2003) and *Religion in the West: A Sociological Perspective* (Macmillan, 2001).

THE NEW SOCIOLOGY

Series Editor: ANTHONY ELLIOTT, University of Kent, UK

The New Sociology is a book series designed to introduce students to new issues and themes in social sciences today. What makes the series distinctive, as compared to other competing introductory textbooks, is a strong emphasis not just on key concepts and ideas but on how these play out in everyday life – on how theories and concepts are lived at the level of selfhood and cultural identities, how they are embedded in interpersonal relationships, and how they are shaped by, and shape, broader social processes.

Forthcoming in the series:

Religion and Everyday Life
STEPHEN HUNT (2005)

Culture and Everyday Life
DAVID INGLIS (2005)

Community and Everyday Life
GRAHAM DAY (2005)

Self-Identity and Everyday Life
HARVIE FERGUSON (2005)

Consumption and Everyday Life
MARK W.D. PATERSON (2005)

Globalization and Everyday Life
LARRY RAY (2006)

The Body and Everyday Life
HELEN THOMAS (2006)

Nationalism and Everyday Life
JANE HINDLEY (2006)

Ethnicity and Everyday Life
CHRISTIAN KARNER (2006)

Risk, Vulnerability and Everyday Life
IAIN WILKINSON (2006)

RELIGION AND EVERYDAY LIFE

STEPHEN HUNT

Routledge
Taylor & Francis Group

LONDON AND NEW YORK

First published 2005
by Routledge
2 Park Square, Milton Park, Abingdon, Oxon, OX14 4RN

Simultaneously published in the USA and Canada
by Routledge
270 Madison Ave, New York, NY 10016

Routledge is an imprint of the Taylor & Francis Group

© 2005 Stephen Hunt

Typeset in Garamond and Scala Sans by Taylor & Francis Books
Printed and bound in Great Britain by MPG Books Ltd, Bodmin

British Library Cataloguing in Publication Data
A catalogue record for this book is available from the British Library

Library of Congress Cataloging-in-Publication Data
A catalog record for this book has been requested

ISBN 0–415–35153–7 (hbk)
ISBN 0–415–35154–5 (pbk)

CONTENTS

SERIES EDITOR'S FOREWORD

'The New Sociology' is a series that takes its cue from massive social transformations currently sweeping the globe. Globalization, new information technologies, the techno-industrialization of warfare and terrorism, the privatization of public resources, the dominance of consumerist values: these developments involve major change to the ways people live their personal and social lives today. Moreover, such developments impact considerably on the tasks of sociology, and the social sciences more generally. Yet, for the most part, the ways in which global institutional transformations are influencing the subject matter and focus of sociology have been discussed only in the more advanced, specialized literature of the discipline. I was prompted to develop this series, therefore, in order to introduce students – as well as general readers who are seeking to come to terms with the practical circumstances of their daily lives – to the various ways in which sociology reflects the transformed conditions and axes of our globalizing world.

Perhaps the central claim of the series is that sociology is fundamentally linked to the practical and moral concerns of everyday life. The authors in this series – examining topics all the way from the body to globalization, from self-identity to consumption – seek to demonstrate the complex, contradictory ways in which sociology is a necessary and very practical aspect of our personal and public lives. From one angle, this may seem uncontroversial. After all, many classical sociological analysts as well as those associated with the classics of social theory emphasized the practical basis of human knowledge, notably Emile Durkheim, Karl Marx, Max Weber, Sigmund Freud and George Simmel, among many others. And yet there are major respects in which the professionalization of academic sociology during the latter period of the twentieth century led to a retreat from the everyday issues and moral basis of sociology itself. (For an excellent discussion of the changing relations between practical and professional sociologies see Charles Lemert, *Sociology After the Crisis*, Second Edition, Boulder: Paradigm, 2004.) As worrying as such a retreat from the practical and moral grounds of the discipline is, one of the main consequences of recent global transformations in the field of sociology has been a renewed emphasis on the mediation of everyday events and experiences by distant social forces, the intermeshing of the local and global in the production of social practices, and on ethics and moral responsibility at both the individual and the collective level. 'The New Sociology' series traces out these concerns across the terrain of various themes and thematics, situating everyday social practices in the broader context of life in a globalizing world.

In *Religion and Everyday Life*, Stephen Hunt makes available to the new reader a range of current conceptual developments and empirical findings from the sociology of religion. In a comprehensive and thoroughly researched book, Hunt maps with great erudition global religious conflicts and pluralisms, the changing nature of religious cults and sects, the intermeshing of religious faith and gender/sexuality, as well as the impacts of contemporary culture and consumerism on religious practices. In this powerful introduction to the transformed landscape of religious beliefs and practices in conditions of globalization, Hunt has much of value to say about the postmodernization of faith and its attendant relativism, rational choice theory and its analysis of today's ever-expanding spiritual marketplace, as well as new religious movements and the discovery of covert forms of religion. He considers carefully the case that current social conditions promote a resurgence of religiosity, especially in the individualized and privatized expressions of new fundamentalisms. But he questions the equation that global space ushers in higher levels of religiosity, and in doing so provides a stimulating integration of sociological and historical perspectives.

Crucially, Hunt links his attempts to situate religion in both sociological and historical terms to present global realities. He subtly considers the social impact of the terrorist attacks on the World Trade Center and the Pentagon of 9/11, and looks at the globalization of terrorism as a central feature of religious fundamentalism in conditions of advanced modernity. Hunt rightly criticises those who portray the radical escalation of religious fundamentalism as something wholly new to our post-9/11 world; among Islamic, Christian, Judiac, Hindu and Sikh religions, as he notes, fundamentalist movements have throughout the history of modernity powerfully influenced the changing realities of social, economic and political life. At stake is developing a critical understanding of the role of faith in public life that will help shape the core concerns of a revised sociology of religion specifically addressed to the global realities of the twenty-first century.

Anthony Elliott
Canterbury, 2005

PREFACE

Not too many years ago the possible inclusion of the theme of religion in a series of sociological textbooks on contemporary everyday life would have been rather remote. Its omission would have proved indicative of the fact that, for several decades, the sociology of religion had gradually but relentlessly slipped from its central position as a key concern for the broader discipline to a rather peripheral specialism. Indeed, the study of religion had undoubtedly been overtaken by other areas of empirical research and theorizing. The substantive topics of globalization, ethnicity, the body, consumption and identity, among others, were perhaps more predictable inclusions in any core text since they could claim a greater social significance and perhaps relevance.

To account for the waning interest in religion it is necessary to understand earlier historical developments. From at least the mid-twentieth century, the secularization thesis had become something of an orthodoxy. The relentless features integral to its processes, namely rationalism, pluralism and the decline of community, all in their different ways, so it was asserted, undermined religiosity at many levels – from the broader social dimensions of its institutional power, to the individual's everyday experience. This apparent decline reduced the sociological enquiry into the relevance of religion and subsequently marginalized its study as a distinct specialism to the extent that it was perhaps facing a more or less permanent extinction.

Now, at the beginning of the twenty-first century, the world appears to be changing once more and in such a manner as to bring a renewed interest in the subject of religion, albeit rather tentatively. Thus, a fairly large number of introductory sociology books discernibly speak of the changing fortunes of present-day religion. There is a good deal of reference to increasing levels of religiosity, a re-enchantment of the world, or the changing direction of religion. The study of the social dynamics of religion has once again become a respectable enterprise. This is a significant sea-change that can largely be attributed to a shift in the core theoretical frameworks which have developed in order to understand current forms of religious expression and in doing so have offered a so-called 'revisionist' line in the long-running secularization debate.

The renewed interest in religious life, then, is clearly contingent upon its perceived resurgence in certain areas. Such a re-emergence may be seen in more conservative and collectivist forms, most notably fundamentalist and ethnic expressions of religiosity. At the same time, many current sociologists are increasingly recognizing that belief and practice may now be largely observable at an individual level, rather than in the social and public sphere or through communal structures. Hence, the title of this book, *Religion and Everyday Life*, might suggest that its task is to explore how and why religion continues to impact in meaningful ways but at the point where religion really matters, in the everyday lives of individuals. It could therefore well be the case that there are now less discernible forms of religiosity, scarcely visible, to be uncovered outside of formal religious institutions, a veritable 'believing without belonging'.

This volume, however, will attempt a more cautious approach and argue that the claim to a resurgence of religiosity via individualized and privatized expressions, at least to the degree of marking a 'return of religion', is largely unsubstantiated. Indeed, it will argue that such claims rest upon far from proven assumptions regarding the nature and extent of contemporary forms, the selective choice of evidence, as well as rather spurious definitions of religion. Moreover, the volume will contend that the impact of even the more 'visible' and collective categories of religion, ethnic variants and fundamentalism among them, is frequently overstated. Claims to their growth and scope need to be carefully examined. Hence, the chapters to come will explore the key debates and issues involved and attempt to present the evidence in conjunction with a measure of empirical analysis. In doing so, the volume will argue that, while significant social changes have occurred in recent decades, and these have impacted on the world of religion, they have not, for the most part, ushered in higher levels of religiosity.

INTRODUCTION

Speculation that religion is enjoying a new lease of life is perhaps understandable in the so-called late or postmodern age where, culturally speaking at least, 'anything goes' and where long-term social trends may be halted or reversed. Ordinary people may continue, in a world of relativism and uncertainty, to seek answers to those 'ultimate questions' of existence and consider the prospects of the afterlife. Such a search is plausibly an inherent part of the human condition. Yet the extent and depth of that search is what really matters, as are the ways in which it is translated into religious expression in a culture that operates increasingly at the level of individual experience and choice, and where the place of religion in constructing identities, both individual and collective, may be given an enhanced scope. This volume therefore explores the alleged search for religiosity and spirituality and its impact on everyday life. The chapters to come endeavour to consider the evidence of their prevalence in Western Europe and North America. In short, the volume will attempt to put a religion of everyday life in its rightful perspective in advanced industrialized societies.

Integrating contemporary developments alongside a comparative and historical approach is a core perspective of this book. Such an approach needs little justification. Historically speaking, it is undoubtedly true that religion would have been one of the first topics on the sociological agenda. It is more than notable that some of the greatest contributions to what has become known as 'classical' sociology focused on religion.

Emile Durkheim's *The Elementary Forms of Religious Life* (1915) and Max Weber's *The Protestant Ethic and the Spirit of Capitalism* (1930) come readily to mind. In the more radical tradition, the inspiration of Marx and Engel's *On Religion* (1957) is also high on the list of contributions. For Durkheim and Weber, and indeed the work of 'early' Marx in his philosophical critique of religion, the subject automatically flagged itself up for description and analysis. After all, for most of human history religion saturated social life and in many developing societies it still does. Either as the upholder of normative values and moralities as Durkheim suggested, or, as in Marx's interpretation, an instrument of ideological oppression and 'the opium of the people', religion could scarcely be ignored by way of its social impact. It upheld and justified social institutions, influenced behaviour and consciousness down to the level of the individual whatever the form of its expression, whether monotheistic, polytheistic, animistic, popular superstition, magic or occultist practice.

While historical and comparative approaches help place religion in Western societies in its legitimate context, they do not necessarily disprove claims to a 'new' religiosity in North America and Europe – claims which are clearly locked in the emerging and increasingly influential sociological frameworks. The most obvious are those of the postmodern perspective and that advanced by North American sociologists – the rational choice paradigm. While these two approaches overlap in their account of religiosity in the contemporary West, most obviously in the commodification of religion in a spiritual marketplace, they also carry contradictory elements, notably in how they deal with the subject of rationalism and its various implications in terms of religiosity. Despite the apparently differing routes taken in exploring religion, both perspectives identify its growth in a number of areas of social life, not least of all at the individual level. In claiming such a growth, these perspectives constitute what may be termed a 'revisionist' approach to the subject of secularization. Given their impact over the last twenty years or so they are theoretical frameworks needing to be thoughtfully considered in their accounts of religion in everyday life upon which they place so much emphasis.

The sociological orthodoxy or near orthodoxy today is to refer to the complexity of religious expression, to detail its resurgence in some quarters of social experience, and to explain stagnation and decline in others. In general, however, such works mark a clear abandonment of the 'hard' secularization thesis which once held sway. The previous fairly universal acceptance of this thesis was forcefully put by Peter Berger who noted some three decades ago that

> ... [i]f commentators on the contemporary situation of religion agree about anything, it is that religion has departed from the world.
>
> (Berger 1970: 13)

This insistence Berger saw as most dramatically stated in such formulations as 'God is dead' or 'the post-Christian era', and the conviction that the decline of religion was a universal and probably irreversible trend. Berger appreciated that the secularization thesis was inherited from the work of Marx and Durkheim, and stated in Weber's discussion of the decline of the 'magical garden' of religion and superstition in the face of rationalism and science. Subsequently the broad secularization thesis has been reinstated in one form or another by a number of more recent sociologists of religion, but they are increasingly a beleaguered minority. This is not only because the evidence apparently does not support their claims, but because the conventional secularization thesis appears to carry so much ideological baggage – born of the Enlightenment, of a hope for a religiousless society and the gleeful triumphantism that religion and superstition were something which the human race was best off without. Eventually, it was assumed, modernity would be synonymous with non-religious principles and, in the words of Nancy Ammerman, religion was designated to eventually become a 'shrunken, emasculated apparition at the periphery of modern society' (Ammerman 1987: 2).

Much has now changed. Discernible in the sociological enterprise over the last two decades are the different and intricate interpretations of secularization or a more radical revisionist line. Today, a new recognition of the vibrant nature of religiosity seems to abound. This is typified by David Lyon's statement that

> ... the religious *realm*, including faith and spirituality, is far from dormant, let alone dead.
>
> (Lyon 2000: ix)

Clearly, the story is now a familiar one. Empirical reality, so it is purported, did not support the presupposition of the secularization thesis, especially in the closing years of the last century. Religion seemed to refuse to lie down and die. Today there is the growing conviction that religious activity is increasing and this is because it is subject to identifiable social change and cultural transformation, notably personal choice, because of voluntarism, and emerging religious identities assembled from a bricolage of beliefs and practices and subject to numerous globalized forces. In short, the contention is that contemporary culture is less hostile to certain types of religion – those forms given to considerable innovation, individual requirements, and linked to identity constructs, which are expressed most obviously in the so-called 'self-spiritualities' and 'quasi-religions'.

Contemporary culture, according to the postmodernist rendition at least, has lost all-embracing myths, not least of all those pertaining to notions of rationalism and progress. Hence, out goes the meta-narrative of the long-cherished secularization theory which was at the heart of classical sociology. It was a theory that rested with accounts of modernity, the analysis of its nature, and the subsequent repercussions for different areas of social life. Here religious belief and practice, particularly in their more conservative forms, were seen as undermined by the onslaught of modernity. However, modernity is not what it was. Quite what is now in its place, or how postmodernity should be defined, is open to interpretation. In some accounts it amounts to a rupture in modernity, marked by substantial and deep changes which exaggerate certain features of the social order. In other renderings it is perceived as a total departure from modernity, the arrival of something profoundly different. Whatever the precise interpretation, most commentators identify change as that pertaining to economics – particularly in the areas of consumerism, culture and technology. It follows that, since religion has frequently conformed or responded to conditions of any given culture, whether that of 'traditional' society or modernity, it comes to reflect a new socio-cultural arrangement in postmodernity but lacks anything approaching a determinist element.

In the new postmodernist interpretation of religion which, in Western Europe at least, has arisen to become something of a new orthodoxy, it is traditional forms of religion that seem to be on the decline or, more specifically, certain expressions – those of an institutionalized variety. It was institutionalized and organized religion which dominated medieval and early modern Europe. This largely meant conventional Christianity with its undoubted influence on social and political spheres and where its cultural dominance permeated down from ecclesiastical hierarchies to impact everyday life, or so it seemed. The arrival of the post-Christian society is now in earnest, one which gives way to a radically different culture with its relativism that eats away at over-arching beliefs and all-embracing theological constructs.

Those religions perceived as growing areas of social life are, in postmodernist accounts, believed to be subject to another feature of contemporary culture – commodification. To be sure, commodification suggests that everything has its price. But it brings more in its wake, including choice, not just in the commodity marketplace but a culture of choice which dovetails with lifestyle preferences increasingly void of the impact of class, kinship structures and the wider community. It ushers in a diffuse and fragmented culture without meaningful tradition, where choice and reflexivity become the reference point of personalized identity and self-enhancement. Here is said to be the nature of the new religious life. At this ordinary, perhaps mundane level, religion is understood to endure and even gain a new vigour. Hence, religion has not just changed, but has changed in direction. It has become individualized and everyday. This is by no means an innovating notion. None the less, postmodernity, so it is claimed, brings new dynamics and new layers of culture, and so deep is change envisaged to be that the term 'religion' is often jettisoned since it smacks of institutionalized versions of faith, of dry ritual and ecclesiastical inertia. In its place comes the more flexible 'spiritualities' which seem void of religion's Christian and ritualized overtones.

The theme of globalization also features in postmodernist accounts of religion, not least of all in areas of claimed resurgence. In the globalized context there may be the explicit or implicit influence of other cultures which can be pre-packaged for a new environment, one of consumption. Whether African-style clothes or Peruvian music, or a whole variety of culinary delights, choice is now available from the global supermarket. It may well be that interaction with these goods takes place in a meaningful way by which identity and lifestyles can be forged. Especially through new technology and modes of communication, people across the world now share many tastes in music, clothes, food, and often the same choices of lifestyles. Religious beliefs and practices are part of this wider picture and have been since the nineteenth century, if not earlier, when

Buddhism and rival forms of Eastern mysticism enjoyed the personalized embrace of the intellectual and bourgeois middle classes. Today, many of the so-called New Religions, and more recently the home-grown New Age movement, are partly informed by beliefs and practices from outside the North American and Western European context, suggesting that Western cultural global dominance is far from complete.

Contemporary theory of religious life does not end there. In their account of religion today, Stark and Bainbridge refer to a growing 'supermarket of faiths: received, jazzed-up, home spun, restored, imported and exotic' (Stark and Bainbridge 1985: 437). This is a statement which encapsulates the thinking of a rival approach to the postmodern perspective, one which also identifies the resurgence of religion, or particular forms of religion, in an ever-expanding spiritual marketplace. Today's rational choice theory of religious behaviour with its emphasis on consumption and a corresponding 'supply-side' has become central to many sociologies of religion. The work of Rodney Stark and his associates is perhaps the most influential. Not all of those who have stressed the alleged significance of a religious marketplace have journeyed as far as Stark's rational choice/supply-side model. However, the link between religious 'markets' and the alleged resurgence of religion has developed into what was termed a decade ago an emerging 'new paradigm' (Warner 1993).

At this point in time there can be no denying the impact of the rational choice/spiritual marketplace model on the sociology of religion in the USA. In Europe, its influence has proved less significant but still discernible in more loosely developed notions of religious 'consumption' and a paralleled development of 'producers' of religiosity in an ever-expanding spiritual marketplace. Much takes its tone from rational choice frameworks. As with postmodernist accounts, that of rational choice suggests a reversal of the orthodox secularization thesis. In short, the rational choice paradigm purports that the deregulation evident in the increasing pluralist context of religion has led to the increase of religiosity, especially at the individual and privatized level. In contrast to postmodernist interpretations, rational choice theorizing emphasizes the rational social 'actor' in his/her pursuit of a satisfying religion in the spiritual marketplace. This implicit refutation of the postmodern insistence on the disillusionment with rationality largely results from the fact that rational choice theorizing is still located within modernist frames of reference. In short, it brings a challenge to the conventional view that modernity necessarily means the demise of religion. Rather, its deregulation in modernity, with its over-arching pluralism, constitutes a resurgence through opening rational choice in religious preferences at the personalized level.

Given the contrasting fresh approaches to the subject, students new to the sociology of religion would be justified in feeling a certain amount of bewilderment. None the less, the sub-discipline, in line with mainstream sociology, has always been subject to rival perspectives. Today, however, theorizing is in a state of flux and the new perspectives are by no means accepted in all quarters. Yet they are gaining ground. Their emergence and increasing influence are understandable. Western societies over the last few decades have undergone considerable change. Classical sociological theory no longer convincingly 'fits'.

New approaches in the discipline may be warranted, not least of all in the sociology of religion. However, what is clear in these approaches is that they have identified a resurgence of religion and frequently associate this with an increased religiosity at the individual and everyday level. Hence, the early chapters of this volume, besides briefly revisiting the 'hard' secularization thesis, where relevant, will overview recent theorizing – offering critiques in terms of their logic and the empirical evidence that often fails to support their speculations. This overview will commence in Chapter 1 with a consideration of rival definitions of religion and how these are embraced by the developing paradigms and inform broader debates regarding the present condition of religiosity – decline or otherwise. This is an essential task since it will set the foundation for what follows in Chapters 2 and 3: the consideration of the merits of the new and emerging perspectives in the sociology of religion, namely postmodernist and rational choice theories.

Chapters 4 and 5 will examine the context of everyday religion, noting its significance at certain times of life. It will consider the importance of religious socialization and the relevance of such variables as social class and gender, concluding that many of these variables are subject to transformation and in such a way as to impact levels and expressions of religiosity. In short, these chapters will argue that many of the structures which once supported previous levels of religiosity have continued to be eroded, making religion at the everyday level less sustainable. The principal contention in these chapters is that contemporary society, however that is defined, eats away at the structures which have long undergirded aspects of religiosity or, in the case of social differenti-ation, carried different levels of religiosity. In short, it will be contended that evidence regarding the changing nature of contemporary society indicates a general decline of religion rather than its growth. In short, these chapters will argue that current sociology has paid too much attention to those changes which are supposed to enhance religion and tended to ignore other variables which undermine it at a more general level.

The chapters following will consider different expressions of religion, each of which provides an index of the alleged increase of religiosity and its impact in everyday life. Perhaps most obviously this commences with a consideration of the state of contemporary Christianity – the theme of Chapter 5. As the historical faith of the Western world, Christianity has clearly undergone profound changes. In Europe it has observably declined at the social and institutionalized level, yet there remains the so-called exclusivism of Christianity USA-style which would seem to mock the conventional secularization thesis. None the less, on both sides of the Atlantic there is good evidence that historical Christian doctrines are being subject to the vagaries of unsophisticated belief systems held by individuals in the pick 'n' mix culture of today. This tendency is also supplemented by another development – the response of Christianity to the challenges of the contemporary world. A discussion of these responses will invariably include an overview of those forms which apparently most successfully adapt to the spiritual marketplace, and highlight what the likely implications are for the broader faith.

Growth areas frequently identified by the new sociological paradigms are those which may be termed 'the religions of certainty'. These are the religions of ethnic communities in the West and religion as expressed through channels of fundamentalism. Clearly there is a link between the two, although this should not be overstated. The function of religion by way of enforcing the boundary maintenance of ethnic minorities may be articulated in terms of fundamentalism. The picture is, however, far more complicated. The apparent growth of Christian fundamentalism, especially in the USA, is largely void of an ethnic basis and would seem to have different origins. The key point, none the less, is that these often controversial expressions of religion would appear to enter the public sphere through such themes as religious liberties and moral campaigns. At the individual, private level they would also seem to have relevance and are additional important components of contemporary spirituality. Appraising their impact constitutes the subject matter for Chapter 7.

Much sociological ink has been spilt on the so-called New Religious Movements. This would seem to be justifiable given their proliferation from the late 1960s. They have been accounted for in various ways in the relevant literature. However, a common theme is that they constitute the 'religions of the gaps' in the growing spiritual marketplace. In short, they fill the gaps left by the decline of traditional Christianity which seemingly fails to be relevant to the everyday lives and experiences of many people. Chapter 8 overviews the new religions; their impact, membership, evolution and, above all, the question as to what extent they have become or will become viable 'alternatives' in Western society.

The final chapter is concerned with more recent expressions of religion, ones which would clearly appear to be in line with contemporary cultural developments and particularly impact on the individual and privatized sphere. These are identified in the form of the New Age and related forms of spirituality – 'self religions', those preoccupied with the 'inner self', self improvement and identity. In short, they are the religions which arguably most readily reflect the nature of late or postmodernity. This is an area of contemporary religion that is fraught with difficulties in terms of not only sociological analysis but by way of theory, measurement and definition. Indeed, these forms of religion would appear to push back the frontiers of traditional concepts of religion and in doing so perceivably counter the secularization thesis with its largely concise and unambiguous definition of religion, one which puts a great deal of emphasis on the belief in the supernatural and the consequences of belief in terms of its outward social manifestations.

New forms of religiosity and the discovery of 'hidden' forms of religion, alongside more traditional expressions, may suggest that religion is alive and well in the contemporary setting. Yet questions still remain. Have recent developments really brought a resurgence of religious life? Do the new forms of religiosity amount to religion in any meaningful sense? Is it not the case that the West still remains a largely secular culture, where religion is reduced to a matter of choice and where the freedom to choose not to be religious prevails? Perhaps most important is the question, where *is* religion in everyday life? It may be that notions of religion at this level can be interpreted in different ways. Religion can be comprehended as having relevance for the individual domain. Yet, more succinctly, it may be argued that such a level is the only one in which religion has any real significance. If so, we may ask how profound is that significance? These are questions which this volume seeks to address and in doing so hopefully provides some of the answers.

1

CONTEMPORARY RELIGION
CHANGING DEFINITIONS

DEFINITIONS OF RELIGION

The matter of the nature and significance of religion in contemporary Western societies, and debates regarding possible decline or resurgence, open up broader questions regarding its definition which, in turn, relate to on-going ideological debates as to the merits or otherwise of religious life. In terms of definitions, the sociology of religion faces a unique set of conceptual difficulties which are enhanced by the increasing variety and ever-changing expressions of religiosity, especially their apparent increasing reduction to the individual and privatized level. Thus, only when it is defined can religion be delimited in terms of the subject matter, the trajectories of its transformation understood, and the conjecture that certain forms are experiencing growth, be put in rightful perspective. This is an important endeavour, especially in relation to current sociological theorizing which departs so radically from the conventional secularization thesis.

To be sure, the human capacity for belief is seemingly endless, and in Western societies today there would appear to be a vast range of belief systems, some very loosely articulated. Alongside mainstream Christianity are the world religions or a particular tradition of them as embraced by many ethnic groups, one variety or another of fundamentalism, New Religious Movements and those not so new, and the diverse New Age phenomenon and related forms of spirituality. To these might be added the 'implicit' or 'quasi' religions – those social phenomena which are 'like' religions in some way but which may not include all the usual attributes and perhaps may not even be accepted as a 'religion' by participating social actors. Such diversity renders a discussion of religion, especially at the level of everyday life, a demanding challenge. To some extent this is because it is virtually impossible to differentiate between what is 'in' and what is 'out', that which can correctly be called religion and that which cannot. This is compounded by the problem of measuring the impact of religiosity at the everyday level – a problem further accentuated by the changing cultural perception of the word 'religion' itself. Put succinctly, the term appears to have gone out of vogue, with 'spirituality' often being preferred, not least of all by those who themselves seek to indulge in new forms.

The current diversity of religion in Western societies may bewilder the contemporary sociologist. Yet, the recognition of a more global diversity is far from new. During the colonial period the discovery of the numerous religions of the world took many of the early anthropologists by surprise. Their sheer variety and expression encouraged the anthropologist to address the question of 'what is religion?' in earnest. Many of the religions encountered in the wake of colonialism and global exploration were in marked contrast to the forms of Christianity that had dominated the West for centuries. Western societies had long been aware of faiths other than their own. Islam, Judaism, the religions of China and India, and a range of so-called 'pagan' religions, were scarcely understood expressions encountered. However, anthropological research of the nineteenth and early twentieth centuries extended the knowledge of religious diversity, of belief and practice. There were clear differences that also interested the sociologist of religion. In the early sociological works perhaps the greatest exposition of a comparative approach was that of Max Weber who, in the early twentieth century, wrote his renowned treatise on the social origins of world religions (Weber 1965, 1970). For Weber, certain cultures, at a particular time and place, will produce belief systems which are unlikely to arise elsewhere. But there were similarities too. Across different parts of world, cultures which had no interaction with each other frequently displayed similar polytheistic beliefs and assigned comparable attributes to a range of gods and supernatural forces, and forged around them common rituals and practices. Indeed, there were sufficient similarities to raise questions related to the definition of religion, although Weber himself fell short of doing so.

Historically speaking, there have been evident two extreme defini-tional poles which are constituted by what have come to be known as functional and substantive approaches. In turn, these approaches are cut across by others which are more phenomenological and interpretive in nature. These contrasting perspectives and definitions are not to be ignored and their significance to current debates in respect of contem-porary religion needs to be explored in earnest, especially since at least some of them are now subject to rigorous critique. However, in this brief analysis I will make some attempt to justify the utilization of substantive definition, rather than others, if for no other reason than it does provide a clear working criterion by which to consider current religious change and its discernible decline from different areas of social life. This is an approach which will be further exploited and defended in subsequent chapters.

Substantive approaches

The substantive approach can be traced back to the early anthropologist Edward Tylor, who outlined his theories of the origins of religion derived from a general study of small-scale pre-industrial societies, *Primitive Culture*, published in 1871. Tylor put forward what he called a 'minimum definition' of religion which centred on a 'belief in spiritual beings' (Tylor 1903: 424). This narrow or substantive definition focus-ing on belief in the supernatural was, he insisted, central to all religions, although the precise beliefs involved obviously varied. The common ground was the faith in spiritual forces; god(s), angels, demons, spirits or other supernatural entities that were perceived as capable of influenc-ing or controlling the world.

Tylor placed an emphasis on supernatural belief systems because, he maintained, they were ultimately derived from the earliest forms of reli-gion. In this respect, Tylor was the first to coin the term 'animism' that was, he conjectured, the most fundamental expression of religion from which all others evolved, and was essentially about 'belief in spiritual beings'. For Tylor, early man attributed supernatural powers to inani-mate objects, to rivers, forests, the sun, and natural forces greater than himself – all of which, according to some reckonings, later evolved into deities of polytheistic systems and eventually monotheistic constructs where the one God becomes the creator and sustainer of the universe.

Tylor's work constituted what was eventually to be known as the intellectualist psychological theory of the origins of religion, one which essentially viewed it as an outcome of the attempt to understand the world through human reason (albeit mistakenly) and the capacity to deduce, generalize and draw conclusions from observation and experience. It was a universal human tendency, so Tylor claimed, to conceive of all beings as being like oneself and to transfer human qualities to a whole range of natural phenomena. Some spirits came to be regarded as more powerful than human beings and therefore able to control their fate. They thus had to be appropriated, persuaded and cajoled in much the same way that powerful and influential human beings were treated – by appeal, entreaty and giving gifts, the religious counterparts of which include prayer and sacrifice.

There are several difficulties related to substantive theories of religion that are significant enough to be noted at this point. One is in allotting which social phenomenon is 'in' and which 'out'. Certainly, there has always been a problem as to whether to include magic or superstition under the rubric of 'religion' since they may relate to the supernatural but are probably more concerned with vague occultist powers than belief in supernatural entities. Given the apparent move in some forms of contemporary religion from the belief in theistic systems to occultism and related expressions, the blanket term 'religiosity' is increasingly difficult to sustain as a cultural idiom in Western societies.

To separate the 'religious' from superstition is, however, probably unnecessary, since almost invariably such a definition is bound to be 'fuzzy around the edges' and not all major expressions of religion display the whole range of supernaturalist beliefs. Indeed, as Kolakowski argues, if we look for a set of beliefs that no religion fails to include, then we will probably be disappointed. In point of fact, if we introduce the idea of a personal god as a candidate for the position of such a constant then a major world religion, Buddhism, does not fit (Kolakowski 1982: 10). None the less, Kolakowski is surely correct in asserting that there is nothing logically wrong in focusing attention on beliefs which include the idea of a personal god and thus regarding Buddhism as espousing metaphysical and moral wisdom, rather than as religion in the full sense despite its other attributes as a religious system.

There is another problem related to the substantive approach beyond the matter of conceptual boundaries. Critics argue that religion may not fundamentally be about beliefs in the supernatural at all. To suggest that this is so, it may be conjectured, is to fail to understand the nature of religion which, at least in its origins, can be traced to an emotional rather than an intellectual or social source. This was the contention of a number of the earliest anthropologists, including R.R. Marett (1914). For Marett, religion primarily centred on ritual behaviour and such behaviour displayed an emotional basis. The source of the emotions which underlaid religious ritual behaviour was the feeling experienced by 'primitive' people of the presence of a strange, mysterious and occult power or force for which Marett used the Polynesian word 'mana'. Mana could be characterized as a mixture of fear and wonder for the natural world and natural phenomena. Religious ritual gave expression to such sentiment and pre-dated man's attribution of mana to special places – trees, animals, rivers, the heavenly bodies and so on – a belief that only later was to be translated through the idiom of ideas related to personalized supernatural entities.

Although this is a valid criticism, such a speculation as to the origins of religion cannot be substantiated by an unprovable hypothesis about its true nature. Moreover, even if Marett's account is correct, then it undoubtedly remains the case that the vast majority of religions display an outward manifestation of such emotions in terms of beliefs and practices which include references to the supernatural and how such forces impinge upon human existence. This may mean that the psychological underpinnings of religion are thus rendered irrelevant to debates regarding its definition. On the other hand, such speculation opens up the possibility that any natural or social phenomenon which engenders an acute emotional response has a 'religious' quality. Hence, the emotionalism generated from anything ranging from beautiful sunsets, romantic encounters, political rallies or sporting events becomes 'religious'. Such a broad sweep, however, is surely unsatisfactory. A more limited approach to religion by way of beliefs in the supernatural would again seem justified because of its conceptual clarity and stringent working criteria.

There is more to consider, however. Perhaps the most telling weakness of the substantive approach is that historians of religion and cultural anthropologists have pointed out that the division of reality into a closed system of rationality that is comprehensible in a natural order and a mysterious world beyond it is a peculiarly modern conception, which is misleading if we seek to understand the religious notions of 'primitive' or at least pre-modern cultures. For example, Evans-Pritchard in his renowned work among the Azunde of the Sudan (Evans-Pritchard 1937) found that the distinction between the natural and the supernatural world, between the sacred and the mundane, simply did not exist. Where people frequently communicate with the spirits of their ancestors or are involved in witchcraft practices, the distinction between the natural and the supernatural may not exist for the social actor. In that sense religion is plausibly only understood in phenomenological terms, since the idea of the sacred or supernatural is one which exists solely in the mind of the observer.

As for the 'hard' secularization theory, it has often held that this fundamental dichotomy between the natural and supernatural world is being eclipsed, resulting in the latter becoming of decreasing importance. This is evident in Bryan Wilson's often-quoted definition of secularization, which centres on the decline of religion from the social sphere and its departure from institutional life:

> In essence, it (secularization) relates to a process of transfer of property, power, activities, and both manifest and latent functions, from institutions with a supernaturalist frame of reference to (often new) institutions operating according to empirical, rational, pragmatic criteria.
>
> (Wilson 1985: 11–12)

It may well be that this inherent dualism in many sociological accounts displays a cognitive source which stems from another origin, one that may be closer to the understanding of the average Westerner steeped in a diluted Christian culture. Such a criticism is a telling one and not an easy one to counter. However, the distinction remains a useful analytical tool by which the sociologist of religion can describe and classify empirical evidence and explain the changing nature of religious life, not least of all in accounting for its possible decline in the contemporary Western setting.

Functionalist approaches

Critics of the substantive approach have often adopted rival stances. These are briefly overviewed here because they have a strong bearing on the current debates about the nature and scope of religiosity in Western societies and how it impinges on particular areas of social life. The traditional major alternative definition of religion, the functional definition, is derived from contrasting views as to the origins of religion, views which lead to a definition not in terms of a belief system but of what it provides in functional terms for society and the individuals that comprise it.

For a good number of years the problem with the 'narrow' substantive definition was said to be that there was too much emphasis on belief systems and not enough on what religion *does*. The assumption inherent in the functional approach is that religion is largely a product of society hence it must be defined in terms of what it contributes at both the societal and individual level. Undoubtedly the earliest contribution from this perspective was the work of Durkheim, according to whom religion worked in a positive and 'functional' way for the well-being, stability and integration of society. In Durkheim's definition, religion is

> a unified system of beliefs and practices relative to sacred things ... beliefs and practices which unite into one single moral community.
>
> (Durkheim 1915: 47)

There are clearly three aspects evident in Durkheim's definition. First, while it entails a belief system, there is no direct reference to a belief in the supernatural. Second, for Durkheim religion stems from the community: it is a *shared* system of beliefs. Third, these beliefs and practices underscore social values. There is certainly merit in the second and third elements of Durkheim's definition, ones which, in fact, may be subsumed, as suggested below, under the heading and scope of substantive definitions.

Much recent theorizing would seem to confirm Durkheim's view that religion in its traditional mode would be of declining social significance. However, he insisted there was 'something eternal in religion'. One of the ways that he believed this would be expressed was via the emergence of secular forms of religion, perhaps an unshakable faith in democracy, social justice and equality before the law. In this way the functional definition is predisposed towards affirming the endurance of religion in the West, albeit in non-supernaturalistic expressions.

Durkheim's approach has periodically been re-stated in one form or another. For example, Ribeiro de Oliveira (2001) has recently argued that the focal point of the sociology of religion should be the study of the 'immanent sacrility' of religion as a Durkheimian social fact. Even though it is increasingly fragmented into personal options, every society is a moral community that requires an ethos of sacred, moral and ethical values which (even if not explicitly religious) penetrate the consciousness of its members. De Oliveira maintains that the immanent sacrality of the plurality of religion (which may or may not take supernatural form) and the transcendent sacrality of religions are not mutually opposed but complement each other as symbolic systems that offer individuals meaning to their existence.

Sociologists who embrace broader functional definitions of religion are thus able to argue that if it could be shown that various social manifestations, while hardly 'religious' in the conventional or supernaturalist sense, may function at the individual if not the collective level, then religion may still be flourishing. This means that social phenomena which substantive theorists identify as non-religious could be defined as such if they performed some requisite. In doing so, the functional definition is predisposed towards affirming the endurance of religion in the West, albeit in non-supernaturalistic forms, and understood as embracing many of the new expressions of religiosity, particularly through self-spiritualities and quasi-religions.

There are problems with the functionalist approach, and these are probably more damaging than those of its substantive rival. A telling criticism is made by Kolakowski, who suggests that, while various definitions of religion are possible, those which imply that religion is merely functional or, in other words, 'nothing but' an instrument of secular, social and psychological needs, are unsatisfactory. Indeed, those commentators who insist that the meaning of religion should be reducible to its function, say that of social integration, tend towards intellectual dishonesty since their endeavours amount to an attempt at an empirical statement which may not be admitted in advance of a definition without a great deal of theoretical contortion. For Kolakowski, the important consideration is to maintain a distinction between the way in which religion may be delineated, more or less arbitrarily, the width of sociological inquiry, and subjective explanatory statements made regarding the nature and function of religious life (Kolakowski 1982: 10). To do otherwise results in calling non-religious institutions and patterns of behaviour 'religious', and this gains very little purpose other than creating contentious theoretical baggage, and loses much analytical clarity.

A related point is made by Bruce, who argues that, far from allowing the study of the 'functions' of religion to be conducted more easily, functional definitions of the phenomenon make it impossible by tautologically mixing into the designation of religion precisely those features of it which we want to establish empirically. Put another way, the substantive definition will normally include functional aspects such as the significance of religion to the community, or answering 'ultimate questions' – an enterprise that is not aided by the sociologist arbitrarily placing anything under the rubric of religiosity (Bruce 1995: ix).

It follows from Bruce's critique that the legitimate interest in exploring functional equivalents of religion can be pursued just as appropriately within a substantive definition. Accepting that human beings always have 'ultimate questions', functional definitions of religion do not permit us to talk of secularization, only 'religious' change. In short, the function of religion for society, whether as an integrating force or in terms of providing an ultimate reality and meaning, is best articulated through a supernaturalist belief system, and a decline in such a system by way of its social functions best constitutes a definition of secularization.

Phenomenological and interpretive approaches

As with the functional definition of religion, exemplified by Durkheim's interpretation, phenomenological viewpoints also offer a wide interpretation and have shown that they are able to enforce either side of the decline-of-religion debate. The most renowned exponent of this approach is probably Peter Berger, whose work became practically the accepted orthodoxy in sociological theorizing until the early 1980s and proved, by way of its consequences, to widen that which could be brought under the remit of 'religion'.

For Berger, arguing from a phenomenological point of view – although his claimed inspiration is Max Weber (Berger 1970: 9) – the sociological enterprise should constitute the study of the nature of subjective reality or the way in which the world appears to human beings. Religion has proved to be, historically and cross-culturally speaking, an integral part of this construction of reality, making the world, including the social world, knowable and accountable to human beings. The sociology of religion thus becomes intertwined with the sociology of knowledge since the essential business of religion is to explain the meaning of life in ultimate terms. In addition, Berger addresses the nature of religion in modernity and, through his own interpretation of secularization, sees religious decline resulting from pluralist tendencies. In particular, pluralism undermines a single plausibility structure which supports a religious view of the world.

From a more phenomenological approach, however, anything may pass as religion if it is meaningful or provides ultimate answers to human existence, supernatural belief systems or not. With this kind of approach some sociologists have come to identify a wide range of religions in contemporary society which include not just traditional religions such as Christianity, but New Age beliefs, secular ideologies, quasi-religions, therapeutic cults and popular superstitions. Furthermore, what is defined as religion may be open to interpretation and, indeed, provide the site of political and ideological struggles. Hence, many New Religious Movements, such as Scientology and the Unification Church, seek, in the face of social prejudice and state regulation to the contrary, to be socially recognized as 'religions'.

According to the phenomenological perspective much is subjective and in the eyes of the social actor. Thus, for example, it is perfectly acceptable for a soccer fan to regard the support of his team as a form of 'religion'. By broadening definitions of religion in this way, the implications for the study of religion in the contemporary Western context are therefore radically rephrased. Whether religion is declining, increasing, or being expressed in different ways, depends on what is meant by the term and, in turn, how its 'believers' define it. The complexity of the discussion of religion in the Western world, particularly in its emerging expressions, thus comes into clear relief and is enforced by more recent approaches, particularly those related to postmodernity and its consequences.

The principal problem with phenomenological perspectives is that, by claiming a given social phenomenon as 'religious', it is possible to apply the definition to social groups who would categorically deny that they have a religious element. For example, it has been conjectured that Alcoholics Anonymous operates rather like a religious sect. There are AA's strict set of beliefs, strong moral codes and a rather vague higher 'transcendental' aim which makes it a religion of sorts, but that is a designation categorically refuted by the organization itself (Greil and Rudy 1984). The current pursuit by contemporary sociologists of 'hidden' or 'implicit' forms of religiosity is thus misguided if it is only they, not the relevant social actors, who define social phenomena as such. Alas, this is what a growing number of sociological accounts appear to do.

Closely allied to the phenomenological approach is the interpretive perspective. The latter has its attractions: not least of all it may allow us to rise above debates over sociological definitions of religion by claiming that religion is primarily what the individual believer or religious community says it is. This is, for example, James Beckford's position, one which he has recently re-stated (Beckford 2001). Indeed, Beckford welcomes the fact that the conceptual boundaries of 'religion' and 'the religious' are currently the subject of renewed discussion, and suggests that from the point of view of the social and cultural sciences, religion is a complex set of phenomena which display continuity and change. Above all, the meanings that people attribute to religion show wide variations and inconsistencies, and are constantly undergoing transformation. There is some merit then, argues Beckford, in following the philosopher Wittgenstein's advice to equate the meaning of terms with the ways in which they are used. It follows that interpretations are situational and subject to the influence of many personal and social considerations, although it is still possible to identify common patterns and regular dispositions. The principal theme for Beckford is therefore not what religion *really* is, but a matter related to historical change and cultural variation in the ways in which human beings interpret objects, situations, dispositions and events as 'religious'.

There is more to this approach since, according to Beckford, scholars should ideally discern patterns in the popular usage of terms and interpret these patterns in relation to their social and cultural context. The position that Beckford thus advocates is not, he claims, a confession of weakness or failure in the sociological discipline. Rather, it marks a recognition that the meaning of religion is the object of constant negotiation, struggle and conflict. Beckford states: 'My position is that every individual decides how to use religion in everyday life' (Beckford 2001: 440). In the final analysis therefore, there is no fixed, objective or privileged point of view from which scholars can identify what is 'really' religious.

Beckford's stance may appear to be fair and reasonable, but it is not without its difficulties, not least of all in that many traditions within sociology have sought to move beyond the subjectivism of those who adhere to a belief system or claim religious 'experiences' in order to establish clear categories. The interpretive approach may allow us to understand changing definitions of religion, above all by social actors, but it is weak in allowing a comparative analysis which can account for wider social influences and social change. The only way that sociology can do so is to move towards a typology of religion. Indeed, Beckford admits that it remains perfectly feasible to stipulate, on a provisional basis, the 'family of resemblances' among features that appear to cohere in some, if not all, circumstances where people consider religious considerations are at work. Taken to its furthest conclusion, this may mean that some form of conceptual dualism is perhaps inevitable and we may be forced, as Dialmy (2001) points out, to acknowledge that the sociological enterprise may legitimately accept the distinction between religion as the specific lived position and adopted attitude of ordinary people on the one hand, and the sociologist's generalized theoretical model which takes into account ordinary definitions of the greatest possible number of religions in their socio-historical contexts on the other.

FROM RELIGION TO 'SPIRITUALITIES'

The matter of the actor's definition is at the heart of present debates within the sociology of religion. In point of fact, recent contentions related to new forms of religiosity come close to turning earlier definitions on their head and profoundly challenge the conventional theoretical and research activities of sociologists. Much of the new debate focuses on the distinction between 'spirituality' and 'religion' – a dichotomy increasingly acknowledged by social and behavioural scientists particularly in relation to transpersonal psychology and the emerging specialty of transpersonal sociology. Typical of recent sociological thinking, McBeis contends that the definitional issue is largely resolved by recognizing that what we actually deal with in the sociology of religion is not religion alone, but religion plus spirituality. Until we have a better label, he suggests, the discipline is best named 'the sociology of religion and spirituality' (McBeis 2002: 137).

A growing realm of spiritualities as distinct from 'religions' has been theorized in several recent sociological accounts. Among the more impressive is Partridge's *The Re-enchantment of the West* (2004). In this work, religion is said to give way to a new spirituality which comes with a re-enchantment of contemporary culture. Partridge argues that a growing non-traditional spiritual vitality emerges from various cultural sources. These include the significance of the self, the priority of experience, the preoccupation of film and literature with the occult and psychedelic, and the embrace of all things culturally Eastern in orientation. For Partridge, the rise of these new forms of spirituality is at the expense of conventional and organized religion.

The distinction between 'religion' and 'spirituality', evident in such accounts of contemporary culture, would seem to be confirmed by some empirical research findings. For example, Paul Heelas (2000) summarizes this shift as a cultural turn from 'religion' to 'spiritualities of life', where the emphasis is less upon religious authorities, established ways of believing, the dogmatic and the formal, and more contingent upon the personal, the immanent, the authority of individual experience and 'life' in the here and now. The significance of this would seem to be endorsed by Heelas's own pioneering research with his co-writer Linda Woodhead. In a book entitled *The Spiritual Revolution: Why Religion is Giving Way to Spirituality* (2004), based on a study of six medium-sized English towns and a comparative analysis with the USA and Europe, Heelas and Woodhead offer far-ranging predictions regarding the future of religion and spirituality in the West and whether new forms of spirituality are overtaking traditional forms of religion.

In the distinction between religion and spiritualities an interpretive approach may seem justified. To be sure, 'spirituality' is how the participants in the new religions frequently define their beliefs and practices. Thus, complicating the problem of definitions of religion is the increasing tendency for at least some of those involved in religious activities to jettison the term altogether. This is made clear by Wade Clark Roof (1994) in his study of the spiritual journeying of America's Baby-Boom generation which found that many individuals did not refer to 'religion' at all but frequently used terms such as 'Eastern spiritualities', 'feminist spiritualities' and 'Goddess spiritualities'. Given this subjective designation of 'spirituality' in preference to 'religion', there have recently been several attempts to clarify aspects of what the term spirituality might imply – largely from an interpretive account. This inference in such research findings that 'spirituality' is what social actors say it is takes us outside of conventional notions of 'religion' as frequented in earlier sociological works. Hence, for example, in New Ageist usage the word 'spiritual' denotes a belonging to a new age of spirituality following the end of the age of 'religion'.

But what does 'spirituality' actually mean? Rose (2001) investigates the term 'spirituality' among professionals drawn from the five major world religions (priests, rabbis and temple presidents) and reveals that, while a great deal of difference exists concerning what is essentially entailed, a basic set of characteristics seems to emerge. Spirituality is not found to be dependent on belonging to a religion. Rather, it is more reliant on a continuous or comparable experience and maintained effort of practice, and the experience of divine benevolence. None the less, while differences are shown to exist between the terms 'religiousness' and 'spirituality', the overall view appears to be that the two terms have similar meanings. Rose found that, in the traditions explored, the 'spiritual' included worship and practice as part of an integrated but central aspect of life. It does not, however, have to include a coherent belief system.

Other studies have identified further dimensions of the 'spiritual'. While Beck (1991) includes among the characteristics of a spiritual person a sense of awareness which he defines as 'awake and enlightened' and a comprehension of the transcendent in life, Evans (1993) describes a set of aspects relating to a spiritual individual and places an emphasis on contemplation – a state where one disciplines the attention so that gradually one moves away from being preoccupied with the self. Newby (1996) also comes close to this when he describes spirituality more as an outcome-based approach; that is, what a spiritually mature individual would look like. He states that, when one has spiritual maturity, one is primarily self-critical and has a desire for understanding and knowledge.

Zinnbauer et al. (1999), in an approach which is primarily concerned with people's perceptions of 'religiousness' and 'spirituality', found that these terms describe different concepts and have different correlates. Religiousness includes personal beliefs like faith in God, organized practices such as church activities, and commitment to a religion's belief system. Spirituality is most often described experientially in terms of faith in God or a higher power, integrating values and beliefs with behaviour in daily life, and sometimes associations with mystical experiences or New Age beliefs and practices.

The self-referential designation of spiritual, as distinct from 'religion', is gaining ground. But is it necessary to separate the terms in the pursuit of what is often perceived as new and growing expressions of religion? The fact remains that the interior spiritual life has long been an integral part of what constitutes religiosity, and does not depart significantly from well-established indexes of faith. The majority of, if not all, religions, suggests McBeis (2002), ultimately rest upon the foundation of an idealized purpose or primary goal of enhancing people's spiritual growth. Religion consists of the institutionalized structures, norms, leadership roles, rituals and the like that have emerged from that basic function. As they develop, religions experience dilemmas of mixed motivation, symbolic dissipation, administrative order, delimitation and power. Thus, admittedly, religions frequently yield to bureaucratic ends instead of retaining their focus as a means to the end of awakening, nurturing and stimulating the spiritual lives of constituents. In this way members become agencies for the end of building religious institutions instead of vice versa, and institutions that ought to support spirituality become its competitor or even its negation. Yet such a tendency should not distract from the primary role of religion in petitioning the supernatural and fostering a sense of divine communication within structured systems of morality, whether or not that is defined as spirituality.

The overlap between religion and spirituality can also be discerned in the relevant academic literature. As Zinnbauer *et al.* (1999) found, there is an integral link between the two. They note thirty-one definitions of religiousness and forty of spirituality in social science publications over the past decade which were fairly evenly distributed across nine content categories. They conclude that spirituality and religiousness overlap so much in human experience that it is usually wise to integrate them in scholarly studies as interconnected phenomena. Indeed, it may be argued that religious activity and faith will necessarily include aspects of spirituality, hence providing one among a number of sources of the measurement of religiosity – measurements which dovetail with definitions of religion. Indeed, this is a substantially grounded assumption and perhaps best integrated in Glock and Stark's (1969) well-known 'dimensions' of individual aspects of religiosity: the '5-Ds' of the ritualistic, the ideological, the intellectual, the consequential, *and* reference to spiritual experience. This still remains a simple but impressive set of criteria. Indeed, Gustavsson states that by the beginning of the 1970s 'Religion in 5-D' had been extensively researched with most scholars supporting the idea of multiple dimensions (Gustavsson 1997:

25). These are by no means foolproof, but still provide indicators by which we might understand the level of religiosity in the mass societies of North America and Western Europe. Notions of spirituality, then, are attributed their legitimate place within the broader field of religion.

SUMMARY

This chapter has attempted to do more than offer a conventional overview of the definitional problems associated with the sociological study of religion, although it may seem that we have come a long way from the matter in hand – the discussion of religion in everyday life. Yet a consideration of its significance must be put in a universal, cross-cultural and historical context. It is not just a matter of defining religion but the question of ascertaining what religiosity in contemporary society is being compared with. At the same time, this chapter has endeavoured to signify change in aspects of religiosity by way of belief, practice and belonging. It has also hinted at the development of new paradigms which have sought to account for many of the changes now observable in religious life.

In order to achieve theoretical clarity and engage with debates regarding the nature and extent of religion in everyday life it is necessarily to reiterate the significance of the substantive definition as the core historical and comparative tool. To be sure, for the most part substantive definitions of religion, as defined in beliefs and practices related to the supernatural, tend to have been previously embraced by those who identified a decline in religion in Western societies, and they are probably correct. Yet we should not totally reject what rival approaches have to offer. Indeed, it is possible to move towards a synthesis of substantive, functionalist and phenomenological perspectives. It is evident that religion stems from the community and is functional in terms of providing a system of shared moral values and 'ultimate reference points'. This gives way to a collective belief in the supernatural and related outward expressions. Much may be generalized by way of practices which may be objectively measured through outward manifestations, including beliefs and the establishment of agencies predicated upon an acceptance of the reality of supernatural entities with powers that impinge upon this world and human affairs, and impose systems of morality subject to reward or retribution.

Given recent debates regarding the nature of contemporary religion, problems related to the broader definition of religion have profound consequences. Above all is the matter of definitions that largely forge each side of the debate about religion in the West and determine whether it is perceived as declining, re-emerging or merely undergoing transformation. This is especially relevant to those social phenomena increasingly designated as 'invisible', 'quasi', or 'implicit' forms of religion which are interpreted as possible growth areas in everyday life. Hence, an overview of these contested areas is vital in our approach and will be the subject matter of the next chapter, where we will consider postmodernist accounts and their critiques.

2

POSTMODERNIST PERSPECTIVES

THE YET BUT NOT YET

CHARACTERISTICS OF POSTMODERNITY

New perspectives in regard to an analysis of religion, as with other aspects of everyday life, are gaining ground. Among them is the postmodernist approach, which has achieved greater legitimacy in the last two decades. Postmodernist writings display a range of theoretical speculations which attempt to explain the rise of new forms of religiosity, as well as providing an account of the eclipse of a number of traditional expressions in some instances and their revival in others. This perceived divergence in religious life stems not only from the complex nature of contemporary social existence, but also from the wide range of themes often developed by the current generation of sociologists of this school. In turn, much reflects the fact that postmodernity is a slippery concept which is open to interpretation and negotiation. In short, postmodernity as a social order (itself a problematic concept) escapes precise definition since its sociological exponents offer different understandings of what it amounts to and what its major characteristics mean by way of their likely consequences.

Although the relevant literature varies considerably, there is a prevailing consensus that the condition of postmodernity is perhaps best conceptualized as a socio-cultural configuration whose principal contours became increasingly identifiable from the 1980s, and whose implications are truly global. Put another way, postmodernity is frequently said to result from the extension of some aspects of modernity, at the expense of others, which serve to render modernity less recognizable as such, and that this has significant repercussions for not only aspects of culture but also for the rapidly changing spheres of economics and technology. In addition, there are a number of subsidiary themes commonly explored by postmodernist commentators which include the reorganization of urban areas, the deregulation of financial markets and public utilities, the by-passing of national-state power, the fragmentation of traditional life courses, global transformation and tourism, and a universal sense of growing social and environmental risk. Many of these developments have particular resonance for contemporary religiosity, including its alleged re-emergence in some areas of social life, although the major repercussions are perhaps mostly derived from the transforming nature of culture, ethics and morality. As a result of this myriad of observable social changes which seemingly depart from modernity, postmodernist writings tend to abandon the secularization thesis and thus seek to find ways of explaining the perseverance of religion in contemporary Western societies in the early twenty-first century, especially in new and innovating forms. Much however, remains speculative. While a more substantive critique of these speculations will be offered at the end of this chapter, further issues will be addressed in the following sections.

Cultural change and religion

Despite the differing accounts, or at least matters of emphasis, offered by sociologists on the subject of postmodernity, there is some common ground to be observed in the acknowledgement of the principal features of the postmodern cultural condition. In this respect, the theme of a cultural 'crisis' remains central to postmodernist concerns and is intrinsically linked to the widening theme of knowledge. Essentially, the source of this crisis is said to be related to the matter of meaning partly engendered by the collapse of meta-narratives. This theme is, for example, a major thrust of Lyotard's work (1984) on postmodernity. While he acknowledges that the post-industrial society and accompanying postmodern culture are essentially associated with a number of important technological, scientific and broad economic transformations, Lyotard suggests that the most significant changes result from the eclipse of mega-narratives, especially those which stress certainty in the world, human emancipation and social progress. Lyotard's contention is that the postmodern situation is one where everything becomes relative. There is, subsequently, a prevailing willingness to abandon the quest for over-arching or victorious myths, narratives or frameworks of knowledge. According to Lyotard, this may lead to the decline of a number of expressions of religion, perhaps most notably those that have historically claimed a monopoly of the 'truth' and which demanded allegiance from the population and socio-political institutions.

While Lyotard identified a 'crisis' integral to the realm of knowledge, the crisis overspills into the cultural realm with a disenchantment with rationality. This clearly tilts at a central core of the classical secularization thesis. Previous accounts of the process of secularization, typified by the work of Bryan Wilson (1966), identified the independent growth of scientific knowledge and method as undermining the credibility of religious interpretations of the world, including the social world. Religion discernibly had less significance with the growing sense of mastery over fate evident in the Western consciousness. The arrival of postmodernity, for Lyotard, brings much of this into question and, as a result, religion may re-enter the void. The collapse of an all-embracing worldview constitutes a crisis of meaning for the individual who will still endeavour to find an ultimate significance in life which only religion can fulfil. If this cannot be provided by traditional religion, namely Christianity, then an ultimate meaning to the world may be achieved by quasi-religions or new forms of religion which carry a strong moral certitude.

Other forms of religion which are attractive, in what many postmodernists identify as an emerging spiritual marketplace, are those which place an emphasis on mysticism and individual 'experience', and these tie in with the relativized nature of knowledge which consequently undermines conventional belief systems. In this regard, Nesti (2002) traces the postmodern landscape of a new religiosity beyond the secularization of modernity and identifies a widespread embrace of the mystical characterized by a cultural nomadism, sensitivity to the environment, and the preoccupation of self which is taken to its ultimate expression in the form of quasi-religiosity. Yet the most obvious home for mysticism is the New Age, alongside re-feminized religions such as Wicca, Western forms of occultism, and the growing popularity of paganism and animism. This emphasis on the mystical tends to undermine conventional religious authority and codified beliefs. Indeed, in his account, Michael York (1995) argues that many expressions of the New Age and neo-paganism have come to assert that *believing* itself is not essential to spiritual orientations. In short, it is individual experience, through various forms of mysticism, which is central. The significance of these developments is that two of the key indices of measuring religion, 'belief' and 'belonging', are automatically short-circuited.

THE INDIVIDUALIZED NATURE OF RELIGION

The conjecture that many of the growth areas of religion take more individualized form and expression is not new. Earlier accounts wedded to the secularization thesis observed that religion was increasingly articulated in the individualized and privatized sphere – a tendency which was indicative of its decline. Again, we can refer to Bryan Wilson's work on secularization, which contends that religion would invariably decline with both a reduction in common social values and the breakdown of communities which uphold shared religious conviction (Wilson 1976). Such a decline of community in modern industrial society resulted from high levels of social and geographical mobility and consequent changes in the nature of social control. In well-integrated communities, authority has a moral and religious foundation, which could no longer be upheld in modernity. Hence, the decline of church attendance and membership, alongside the decline of rituals such as infant baptism, would be part of the evidence of secularization. A repercussion of the decline of community was, therefore, the reduction of religion to the private sphere of atomized individuals, but only as a matter of choice. Moreover, because Wilson saw religion as essentially rooted in the community, he could not see how it could ever make a comeback. Privatization of religious practice and belief, as Wilson interpreted it, would not keep religion afloat and, moreover, displayed a certain superficiality.

A contrasting approach related to the reduction of religion to the individual and everyday sphere was offered by those such as Thomas Luckmann (1967, 1990) who suggested that the concept of secularization should be re-interpreted as the growing privatization of religion. The term 'secularization' thus denoted the transference of religion, from the social context as a collective expression, to the private realm. It was simply that traditional forms of religion were being transformed into new manifestations at the individual level. Void of institutional and conforming pressures, people were thus free to follow a personal quest for 'ultimate meaning' which endured as part of the human condition.

Luckmann also noted the emergence of new expressions of religiosity. Modern societies had no need for an overarching system of values framed in religious terms. Subsequently, religion become an aspect of private life and engendered individual choice from a variety of alternatives which could be constructed into a personally satisfying system of beliefs. In this way Luckmann pre-dates postmodern theories and, like them, argues that contemporary societies are witnessing a profound change in the orientation of religion, away from the 'great transcendences' concerned with other-worldly matters of issues of life and death, and towards new forms expressing the 'little transcendences' of earthly life which involve self-realization, self-expression and personal freedoms. These are not forms of religion that are necessarily easily observable. Indeed, many constitute an 'invisible religion'. More recently, Luckmann has re-stated his case by relating privatized expressions of religion to the emerging culture which is identified with characteristics akin to that of postmodernity in other literature. In short Luckmann argues that, where privatized forms of religion are characterized by the absence of obligation, they will tend towards self-realization through concepts of wholeness. Alternatively, the search for 'ultimate meaning' may also be expressed in terms of religious fundamentalism. What both fundamentalism and holistic new spiritualities attempt to do is to satisfy the desire for all-embracing belief systems that provide a meaning to everyday existence (Luckmann 2003).

RELIGION, CONSUMPTION AND IDENTITY

While many commentators explore notions of individualized religion, in postmodernist accounts it becomes enmeshed with additional themes which recognize further developments in the cultural sphere. According to much of the literature the emergence of consumerism as a cultural expression, and not just a component of the present-day economic system, is another principal feature of postmodernity, forging relevant lifestyles for large sections of the population. Since religion follows the contours of contemporary culture, it is invariably influenced by consumerism and commodification. Such a development would seem to dovetail well with notions of the growth of a spiritual marketplace, as well as reflecting the individualized nature of contemporary religion. Quite what the social significance of a consumer culture amounts to and how it should be appraised has, however, been open to debate – a debate which has considerable resonance for evaluating the nature of religion in postmodernity.

Here, much of the relevant literature has focused on the leading question as to whether consumerism is a liberating experience or whether it is imposed by dictates of corporate interests, and what the implications of either amount to. When the question is applied at a broad level to the nature of the spiritual marketplace it is difficult to see religion as something pre-packaged, as a top-down process, in the same way as other forms of consumption. Yet there is little doubt that the emphasis on a 'brand image' carries over into some fields of religiosity. The 'selling', literally and metaphorically, of a pre-packaged and simplified set of beliefs and practices is discernible in several quarters. Such a development obviously brings us close to notions of McDonaldization as applied to religion – a rationalized expression of religion that does not rest well with postmodernist paradigms, although the theme is often explored in postmodernist writings and, paradoxically, amounts to a process which cuts across the stress on unmediated individual subjective spiritual experience.

First coined in the early 1990s by George Ritzer, McDonaldization denotes the global patterns of consumption and consumerism and is a process of rationalization exemplified by the American fast food company McDonald's (Ritzer 1996). On a global scale, McDonald's is a major stakeholder in the burger-and-fries market, and what is produced is a fairly standard package. Moreover, the principals identified with McDonaldization are increasingly applied to other areas of life; education, work, healthcare, travel, leisure, dieting, politics and the family. That McDonaldization has impacted religious life is more than conceivable. Hence, the standardization and commodification of religious 'products' may be on a global scale through the use of literature and the plastic media of audio and visual communications technology as perhaps exemplified by American evangelizing ministries with their enculturated Christian gospel (Coleman 1991). However, like 'fads' in the commodity market, the 'shelf life' of these forms of religion might be limited, while the standardized and simplified pre-packaged belief systems offered rarely constitute a doctrinal culinary delight.

At least some expressions of commodification clearly do more than hint at a certain superficiality, although this may be best appreciated in terms of the razzmatazz element of some forms of contemporary religion typified by tendencies towards 'Disneyization', a term first coined by Bryman (1995). For Bryman, Disneyland is a social and cultural symbol of our times. It points to the ambiguities and ironies of postmodernity, as well as the proliferation of new communications media and the growth of consumerism. It is a symbol which is aimed at matters of authority and identity, of time and space. According to Lyon (2000: 10–14), all these elements of Disneyization are critical for a contemporary understanding of religion, spirituality and faith. The processes involved break down cultural differences, create a depthlessness, deal in cultivated nostalgia and bring a playfulness regarding reality and how it is perceived. The possibilities for the Disneyization of religion, then, are practically limitless in the postmodern environment.

There is more to consider in a dicussion of the 'consumption' of a relgion. Where the consumption ethic of postmodern religion may impact most significantly is in the area of identity. The 'consumption' of a religious identity in constructing a meaningful self comes in reaction to a society that finds it difficult to provide one. Multiple careers, unemployment and economic uncertainties have plausibly led individuals to regard the public sphere as a source of fragmentation, one compounded bu discontinuities in private life – a development exemplified by the temporary nature of many close relationships. Hence, as Phal has explored at length, people are now often alone in constructing self-identity and, in their own way, are in a culture which is unable to provide moral guidance (Phal 1995). A religious identity, however it is constructed, plausibly has tis attractions as part of a coherent and distinct lofestlyle, and the meaningful pursuit of idenitity may or may not lead to the search for a distinct subculture to provide its expression

According to postmodernist readings the contemporary market economy has increasingly encouraged a culture of consumer choice, and accompanies the fragmentation of occupational specialism and the pluralism of life-experiences. Mirroring cultural change, the sphere of religion tends to take on attributes of marketability. In short, the spiritual marketplace encourages people to pick and choose until they find a religious identity best suited to their individual, rather than collective, experience – a freedom to seek a religious faith which reflects, endorses and gives symbolic expression to their everyday social familiarities. The contemporary religious milieu therefore permits individuals the freedom to discover their own spiritual 'truths', their own 'reality' and their own 'experience', according to what is relevant in their lives, and provides a means by which to create a new self. Religion, in the postmodernist account, thus aids the construction of identity and lifestyle preferences as a subjective act of becoming what the individual aspires ideally to be.

By offering a sense of identity, the crisis of meaning and the problems of establishing an integrated concept of self synonymous with post-modernity may be overcome by a chosen form of religiosity. As noted above, with reference to the New Age and related spiritualities, it is innovative forms of religion which come to lend themselves best to this task. In this context, Castells identifies a 'conspicuous consumption of religion, under all kinds of generic and brand names ... (where) all wonders are on-line and can be combined into self-constructed image-worlds' (Castells 1997: 375). New expressions of religion may, from this point of view, restore a concept of self and identity by linking them to a moral system and over-arching cosmic order, but they are essentially personalized expressions and generally void of collective forms, and therefore tend to deny the traditional authority of the church, mosque or temple.

While such forms of religion plausibly have implications for the individual, their wider social significance may be diminishing. In stratified societies religion is frequently closely linked to status, whether expressed in the rites of passage of pre-industrial communities or, as in seventeenth-century England, in the possibility for wealthy people to reserve their pew at the front of the church in order to display their social standing. It is hard to imagine that in contemporary society religion operates in this way. A person's chosen religion, the church they subscribe to or the New Age paraphernalia they buy, may tell others about the type of lifestyle which an individual wishes to project. None the less, in a secular society religious preferences are unlikely to be important social markers of anything in particular.

Mix 'n' match spirituality

Postmodern culture also displays another dimension which may impinge on contemporary religious life: its syncretic nature – a development that also sits well with aspects of consumption and identity construct. For Lyotard (1984), the collapse of modernist social and cognitive structures means that postmodernity involves a desire to combine cultural symbols from disparate codes or frameworks of meaning, perhaps from different parts of the globe, even at the cost of disjunction and eclecticism. At the same time, diversity of discourse and the abandonment of universal and unitary meanings allow syncretic elements of religion to flourish – a tendency enhanced by the collapse of the boundaries between 'high' and 'popular' forms of religion which mirrors the disintegration of distinctions separating different cultural systems in Western societies.

This innovating aspect has been enhanced by the consumerist postmodern condition so that the new religions often constitute a mix 'n' match religiosity where many forms develop belief systems which are enhanced by reconstructing past religious myths. Here, much reflects the consumer ethic that brings a fragmentation according to a customized requirement. Such a process is plausibly also at work in a religious identity construction, especially in the way people may make sense of life and forge a meaningful existence in religious terms at the ordinary, mundane and everyday level. This development is obviously a challenge to traditional religious institutions, since cultural and religious monopolies are being dismantled and a deregulated spiritual market is emerging.

There is more than consumerism evident in these syncretic trends. For Fenn (1990: 101), the very speed of social change and decline of cultural continuity in the postmodern world breeds an ignorance of history, including religious history. Thus religious chronicles are frequently re-invented through new narratives, with individuals and collectives perceiving themselves as restoring, reforming or reviving the 'true' faith. Also evident is the breaking down of cultural and religious boundaries by the processes of globalization. Such developments have proved conducive to what Featherstone (1995: 11) refers to as 'cross-overs', and there is ample capacity for such cross-overs in the sphere of religion. Beliefs and practices which were once sealed within institutionalized cultural forms now freely flow across hermeneutical, organizational and international boundaries. New possibilities emerge in what Lyon cogently refers to as 'liturgical smorgasbords' and 'doctrinal potlucks' (Lyon 2000: 43). Here, the link with identity construction would seem to be imperative. Believers may construct their identities from various resources, depending upon the availability of symbols and the capability to hold together fresh combinations of ideas and beliefs once thought of as incompatible.

Globalization has opened the West to beliefs and practices from elsewhere, but those most readily accepted, notably those derived from Indian and Far-Eastern religions, would seem to enhance contemporary cultural attributes. While often mystical in orientation, they are frequently transformed for this-worldly purposes. This is part of a process of what Colin Campbell (1999) has referred to as 'Easternization'. The significance of this development, argues Campbell, is that it has undermined the traditional Western cultural way of seeing the world. Easternization has arrived in the wake of the decline of Christian culture, and challenges rationalism as the dominant paradigm. Campbell argues, however, that the postmodern culture brings a confluence of Eastern influences and internal Western developments. Much here indicates the significance of 'glocalization' (Robertson 1995) – that global incursions may be subject to localized meaning systems and infused with indigenous ideas and cultural trajectories.

For Campbell, this has occurred in the arena of religion. In the West, changes in consciousness include beliefs in the unity of man and nature, holistic views of the mind, the unity of body and spirit, the limits of science and rationality, and the alleged virtues of meditation and other psychotherapeutic techniques. The irony, for Campbell, is that contemporary religion becomes increasingly secularized. Behind the concern with the environment and popular beliefs in reincarnation is the preoccupation with human potential in this world, and with 'life-affirming' techniques. Eastern mysticism thus dovetails not only with present-day alternative thinking, but with the development of core values of the West.

The new technologies

Transformations related to technology have obviously occurred rapidly over the last few decades, and continue apace today. While much in the postmodernist writings puts an emphasis on the link to the restructure of capitalism evident in post-Fordist production and consumption and its accompanying culture, such accounts again tend to play down the significance in terms of rationalizing impulses and scientific advancement. Here, there appears to be a contradiction that is rarely addressed in postmodernist writings. Contemporary society *is* predicated on science, rationalism and reflexive calculability that is also abundantly evident in technological advancement whatever the cultural consequences may be.

Perhaps the most important dimension of the new technologies has been the development of the 'information age' – a term usually attributed to Castells (1989). For Castells, the information technology revolution has an impact upon everything else in the 'network society'. Postmodernity, then, constitutes a society saturated with technological growth and media images. It has ushered in a new form of economics, culture and polity, not least of all the niche marketing of commodities and enhancement of wide-ranging globalization processes. It is less plausible to see the new technologies as impacting upon religion, let along revolutionizing it. However, technological developments do have implications, arguably best appreciated through their mode of communication via supply-side religiosity and repercussions in terms of religious 'consumption' (Dawson and Hennebry 1999).

Contemporary writings have tended to take the significance of technology and religion to rather questionable lengths. This is evident in Turkel's (1996) insistence that there is a sense in which cyberspace displays its own 'religious' element. The internet has become a new metaphor for God. Websites, driven by commercial and personal interests, are 'visited' as part of a centralized but global system which overcomes geographical boundaries. It is universal, all-knowing and ever-present, a 'god' that *is* the distributed, decentralized system. This is truly 'implicit' religion writ large and perhaps taken to its ultimate conclusion.

Cyberspace is also the means by which conventional and new forms of religion utilize the new technologies and attempt to keep in step with recent innovations. There may be some Christian sects that distance themselves from such devilish developments, but for many people cyberspace, once a notion invented by science fiction, has come to produce a new 'reality'. It has opened up a world with immediate and direct access to an endless realm of information. A good number of the New Religions have their own sites, as do a fair few anti-cultist groups. Hence, information technology in respect of religion can perhaps be taken seriously in the way that it has become a powerful means of advertising in the postmodern age dominated by the visual image. Mainline religion has also woken up to the possibilities. In 2004, the Church of England advertised a post to be filled by a clergyman who would 'go on-line' for anyone who wanted to speak to him or her. This is another variation of the philosophy that, if people will not go to Church, then the Church must go to the people.

For some religious believers there may be an opportunity on the internet to meet people in another dimension as a kind of disembodied entity to discuss special interests and specialized tastes. One can 'surf' the net for a religion of one's choice, since major religious groupings will attractively present their 'wares'. In cyberspace, the beliefs and practices, and all other information required by the religious seeker, are available for perusal. One can enter 'chat rooms' to converse with others over controversies and doctrines – a radical departure from the reality of religion in its traditional community setting. This is perhaps privatized religion taken to its ultimate conclusion but one where the 'site' of religiosity is restricted to the home even if the technology seeks to unite individuals, albeit temporarily, across the world.

That such 'sites' are winning a substantial number of converts for religious organizations or bringing a wide spiritual awakening is unlikely. Just as on-line shopping has not quite taken off, partly because the products cannot be seen or experienced at first hand, advertisements by the New Religions are a poor substitute for the real thing. There may be plenty of information, but few who 'buy' the wares. Moreover, it is far from proven that those who meet in virtual reality subsequently engage in face-to-face activities and establish collective practice on any significant level. More plausibly, users may merely be seeking a means of reinforcing their beliefs, already subscribing to the views espoused. Thus the internet may be restricted in its impact to providing an opportunity to meet with the like-minded in a niche in the spiritual marketplace, and little more.

THE LIMITS OF POSTMODERNITY

Is there a justification for such a radical new approach to religion as that advanced by theories of postmodernity? The throwaway answer is perhaps 'yes and no'. Yes, if older perspectives are redundant and can no longer convincingly describe, analyse and account for emerging and changing social phenomena. No, if a new perspective makes assumptions which are unwarranted or hard to substantiate – and a number of such assumptions have been critiqued above.

More specifically, we might question the common conclusion found in the extant writings that the emergence of postmodernity is significant because it may suggest the resurgence of religion at different levels. Hence, we should not expect to find ever-diminishing dried-up pools of religiosity in the postmodern world, but to see it as expressed, utilized and forged in a variety of ways. This is a popular approach which discerns a resurgence of global religiosity in different forms: civil religion, fundamentalism and innovating new cultist orientations. Put succinctly, a fair number of postmodernist writings insist that, despite the variety and increasing fragmentation, it is clear that in the West, as elsewhere in the world, religion is emerging with a new vigour and through new expressions.

Ingelhart (1997), however, is not convinced of the link between postmodernity and a possible resurgence of religiosity. It is a forceful contention. He commences his argument by insisting that the most important consideration is that postmodernity should primarily be understood in its relationship to prosperity and security. Above all, postmodernity and the values which it engenders rest on a new stage of economic development. In short, the shift towards postmodern and indeed postmaterialist values is based on a rising sense of mass security. In this analysis Ingelhart falls back on Maslow's 'hierarchy of needs'. Hence, Ingelhart explains that the exploration of new forms of religion is predicated on a high level of material prosperity. It may be argued, then, that those related to identity and self-fulfilment, to potential and self-discovery, rest upon assurances of the satisfaction of material necessity. Only when these are guaranteed can such 'higher' indulgences flourish. Moreover, an appreciable standard of material satisfaction leads to a decline in conventional religion concerned with divinely imposed moralities which centre on the petitioning of supernatural entities to ensure favourable outcomes that sustain human life. Indeed, despite the postmodernists' insistence of disenchantment with rationalism and science, it is their achievements in modernity that have guaranteed the fulfilment of materialist needs in the first instance.

Ingelhart does not deny that, in this world of materialism and the emergence of a new cultural order, there may well be a search for meaning which only religion can deal with. However, the question is how *widespread* this religious searching is and what is the *depth* of its expression. Given the evidence, both may be doubted. Furthermore, the *way* that religion is expressed in postmodernity is frequently through values in keeping with the dominant cultural idiom, those of self-improvement, identity constructs and therapeutic techniques. Here, religion is reduced to individualized this-worldly needs rather than based upon 'externally' imposed systems of morality.

While the desire for a religious identity does not, in itself, suggest a level of superficiality, the search for 'experience' and its link to consumption may more than hint at this. Related to the growth of the commodity culture and perhaps, in some forms at least, enhanced by a disenchantment with rationalism, is the tendency of religion in the emerging age to be expressed in terms of an individualistic religious 'experience' which is fleetingly dramatic and transitory. Moreover, the extent of the search for a religious identity is virtually unquantifiable. Certainly, in its individualized expressions, void of institutionalized allegiance and codified belief systems, levels of contemporary religiosity are hard to evaluate since they commonly amount to Luckmann's 'invisible religion' (1967) and, as Cipriani (2003) suggests, this is not a form of religiosity which can be empirically measured and certainly not one easily susceptible to systematic field research.

The future of such religion is also hard to anticipate. With the decline of religious monopolies, religious activity is affected by a culture in which 'anything goes'. The consumer marketplace of religiosity encourages an interchange of beliefs and practices, so that elements from one meaning system flow into another, perhaps devaluating religion. Furthermore, religion can now be mixed with just about anything else. Thus, practically anything can be transformed into an expression of religion or grafted on to more traditional forms. Indeed, as Milbank notes, the evidence of postmodern theorizing is one which necessarily expands definitions of religion, reducing religion to more world-accommodating forms and accentuating the significance of quasi-religions in particular (Milbank 1992: 30).

Finally, do the new forms of religion suggest a future vitality? It may well be that people seek a mystical and meaningful spirituality beyond the limitations of the secular and rational world, constructing their own syncretic set of beliefs. However, the difficulty is that without institutional expression and belief codes it is practically impossible to sustain doctrinal systems over the generations in the way that traditional Christianity in the West has historically been able to do. The popular academic image of the postmodern setting is of people flitting from store to store – literally or as a metaphor – and from one image to another, constantly constructing and reconstructing themselves through experimentation with fashions and lifestyle. If religion now operates in this way, there is much which does not augur well for the future or the long-term endurance of religiosity, whatever its expression.

SUMMARY

If at one time the context for understanding religion in modernity included a reference to its decline in the face of science and rationalism, industrial development, urbanization, the growth of the nation state, bureaucratic organizations and notions of progress, then postmodernity, according to contemporary accounts, would seem to reshape religion in a radically different way. The key issues are related to the new technologies and consumerism, with changing experiences of time and space, with emerging social movements, with the focus on the body and identity, and with a sense of fragmentation and its complex repercussions. Despite these principal themes, there are divergent views concerning the nature of religion in the postmodern world, and disputes about which forms are expanding and which are experiencing decline. In some interpretations the subject of religion appears to be discussed in rather contradictory ways. What is clear, however, is that in the postmodernist account the 'hard' theory of secularization, which is viewed as a defunct mega-narrative, has been jettisoned in favour of a far more complex approach that stresses areas of religious resurgence as well as decline.

It is evident that theories of postmodernity attempt to grapple with the significance of current economic, technological and cultural transformations which are so far-reaching that it is difficult to predict future developments. Plausibly, then, postmodernity might mark a kind of interim condition where some characteristics of modernity have become so exaggerated as to be rendered scarcely recognizable. Indeed, there is a 'yet but not yet' in postmodernist theorizing regarding long-term developments including religion. With such an elucidation of postmodernity, Andrew Walker has written

> Postmodernism is not the ideology of the future, of the Internet, mass culture and mass pluralism. Instead it is the language of limbo;

the go-between gossip of transition; the discourse of leave-taking,
traveling from modernity to the not yet.

(Walker 1996: 180)

Whether current developments by way of culture, economics and the
impact of new technologies will prove to be long-term is rarely discussed in the relevant literature. Thus the predictive element tends to
be weak, and this includes speculative appraisals of the future of religiosity given the contradiction of postmodernity itself. Such is the
nature of the postmodern world. Ironically, then, the postmodernist
paradigm which suggests that over-arching mega-theories cannot be
sustained, since all frameworks of knowledge are subjective, faces its
own problems of internal logic.

3

RATIONAL CHOICE THEORY
AND ITS DISCONTENTS

It has long been discernible that theoretical frameworks and prioritized areas of sociological concern have not infrequently diverged between the USA and Western Europe. This is not to suggest that there are no fields of overlap or interplay between the two traditions which have emerged on either side of the Atlantic. After all, they are both inheritors of classical sociology even if they may make radical departures from it. None the less, cultural and political factors have created contrasting backdrops against which the discipline operates. More recently this has proved to be the case in the sociology of religion, where competing theoretical paradigms have emerged. In the USA, schools of sociology have produced their own revisionist theories of secularization as a counterpoint to the postmodernist writings of the Europeans (although postmodernism has notable exponents in North America). The major contribution is that of the rational choice school which has been so dominant since the 1980s.

There can be little doubt that rational choice theory has emerged as a major item on the agenda for a good number of social scientists in the USA across a range of disciplines. However, what appears at first to be a coherent and self-contained paradigm is, in fact, part of a wider approach to the field of economics which has been subsequently applied to a study of religious life. In this regard, its potential for the sub-discipline was greatly lauded in the early 1990s. Much was evident in the claim of Iannaccone, one of the leading exponents of rational choice theory, who stated that 'the logic of economics and even its language are powerful tools for the social-scientific study of religion' (Iannaccone 1992: 123). In terms of its broad orientation, a major thrust of the new paradigm was directed towards challenging the long-standing secularization thesis in the light of the growth of new forms of religion. However, it also dovetailed with a more generalized theory of religion and philosophy of social action. In developing such a stance, rational choice theory has emerged in radical contrast to some of the assumptions grounded in postmodernist thinking that rest upon a rejection or at least a perceived limitation of rationalism in contemporary culture. In Europe, few sociologists of religion have utilized the more extreme rational choice theorizing that has come out of some North American circles, although European sociologists, even those of a postmodernist persuasion, will subscribe to a number of core concepts and assumptions, especially notions of a religious 'supply-side', which denote those organizations and movements which adapt and emerge in response to the needs of religious 'customers' and 'seekers'.

RATIONAL CHOICE THEORY IN CONTEXT

The rational choice paradigm is built upon the assumption that human beings have always acted out of enlightened self-interest and are motivated by achieving 'rewards' and avoiding 'cost'. Put succinctly, individuals seek what is to their advantage and give a wide berth to what is not. The theory presupposes that people treat religion in the same way as they treat other matters of choice: they weigh up costs and benefits and act accordingly in the attempt to maximize their net benefits. However, a purer form of rational motivation in all areas of social life, including religion, is discernible in the contemporary age. Hence, the distinctive tone of rational choice theory and its broader reference point of USA-style market accounts of religious activity would seem, almost by definition, to focus upon some of the key developments of advanced industrial societies and the logical extension of *modernity*. In particular, there is the taken-for-granted view that the modern world encourages rational, means–end thinking through calculability and instrumentalism. It is a world which undermines tradition and social hierarchies, and where the erosion of primary allegiances allows an emphasis on individual motivation and the core value of individualism – all of which are conducive to rational social action.

There is also another source of origin in the development of rational choice theory as applied to religion. The key figure in the early theoretical speculations was the leading sociologist of religion, Rodney Stark, who was later to write in conjunction with a number of associates. Much of Stark's work regarding the nature of religion in contemporary society can be seen as rooted in his broader analysis of religion that developed over a period of time with William Bainbridge – a framework which is most comprehensively articulated in their influential work *A Theory of Religion* (1987). For Stark and Bainbridge the origins of religion are to be found at the individual, rather than the social level. It is the universal psychological need for religion which ensures its survival in advanced industrial societies. This is a theory which, as Mellor (2000) points out, stands in clear relief to the Durkheimian interest in a societal reality transcendent of the individual which informs the nature of religiosity. In contrast, rational choice theory discusses the fundamentally non-social character of religion in clear favour of the revitalization of individualistic and rational conceptualizations of the social order. The important point inherent in this approach is that profound social and cultural change does not undermine this basic human necessity for religion, although it may shape the nature and extent of religiosity. For example, a person may join the Nation of Islam because of a general antipathy towards Jews and as a result of his pro-Muslim upbringing, rather than as a totally 'free' choice in the spiritual marketplace (Granovetter 1993).

In *A Theory of Religion*, Stark and Bainbridge explore their notion of 'rewards' and 'costs' as part of a deductive theory of human nature and action. Rewards are those things which humans desire and are willing to incur some cost to obtain. These may be related to specific goals such as good health, status or material enrichment, which are often unattainable because they are always in short supply. Individuals frequently then turn to 'compensators' to deal with such deprivations. A compensator constitutes the belief that a reward will be obtained in the distant future or in some other context which cannot be verified. It amounts to a kind of 'IOU'. In short, individuals believe that if they act in a particular way they will eventually be rewarded. This is the essence of religious belief: it provides an unverifiable future – especially after death, compensating for what cannot be obtained in this life. At the same time, a more generalized desire that religion deals with are the ultimate questions which have plagued humanity from time immemorial. Why is there suffering? Is there an existence after this life? These questions constitute a search for meaning to life that only a belief in supernatural entities can provide answers to. Thus, Stark and Bainbridge's theory would appear to be utilizing substantive definitions of religion, although there are clear functional and phenomenological overtones to be observed.

The spiritual marketplace – rational choice style

Rational choice theory lends itself well to notions of a spiritual marketplace, but in doing so it gives a unique twist to earlier theorizing related to the link between pluralism and religious participation. The 'hard' secularization thesis included the assumption that pluralism undermined participation. This was most cogently explored in the work of Peter Berger (1967), who argued that religious pluralism reduced religious vitality through its effects on 'plausibility': the more worldviews there are, the less plausible each seems, and the less religious belief and activity there will be.

Finke and Stark, in their elaboration of notions of a spiritual marketplace, argue to the contrary and associate religious pluralism with religious participation. For Finke and Stark (1988: 42), the principal determinant is not plausibility but competition. Starting from the basis that 'religious economies are like commercial economies', they argue that competition among religious groups enhances the quantity and quality of religious 'products' available to rationally motivated 'consumers' and, so it follows, the total amount of religion which is 'consumed' increases accordingly. Although religious pluralism is not identical with religious competition, it has commonly been treated as an indicator of competition in rational choice theorizing, and surveys of the relationship between religious pluralism and participation have been the primary source of evidence offered in favour of the idea that competition leads to an increased religious vitality (Hechter and Kanazawa 1997: 198).

According to rational choice theory, given that people approach all actions in the same way, evaluating costs and benefits and acting so as to maximize their net benefits, they choose what religion, if any, they will accept and how extensively they will participate in what it has to offer. Over time, most people modify their religious choices in significant ways, varying their rates of religious participation and altering its character or even switching religions altogether. Given the assumption of stable preferences, the rational choice theorists are rarely content to account for such changes with reference to altering tastes, norms or beliefs. This is, in many respects, in stark contrast to postmodernist accounts of a spiritual marketplace. Rational choice theorists seek instead to model behavioural changes (and interpersonal differences) as optimal responses to varying circumstances – different prices, incomes, skills, experiences, technologies, resource constraints and the like.

The essential market dynamic of contemporary religion, according to Stark and Bainbridge (1980, 1985), is that if religious meaning cannot be satisfied by traditional expressions of faith, and in particular by established forms of Christianity, then new types of religiosity will emerge that can satisfy it. Given the nature of religion, the 'demand' for what it has to offer should be more or less universal and stable. Principal contemporary evidence for this is said to be the appearance of new cult movements which, generally free of the deficiencies of the older religious traditions, are in line with the needs of individuals in Western societies. The growth of the 'supply side' of religion can thus be discerned whereby traditional religious structures adapt to the needs of religious 'consumers' (Stark and Iannaccone 1993).

Stark and Bainbridge argue that the fact that their own survey evidence proves those who report no religious affiliation or belief are more likely to show interest in some form of unorthodox or fringe supernaturalism, such as astrology, yoga or transcendental meditation, is an indication of the endurance of religion. Facing life's dilemmas without the benefit of religious interpretations, people have always turned instead to other sources of explanation, justification or hope. Today, however, life's dilemmas are different. Hence some cults will include self-improvement techniques to enhance the worldly conditions of their members. These new religions and cults, according to Stark and Bainbridge, must be taken seriously. They are not superficial and insignificant forms of spirituality. Rather, they have meaning and relevance in supplying the universal functions of religion. At the same time, although the more secularized American denominations are in decline, the least secularized or conservative forms are not, since they provide more meaningful expressions of Christianity and effectively offer what religion is supposed to provide universally.

SUPPLY-SIDE RELIGION

Stark *et al.* maintain that, free of the ecclesiastical monopolies or state involvement so evident in European history, the spiritual marketplace of today increases religious activity as 'consumers' are now liberated to express their religious requirements in a variety of ways (Stark *et al.* 1996). In the contemporary marketplace so-called 'client cults' emerge to fulfil specific needs while older religious institutions are obliged to adapt in order to retain and attract clientele. In this way, explains Iannaccone (1997: 27), religious 'producers' must be viewed as optimizers – maximizing members, net resources, government support and a number of other basic determinants of institutional success. Even if religious 'firms' do not consciously strive for 'success', the individuals, organizations and policies that yield greater resources are more likely to survive and grow in the contemporary religious marketplace. The actions of today's churches are thus modelled as rational responses to the constraints and opportunities found in the religious marketplace. The combined actions of religious consumers and religious producers form a 'religious market' which, like similar markets, tends towards a steady-state equilibrium. As in other markets, the customer's freedom to choose constrains the producers of religion. A 'seller' cannot survive long without the steady support of 'buyers'. Customer preferences thus shape the content of religious commodities and the structure of the institutions which provide them.

Notions of a supply side have led to discussions of variations on a theme or taken exponents off in different directions in explaining the success of some 'producers' in the supply side and the failings of others. For example, Ammerman (1997) and Iannaccone (1994) have discussed the nature of church congregational growth and see it as resulting from a two-way bargain. Members can expect to receive all kinds of benefits since churches help meet a variety of needs, some spiritual, some much more mundane such as friendship, enhanced social status, and collective activities. In return churches will obtain the service and dedication of members. On the other hand, some religious organizations and movements fail because they do not adapt. Bibby, for instance, sees the current difficulties of religious suppliers in Canada as being one of 'product, promotion, and distribution problems'. The religious demand is there but the organizational response is not (Bibby 1993: 169).

Rational choice, modernity and the secularization thesis

Some of the broader assumptions made by rational choice theorists concerning the nature of contemporary religion would seem to dovetail with a number of the major themes advanced in discussions of modernity, pluralism, rationalism, reflexivity, individualism, choice, advanced capitalism and consumption. A few rational choice writers have developed specific areas of concern. This is exemplified in the work of Tamney *et al.* (2003) who posit their research on supply-side religion and congregational growth within 'modernization theory'. In short, they argue that strict conservative churches are growing because they have certain elements which are attractive to religious 'seekers'. These include authoritative structures and ascetic strictness, features which Tamney *et al.* see as components of modernity which have been transplanted into the religious sphere.

Despite arguing within the context of modernity, rational choice theorizing opposes the 'hard' secularization thesis which originally evolved within the modernist frame of reference. Secularization, according to Stark and Bainbridge, should not be seen as a smooth and continuous process. Historical evidence shows that religion has its peaks and troughs of revival and decline. Moreover, there is no inevitable spiralling decline of religiosity. While acknowledging that the rise of science stimulated an unprecedented, rapid degree of secularization, Stark and Bainbridge (1985) argue that science itself cannot fulfil many of the core needs and desires which religion provides. It cannot remove all the suffering and injustice of the world or man's mortality, and fails to give significant meaning to human existence.

In some accounts provided by the rational choice theorists the critique of the 'hard' secularization thesis is countered head-on. For example, Finke (1997), quoting Bryan Wilson (1966, 1982), maintains that the orthodox secularization model is based on the premise that religion will decline as modernity erodes the demand for religious belief with the advance of rationalism and science. The problem of this approach for Finke is two-fold. Since the model forecasts only a decline in religious demand, it fails to explain increase in religious activity. Second, it is unable to address the impact of changing supply. What happens when the number and type of available religions change? Indeed, Finke argues that the most noteworthy transformation in recent times is observable in the change in demand.

Another part of the conventional secularization equation is contended by Stark (2001), who purports that there never was a 'Golden Age' of religion in Europe. Contrary to received wisdom, belief in secularization is not supported by declining religious participation in Europe (Stark and Iannaccone 1994). Although current levels of participation are low on the Continent, the situation needs to be put into historical perspective. The fact is, according to Stark, in most of Europe the average person was *always* absent from the pews on the Sabbath. There never was any Christianization of Europe in the first place, merely a monopoly at the ecclesiastical and state level. If a person was converted, it was only in the most superficial ways. America, by contrast, had more religious vigour because it was the first modern nation to sustain a highly competitive religious free market. Socialized religion, then, destroys the religious initiative that it imposes through the state's demythologized translations of sacred scripture (Stark and Finke 2000). It follows that the clergy in these state religious monopolies were thus little more than civil servants. The USA, contends Stark, never allowed a state monopoly of religion, hence its higher level of religiosity. On the other hand, it has displayed a civil religion whose decline has further encouraged the proliferation of a religious marketplace (Stark *et al.* 1996). Stark concludes that religious monopolies (especially state-sponsored ones) dampen the demand for religious products. The competitive free market which comes in the wake of a pluralistic modernity offers a wide variety of religious products at low cost and thus increases consumption. Hence, there should be a strong positive correlation between religious diversity and religious vitality.

Critiques of rational choice theory

There can be little doubting the impact of the broader rational choice paradigm in the sociology of religion, especially in North American circles. Indeed, its proponents across the sub-disciplines have formed a section within the American Sociological Association. Its potential has been heralded as practically limitless. As a leading journal in the area relates:

> The paradigm of rational action is the one paradigm that offers the
> promising of a greater theoretical unity among social science disci-

plines such as economics, sociology, cognitive psychology, political
science, moral philosophy and law.

(quoted in Young 1997: xi)

Whether it is applicable to the study of religion in the same way, given
the nature of the subject, is open to serious questioning. For those with a
religious conviction this kind of theorizing may be objectionable, since
religion is reduced to the status of a commodity where the language of
economics and an instrumental pragmatism may be deemed as seriously
restricting an understanding of the complexities of religion. What is
missing is the social actor's experience. To be sure, it is clear that Stark
recognizes the failure of previous theorizing to acknowledge the 'human'
component' of religiosity, and this is discussed in his more recent work
with Roger Finke, *Acts of Faith: Explaining the Human Side of Religion*,
which modifies rational choice theory (Stark and Finke 2000). Whether
it improves on the basic theoretical model is a matter of debate.

While the theory has proved to be influential in the USA, its popularity has perhaps already begun to wane. In recent years there has been a
spate of books and articles that have offered quite damaging criticism of
the rationale upon which it is based and on the failure of empirical
research to confirm its major propositions. One set of criticisms has been
directed at the internal logic of rational choice theory, including that
aimed at the general theory of religion developed by Stark and
Bainbridge from which rational choice theory is ultimately derived. For
instance, Wallis (1984) questions the whole notion of a religious 'compensator'. Wallis suggests that it is not at all clear in Stark and
Bainbridge's writings why many religious beliefs should constitute compensators of some kind and in what sense a faith in immortality provides
a compensator for anything. While beliefs may give comfort in the face
of the meaninglessness that death presents, this is very different from the
alleged purpose of a compensator for the fact that human beings do not
live forever or the significance which it might otherwise have.

In terms of more specific theories of rational action, Bruce (1993,
1999) accepts that religious behaviour may be rational in the most general sense of being reasoned and reasonable. In short, people have always
adopted religion for fairly commonsense and subjective reasons.
Nevertheless, rational action in the religious sphere is not particularly
illuminated by the application of rational choice and supply-side mod-

els. Indeed, such an approach would be meaningful only in a society that was entirely secular and 'rational'. Moreover, Bruce detects an ideo-logical view underpinning the emphasis on a supply side of the spiritual marketplace, since it sounds like propaganda for *laissez-faire* capitalism whereby free markets are supposed to be better at meeting not only material but also spiritual needs (Bruce 1993).

A key premise advanced by rational choice theorists is that increas-ing choice stimulates the amount of religious activity. This is a forceful claim which, however, is most forcefully contended by those who hold a more conventional secularization line. In criticizing the supply-side argument, Bruce (1999) argues that there is little indication of the sup-posed increased religious activity in the majority of Western societies. This also brings us back to the historical testimony advanced by Stark *et al.* in suggesting that the past was not a Golden Age of religion, while religion today is enjoying something of a revival.

Bruce maintains that the weight of historical evidence simply does not substantiate such a claim. Moreover, two 'master trends' of moder-nity continue to work against a revival of religion: cultural diversity and individual autonomy. The first suggests that, even if existential ques-tions are somehow biologically given, the answers are not. Rather, they are culturally produced and, in the context of modernity, pluralism mit-igates against the strength of religiosity. The second, individuality, means that individuals are at liberty to choose their answers to life's ultimate concerns. Thus, individuals today cannot agree on the formula-tions of these essentially 'religious' questions or what would count as acceptable answers. The common values and assumptions that give legitimacy to a divine authority upon which a truly religious society is built have therefore been eroded (Bruce 1999: 185).

In considering the claim that a social decline of religion has not been apparent, a broader historical sweep is necessary. It may be incorrect to assert that some 'Golden Age' of religion ever existed. However, the evi-dence suggests that there has been a steady if uneven decline in religion in the social sphere, and this has had further impact at the individual level. At least this is Bruce's account of the situation in Britain (Bruce 1997). Bruce endeavours to trace the declining political power of the Christian Church in recent centuries as an example of its broader decline in Europe. Moreover, by using a largely substantive definition of reli-gion, i.e. the beliefs and practices of Christianity, Bruce suggests that, in countries where Christianity was strong, ordinary people saw religion in terms of such a set of beliefs and practices related to the supernatural. At one time the Church was an institution deeply embedded in social, economic and political life, but since the Reformation it has lost popular support. In some parts of Western Europe it quickly recovered; in others it did not. None the less, the general trend is the identifiable decline of an all-pervasive worldview – whether predominantly Christian or the magic and superstition which frequently gained greater popularity when the faith experienced periods of decline. For Bruce, such a tendency was accompanied by another: the role of diversity in removing communal and institutional support for particular religious beliefs (Bruce 1996).

In his aptly entitled paper, 'Christianity in Britain, R.I.P.' (2001), Bruce takes Rodney Stark to task on his claim that secularization is a myth based on exaggerating the religious vitality of the past and underestimating that of the present. Bruce contends that, in the case of Britain, even if the evidence is confined to comparisons of religiosity in 1951, 1900 and 2000, the trend is of clear and dramatic decline. Given up-to-date data on church membership and attendance, the long-stable trend shows that the major British denominations will cease to exist by 2030. Bruce argues that no amount of supply-side revisionism will change the fact that 'organized Christianity in Britain is in serious trouble' (Bruce 1999: 1). Bruce then turns to the supply-side model. If, he asks, there is such a 'free' marketplace for religion and no potential shortage in the variety of Christian organizations, surely there are those who offer or could potentially offer various preferences, perhaps by gender and conservative or liberal orientation. Given that Christianity has always valued collective acts of worship, it should be expressed in some way. However, actual and possible new churches do not make up for those lost to the more traditional denominations.

A review of the vast amount of literature produced in the USA and elsewhere testing the hypothesis of rational choice theory is not attempted here. None the less, cross-national research tends to find little general correlation between religious pluralism and religious participation (Verweij *et al.* 1997). Furthermore, the evidence suggests that this is not even the case in the USA where, using data from several US counties in 1980, Breault (1989) found a negative relationship between religious pluralism and religious participation.

These critiques led to a flurry of further detailed writings overviewing the evidence from various times and places, advancing evidence on both sides of the debate throughout the 1990s. Few scholars have been able convincingly to verify the equation that pluralization increased religious activity, or in positive cases could not identify the key supplementary variables involved such as denomination, urbanization, population density and transience (for example Olson 1999, Petersson and Hamberg 1997). The case of the rational choice theorist, then, remains to be proven.

THE NEW PERSPECTIVES: AN APPRAISAL

Like aspects of postmodernist theorizing, not all of the rational choice speculations can be ignored. There are some significant and valid insights provided concerning the nature of religion today. Contemporary society, however it is described, is circumvented by radical change in the spheres of economics, technology and culture. They have all left their mark on religious life. These are transformations so far-reaching that classical sociological theorizing struggles to catch up.

Part of the difficulty for contemporary sociology in attempting to apply classical theory is derived from the long-founded twin typologies of 'traditional' and 'modern' society. While certain characteristics separating the two, including the nature and extent of religion, may be fairly clear, modernity is an ongoing process which has developed in ways that the early sociologists did not anticipate. Hence, consumerism, a relativizing mix 'n' match culture, ever-expanding choice, individuality in many areas of social life, subjectivism, issues related to the self and identity, changes in the family structure and the life course, and the far-reaching consequences of globalization, are outcomes of a later stage of social development – if 'development' may be retained as the operative word.

Despite contrasting areas of interpretation, the overarching generality of postmodernist writings is predicated on the belief that Western societies have moved beyond that previously understood to be denoted by the processes of modernization and industrialization and most of what these processes entailed. Some of the literature suggests a new epoch in Western societies and indeed in global terms, while other writings do not contend that modernity has, for whatever reason, abruptly ended, to be replaced wholesale by postmodernity with all its attendant features. In the latter interpretation the prefix 'post' suggests that modernity itself is being transformed, and subsequently how it is defined is brought into question. By contrast, Giddens (1990, 1991) and other sociological theorists couple 'late' or 'high' to 'modernity' in order to discuss social changes in advanced industrialized free-market nations – identifying some social phenomenon that could otherwise be described as 'postmodern'. None the less, the task in describing and accounting for the contemporary order is not an easy one, whichever prefix is preferred. Indeed, such concepts as 'late modernity' or 'postmodernity' remain problematic. Davies puts the central dilemma in this way:

> we can be certain, and have long been certain, that there will be further major advances. This is the key, indeed the only, defining characteristic of modernity, the one sense in which we know that today is more 'modern' that yesterday … Where our ability to understand the material world is concerned, there is no late modernity and no postmodernity for there is nothing to be 'post' to and late implies an approaching terminus for which we have no evidence.
>
> (Davies 2004: xii)

The key point, however, at least regarding the subject of religion, is whether the profound cultural, economic and technological transformations observable in society today warrant a revisionist line to the secularization debate. Both the postmodernists and the rational choice theorists throw a measure of light on contemporary religion. Above all, it should be noted where they seem to converge: on the commodification and instrumental nature of a good deal of religion. Above all, it is clear that the various trends of religiosity follow the major contours of society, not least of all the tendency for just about everything to be open to commercialization and marketability. The strength of such theorizing, then, is at this point of convergence on the spiritual marketplace and its accompanying commodification. The central question, nevertheless, is whether that marketplace has an increased level of religiosity at the individual, or indeed at any other level.

SUMMARY

The marketability of religion and its consumerist aspects have been recognized for some time. It is, for example, to be found in such earlier works as that of Berger (1970), who discussed commercialization in terms of secularization, rather than the enhancement and growth of religiosity. For Berger, the development of a spiritual supermarket prefigured a situation of increasing pluralism which would irreversibly undermine conventional forms of religiosity centred on institutions and, in doing so, accelerate secularization processes. In short, Berger suggested that in the pluralist situation religions would have to compete in a 'marketplace' of religions and that this might lead to a degree of commodification. The important observation, none the less, was that this competition was derived from the pluralist context and, ultimately, this would weaken the social importance of religion.

Although there may be nothing new about identifying a spiritual marketplace and all that that entails, particularly in terms of privatized aspects of religion, there is now a far greater emphasis placed on these aspects of religion in current sociological thinking. Yet the privatization of religion antedates the consumer society. Such a development was a response to the withdrawal of institutional religion from many areas of modern social life. Agencies born in a religious context – law, education, health and welfare – are now part of the public secular realm.

Individualized religion remains a central feature of religious life played out in the spiritual marketplace. In the postindustrial society, however it is conceived, consumerism, rather than production, has become the dominant economic and cultural mode. Religion comes to partake of the consumer ethic. It is now increasingly a matter of choice, fashion and lifestyle. Certainly, from both a rational choice and a postmodernist approach, the implications of consumerism are immeasurable and the potential for fresh speculations as to the nature of religion today now seems endless. The postmodernist account is, however, more ambiguous. In the postmodern usage of the term, on the one hand 'religion' may be reduced to a mere leisure pursuit, or on the other, the increasing economic and cultural importance of leisure time may mean that religion is just relocated to an equally significant sphere. It may also mean that other, more secular avenues and expressions of meaning compete with greater success in the free-market setting, reducing religion's market share and transforming its nature to more quasi-religious expressions.

An analysis of the spiritual marketplace advanced by rational choice theorizing is fairly clear. Competition increases the level of religiosity through the law of supply and demand, although such theorizing is ultimately built upon the assumption that there is a human predisposition to be 'religious' since certain 'needs' are universal. Thus there is a thriving or at least a potential religious 'seekership' to be discovered. However, we are faced with a number of problems linked to proving such speculations. How do we measure consumption or 'seekership' – the number of New Age books sold, and conventions, seminars, retreats visited, or churches attended? What does it mean, moreover, to 'consume religion', and are consumption and commodification applicable to all forms?

Above all, religion is not like other social phenomena. There are too many dimensions of religion, which, by its very nature, cannot simply be reduced to the marketplace and consumerist forces. Thus notions of competition in the field of religion are not particularly well placed to account for the religion of ethnic communities nor the source of religious fundamentalism, even if, over time, they will be forced to compete in the spiritual marketplace. To conjecture within rational choice constraints is to profoundly limit our understanding of religion. Nevertheless, it is possible to suggest that its exponents are correct in suggesting that many forms are now directed to the benefits in this world, to human potential regimes with a spiritual gloss, to therapeutic techniques with little reference to the transcendental or supernatural entities.

While notions of a spiritual marketplace may illuminate aspects of religious change, there is also the danger of overlooking other long-term and profound social changes which have impacted upon and weakened religiosity in its various manifestations. Individualism, choice, the disintegration of communities, declining structures such as the family and social class, have all taken their toll. These topics are engaged in the postmodernist and rational choice literature, but are frequently seen as liberating the religious consumer from convention, and engendering choice in spirituality and generally enhancing the levels of spirituality, as if spirituality rests with the autonomous consumer. Such an approach tends to downplay the significance of reinforcement of belief and practice over the life course and over successive generations through social mechanisms of religious socialization. Moreover, it is an approach that is inclined to neglect the implication of the nature of religious adherence. These aspects of religion have been subject to considerable changes upon which the culture of choice and the spiritual marketplace are at least partly contingent. The next two chapters address some of these wider changes, changes which more than hint at ongoing decline.

4

THE CONTEXT OF EVERYDAY RELIGION

The ever-increasingly complex levels on which individual religiosity takes place should not distract from its discernible decline in many social domains pertinent to belief and practice. Perhaps the most obvious modes of religious expression by way of measurement are through institutional allegiance. Long recognized, particularly in the Christian tradition, is the link between beliefs and institutional belonging, alongside the ritualization of life-course transitions. A consideration of this relationship today would be forced to recognize that the institutions that carry beliefs have been subject to long-term disintegration. There are, of course, variations in attendance and membership in the Christian churches in North America and Western Europe – a theme which will be explored in Chapter 6. However, the general observable trend is there to be seen. So are the consequences, especially in terms of the more voluntaristic nature of belonging.

While individuals may freely choose belief and practice, such expressions of religiosity need to be preserved. The institutional mechanisms must remain in order to provide future generations with the options of religious life if they are not to be otherwise purely reduced to the vagaries and instability of the pick 'n' mix religiosity of the spiritual marketplace. These mechanisms are also enforced by aspects of religious socialization such as that of the community, locality and kinship structures which have also been subject to steady but continued erosion.

The importance of religious socialization still prevails. Indeed,

Sherkat and Wilson (1995), in an article entitled 'Preferences, Constraints, and Choices in Religious Markets', show that in the case of the USA there is not an entirely competitive spiritual marketplace, although in theory it is the most advanced of Western societies. Socialization continues to influence religious choice in terms of social variables such as ethnicity and class, alongside denominational affiliation. In defence of rational choice theorizing it might be contended that religious socialization is declining and that this will, in time, lead to an entirely 'free' market. Yet such a free market would undermine a major source of the transference of belief and practice which has historically been shown to be a powerful mechanism behind expressions of religiosity. In that sense, an entirely open market reduces the level of religion rather than enhancing it.

RELIGIOUS SOCIALIZATION

Despite the propensity to adhere to an infinite variety of beliefs, and while there might plausibly be a human 'need' for religion in satisfying a range of deprivations whether social, psychological or emotional, or, alternatively, in satisfying intellectual needs, people are not obviously born with an inherited religious conviction. Furthermore, while individuals may lay claim to a conversion experience, that experience is likely to be mediated through religious beliefs and practices already instilled at an earlier age. This is not to suggest that conversion may not sometimes be in respect of a previously unknown faith, but it is likely to include a process of socialization into the religious collective (Beckford 1975; Bromley and Shupe 1979).

The broader framework which embraces such social influences of religiosity is usually termed social learning theory. It is one which views religious orientation as largely a learned behaviour arising out of a particular life context. Hence, there is considerable emphasis placed on demographic variables such as class and gender which permit an understanding of characteristic trends including a greater participation and church attendance among women compared to men, and among more affluent social groups compared to those less well-off.

Social learning theory suggests that, as life environments change, people change, primarily by observing role models and practising new modes of behaviour (Bandura 1977). This is born out by O'Connor *et al.*'s recent and sizeable survey of over 200 adults of different denominations, which found that measurements of personal spirituality including private prayer, attending Bible classes and reading religious material, are linked to the denominational background in the years of youth, church youth-group participation, experiences since school which change feelings about church life, and attending church with one's spouse (O'Connor *et al.* 2002). The precise variables involved in social learning, however, are complex and cross-cutting. For instance, the influence of family life may be gender specific. Since men's religious roles are less institutionalized or socially defined than women's, the former's involvement in church may depend more on non-religious factors such as changes in family status. In turn, this may lead to a greater or lesser involvement in religious practice and affiliation (Wilson and Sherkat 1994).

The matter of religious socialization in the late-modern/postmodern context, or however contemporary society is conceptualized, should not be underestimated in accounting for the decline of religious belief and practice, at least in terms of conventional Christianity and plausibly, in future terms, the fate of those religions embraced by the ethnic minorities – those which have a more communal and historical context. In this respect, two broad and complementary themes present themselves. First, the breakdown of social structures, such as the family, that more informally carry religious attitudes and orientations. This accompanies, second, the decline of formal religious institutions, typically established denominations or comparable institutions, which transmit religious belief and practice over the generations.

In respect of formal agencies, religious socialization will invariably vary from one denomination or religious group to another depending on the kind of religious modelling and practices that are most prevalent for each. The culture of the collective in which the person was raised, including its teachings and habits, along with the amount of involvement encouraged through organizations such as church youth programmes, frequently impacts upon church participation, and even upon levels of religiosity if a church is not attended. These variables, along with early family socialization, are evidently more important than changes discernible across the life course (O'Connor *et al.* 2002).

It follows that it is the more conservative and sectarian forms of religion that are most strict in early religious socialization. This may at least partly explain the alleged success of conservative churches in the USA. Hence it has been calculated that the high level of church growth experienced by fundamentalist Baptists has less to do with evangelism and much more to do with their higher birth rate and the evident ability to retain their children within the church through socialization (Smith 1992). These churches, however, are also equally strict in insisting that, on reaching adulthood, the individual should demonstrate all the marks of commitment or leave. By contrast, mainstream religion, by which is generally meant liberal or middle-of-the-road Christian churches, are more likely to be tolerant of divergent religious views or secular influences and less strict in terms of religious socialization. This more than suggests that such churches will invariably decline over time and at a faster rate.

Formal and informal agencies of religious socialization

Outside of the specifically religious institutional setting, initiation into a 'religious' environment via socialization can occur at various levels. In its broadest sense religious socialization may be with reference to one variety or another of civil religion, and perhaps more obviously in the family or through formal education (Hoge *et al.* 1982). The decline of all of these in performing such functions scarcely argues for the transmission of traditional religiosity. Thus, religious values in a society void of stringent moralities and identified by relativizing impulses are difficult to sustain over successive generations. Moreover, in a globalized environment there is a tendency for belief systems to break down or at least to be rendered subject to modification and syncreticism.

Notions of a civil religion, from the influential work of Bellah (1967) onwards, constituted an attempt to identify the significance of religion at a collective societal level. The existence of a civil religion suggested a degree of common religiosity in which individual religion is anchored and subsumed, although a personalized system of belief may run alongside it. The apparent decline of civil religion in Western societies as a broad and loose form of religious socialization and means of social integration has been noted for its negative consequences. In exploring links between the decline of civil religion and moral decay, Anthony and Robbins (1990) list some of the negative implications for Western society, particularly for the USA. These include a crisis of moral meaning and boundaries leading to uncertainties in basic guidelines of behaviour, e.g. sexual permissiveness, lack of faith in traditional social and political institutions, the internal dysfunctioning of these institutions – perhaps displayed in corruption of government, increase in the divorce rate and family disintegration, rising crime and shrinking voting turnouts. While the attempt to establish a link between declining civil religions and morality may constitute something of a tautology, evidence of the decline of shared religious commonality is certainly evident.

It is noteworthy that some of the traditional agencies of childhood religious socialization are also breaking down and, in fact, this is a long-term trend. Perhaps most obvious is the decline of the Sunday School movement. This movement of the nineteenth century with its focus on specialized religious knowledge was felt by many churches to be neces-sary in an increasingly secular and differentiated society. In 1911, over half the children in England and Wales attended Sunday School. This figure was down to 20 per cent in 1961 and 14 per cent in 1989. At the peak of their influence in the late nineteenth and early twentieth cen-turies the Sunday Schools reached a very large number of young people and a very high proportion of their age group. By the year 2000 fewer than 10 per cent of children attended a Sunday school (Brown 2001).

Davies suggests that this decline in the Sunday School movement means that in terms of the Christian faith an 'entire culture had been lost' (Davies 2004: 66). Moreover, he argues that the lack of moral instruction has contributed towards a rise of deviant behaviour, at least in the UK. Hence, it is not surprising that rising crime statistics and drug and alcohol abuse have become serious problems in UK society. Church leaders of previous generations, Davies recounts, knew that they had not created a devout church-attending population, but nevertheless they instilled standards of morality and a public spirit (Davies 2004: 66–7). Such sentiments may sound somewhat reactionary in a society of choice where systems of morality are contested, but rightly or wrongly the declining impact of Christian instruction must be used as an index of religious life. In short, the decline in the Sunday School movement provides an indication of the ongoing process of secularization through increasing pluralism and social diversity.

Christian-based youth organizations have also experienced a reversal in fortunes. For instance, the number of Scouts and Guides meeting in churches in the UK decreased by 15.8 per cent between 1987 and 1993. The decline had, however, been set in motion several decades earlier.

The Church of England report, *Youth A Part*, attributed this to a general social trend of 'similar patterns of declining attendance ... in secular organisations' (1996: 13). The report also took comfort in what it believed was the sensitivity and commitment of many young people to the issues of justice, peace and the environment, but stopped short of attributing such sensitivity to any meaningful religious sentiment.

There is more to consider. In many Western societies, gone are the days of systematic Christian instruction in the public educational system. Considerable debate has followed as to what should replace it. A broader curriculum that endeavours to teach the basic beliefs and practices of the world religions is common in many Western schools, but the general orientation is more towards the virtues of a liberal education and the fostering of tolerance in a pluralist and ethnically varied society than spiritual edification or doctrinal instruction. This is not to suggest that there may not be some intent to instil a system of moral values. In the UK, for example, the 1988 Educational Reform Act requires that the curriculum makes a contribution to the spiritual enrichment of schoolchildren. As Duff (2003) notes, however, great uncertainties prevail in encouraging spiritual development in the secular and pluralist society of the UK. Similarly, Souza argues that in Australia the formal public education of the child in new curricula of spirituality allows little by way of connections between mind, body and soul; the mental, physical and spiritual world. The tendency is to ignore the inner reflective life altogether. The focus instead remains on the 'gaining of knowledge with less attention being given to the gaining of wisdom' (Souza 2003: 272).

We may now turn to the family as a carrier of religious socialization and the processes that it has been subject to in recent decades. Religious socialization is most likely to be successful when parents are openly committed to their religion, where they make a conscious effort to inspire religious values in their children, and when relationships between child and parents are cordial. People brought up in a religious family learn to be part of a religious subculture with a particular worldview and set of moral standards. However, the impact of familial religious socialization may vary over time. Religious disaffiliation and reaffiliation are influenced by the strength of family ties, marital history and attitudes to family life throughout the life course. The foundations of churchgoing or church-leaving, by way of illustration, are laid in a person's childhood, during his or her most formative years.

Where parents are successful in transmitting faith to their children and are themselves good churchgoing role models, there is much less likelihood that their offspring will drop out of church life. This tendency has been explored by various studies. For example, Hunsberger (1983: 34) found that church-leavers are less inclined to report that there has been emphasis placed on religion in families while they were growing up than are church remainers. Thus, home environment is at least part of the church-attending or leaving process. There are other indices besides church attendance, such as the American family tradition of saying grace before a meal which may also predict a person's future level of religiosity. Significantly, Hadaway (1990) identifies a rapid decline in parents providing these religious examples in the USA, or, alternatively, that such examples are being trivialized; this, he predicts, scarcely bodes well for the future.

If religious activity recedes in the teenage years the tendency is sometimes reversed in mature adulthood by treating parents as role models (although parental overenthusiasm can have a negative effect) – particularly if they marry and have children of their own (Wilson and Sherkat 1994), since churchgoing may fit into what makes the 'good parent' (Roof 1994: 151). Such trappings of respectability and markers of adulthood are not, however, indices of a high level of religiosity, nor do they run against generalized tendencies of decline. The increasing breakdown of family structures, the decline in broader religious instruction, and a culture of choice, mitigate against continuity of belief and practice over the generations.

In a two-parent family, only one parent may choose to go to church. The other may be a non-believer, or belong to another denomination or even to another faith. Sandomirsky and Wilson (1990: 1215) have pointed out that the result of this kind of cross-pressure is more likely to lead the child to withdraw from religious commitments altogether rather than choose one parent's religion over another. Plausibly, such factors may be accentuated in the so-called 'restructured' or 'blended' families which result from the increasingly common re-marriage situation. Indeed, the breakdown of family structures and family life today may suggest that religious socialization is undermined in various and far-reaching respects.

These social developments working against high levels of religiosity are common to most Western societies, even to the USA. While the USA appears to be a more 'religious' society than European nations, the reduction in specifically familial religious instruction (in conjunction with more formalized instruction such as Sunday Schools) as a principal carrier of religious socialization was particularly marked from the middle of the twentieth century. In 1952, in the USA, only 6 per cent of people had received no religious training as a child. In 1965, this had risen to 9 per cent and in 1988 to 18 per cent. This does not augur particularly well for the level of belief and belonging in the future – a fact explored by Reginald Bibby in *Fragmented Gods* (1987), where he argues that the principle reason for decline in church attendance is the lack of religious socialization. People who attend church as adults are primarily those who attended as children. Active churchgoers seldom come out of nowhere: they are home-grown. However, the proportion of children being exposed to religious instruction outside of Sunday School is estimated by Bibby to have now dropped from three in four to less than one in four.

FROM LOCALISM TO VOLUNTARISM

The dimension of localism presents another slant to the significance of religious socialization. Localism denotes a 'local orientation' characterized by involvement with local institutions and networks of friends and family (as opposed to a 'cosmopolitan' orientation) which typically predicts higher rates of religious activity. It follows that church attendance tends, for example, to be higher in small-town America and rural England than in inner-city areas which are typified by social disintegration, or suburban areas with a high degree of population mobility. In the more static communities church attendance may be high as a result of a constant reinforcement of 'plausibility structures' (Cornwall 1989). This tendency is perhaps most obviously the case with settled ethnic communities where it has been found that allegiance to a religious system frequently depends on the stability, density and size of any given community in a geographical area. The key factor is that religious socialization not only takes place over generations but spatially via a continued reinforcement on a day-to-day and face-to-face basis within a locality. In a highly differentiated and pluralistic society, the maintenance of a particular religious worldview requires that members of a community continuingly support one another's belief in daily interaction (Roof 1987).

The pluralist nature of society in the West, and the lack of a sense of community due to the disintegrating forces of social and geographical mobility, mean that the 'religion of the community' in the Durkheimian sense is increasingly unsustainable. The differentiation of modernity fragmented the community in terms of life experiences, urbanization similarly undermined them, while the community sentiment upon which collective symbols of religion were based was also eroded. These are processes complicated by the dynamics frequently identified in late-modernist/postmodernist writings with their emphasis on relativism, choice and individualism, all of which destroy the communal and public moralities which were once informed by aspects of religiosity. However, the disintegration of this basis of community is likely to lead to a decline of belief and practice whatever the religious tradition. Moreover, this tendency also suggests that new forms of religion or spirituality will not endure unless they transmogrify in shape or form or can gain adherence at some other societal level, perhaps increasingly displaying an anchorage in secular, rather than religious culture, especially where they are linked to lifestyle choices. Indeed, while localism is increasingly undermined, it is further impacted by change, discontinuity and mobility. For example, college experience, geographic relocation, inter-faith marriage or other shifts in the life course may disrupt the individual's interactions with earlier practices and networks and so lead to lesser involvement in conventional religious life (Roozen 1980).

Voluntarism and identity

With the decline of community there may have arrived a new underpinning of association and belonging to religious organizations and movements. A growing body of literature, especially in the USA, has focused upon the so-called 'new voluntarism'. This term implies that the basis of joining any sphere of social activity now relies on voluntary choice on the part of individuals. This is clearly a consequence of the increasing social and geographical mobility which has occurred in the wake of the breakdown of communities and primary group association. Free from community obligations and conformity to group norms, the individual is uncompromisingly exposed to the values of an achievement-oriented culture and accompanied by purposeful, instrumental and self-advancement strategies that have come to encompass so many areas of social and economic life (Warner 1993). The new voluntarism is now evident in religious life, where 'choice' is the operative word. In the culture of choice people are more likely to join a group for personal advantage and instrumental reasons. This is in marked contrast to the previous basis of belonging: social pressure, altruism, convention and collective concerns. Thus, the contemporary world heralds a more profound individualism and utilitarianism that overspills into the religious domain, whatever the form of spirituality preferred (Wuthnow 1993: 39–40). Such developments mark a distinctive departure from 'collective-expressive' to 'individual-expressive' religious identity (Roof and McKinney 1987) and invariably accompany the general erosion of religious commitment in cosmopolitan, multi-cultural Western societies. Indeed, religious activity can be said to be particularly challenged by contemporary transformations since both social and geographical mobility have undermined the 'religious culture' and the community where it has historically been embedded and thrived. The outcome is that there is little or no social pressure on the individual to convert to a faith through the proselytizing efforts of the religious collective since, ultimately, the momentum is derived from the religious 'seeker'.

Hammond (1988) suggests that there is now an increasing link between identity and voluntary religious belonging. This is clear in the case of church membership. Previously, people were largely influenced in their religious affiliation by primary group pressure such as that from the local community or the family. The membership of such primary groups has historically been involuntary. Today, however, secondary group membership is becoming increasingly important in determining institutional membership. These are voluntary associations which more obvious, including age, gender and occupation, associations that are more amorphous and arguably weaker sources of membership. Allegiance to such associations, whether church or cult, is freely chosen and relates to the construction of personal identities which are a vital ingredient of lifestyle choice. While the tendency to adhere to a religious collective of one's choice, rather than as a result of social pressure, may be a growing phenomenon (Bibby 1993; Wuthnow 1994), it may also be the case that people are inclined not to belong at all – a long-term trend in Western Europe. This reflects broader changes in the secular sphere where membership of political parties, trade unions and other forms of organization has rapidly declined. Such a trend is also increasingly observable in the USA. The change in the latter is recognized in the so-called Putnam thesis. Putnam's (2000) indictment of developments in the USA focuses on the demise of a core cultural attribute, the great love of Americans to belong, a dimension which plausibly partly explains the high church attendance rate. The desire to belong to a multitude of associations, from political associations, to the bowling club, to the boy scouts, once supplemented the excesses of American individualism. The latter has now increasingly replaced the former, and with it, according to Putnam, has gone social concern and a public spirit. Religion is arguably moving in the same direction. The individual spiritual quest, where it exists, is inward-looking and tending towards narcissism and egoistic desires rather than being expressed in terms of communities or through institutional settings.

THE LIFE COURSE: FRAGMENTATION AND CHANGE

Varying levels of religiosity have long been associated with the life-cycle through the different age categories. Their significance will be considered in the next chapter. They are also observable through rites of passage, at least in pre-modern cultures, and are invariably tied up with dimensions of religious socialization – over time as well as spatially and through organized aspects of ceremonial ritual. Indeed, a primary theme of anthropological studies of religion in non-industrial societies is related to those rituals designating the transition of one clearly demarcated 'stage' of life to another, whether biologically defined stages such as birth, puberty, pregnancy and death, or those socially constructed – marriage perhaps being the primary example. Compared to contemporary societies, pre-industrial societies displayed a less complex and relatively undifferentiated 'cycle-of-life', and typically involved merely pre-adult and adult 'stages' – a simple distinction that was largely unchanging over the generations where such rites of passage marked community-imposed expressions of religiosity in the individual's experience of the lifespan.

In the past, as in many less developed societies today, rites of passage were often tied to one of the most important forms of social stratification, age. Unlike Western societies, social structures and culture in pre-industrial societies are usually static or undergo transformation very slowly. The generations that pass through the age categories will invariably be subject to similar experiences. This is far less the case in the contemporary West, where life experiences are extraordinarily varied and where the notion of age cohort is more relevant and denotes those born in a distinct historical period, which may forge very different experiences when compared to past or later generations. This contrast serves to highlight the fact that traditional societies, culturally and structurally speaking, were built upon a high degree of predictability. Individuals knew with assurance which age sets they would belong to in the years to come and what this entailed by way of expected modes of behaviour.

The advent of modernity brought a more complex life-cycle, giving new meaning to some stages of life such as childhood, while creating new stages including adolescence and youth. At the same time, the life-cycle engendered its own clearly structured round of life which reached its greatest complexity in the mid-twentieth century. Also characterizing modernity was the emergence of the nation-state that ushered in alternative forms of social control and that itself contributed to the industrialized society by educational and welfare reforms and by extending the rights of its citizens through democratic processes and institutions. In this way the state, as well as the onset of the industrial–capitalist order, brought the growth of bureaucracies which were identified not only by certain 'internal' arrangements such as a pervading rationalism, hierarchy and division of labour, as Max Weber (1978) noted, but by the regularized control of social relations of time and space – implementing a regularity and regimentation epitomized by the factory system.

Under the impact of industrialization and the demographic changes of the nineteenth century a gradual differentiation in age groups and a greater specialization in age-related functions began to emerge, although it was by no means complete by the end of the century. Paradoxically, the same modernity which increased the number of 'stages' of life also stripped them of rites of passage. Rationalism and science secured many of the 'crises' of human existence: childbirth lost most of its dangers, while everyday life became safer and more predictable as the environment was increasingly mastered. In the contemporary context, then, many of the social and psychological underpinnings to the rites of passage have undoubtedly been undermined, not least of all uncertainty and crisis even in the so-called 'risk society'. As a result of scientific advances and improved living conditions, the majority of the populations of Western societies may now look forward to completing an ever-extending life-span. The decline in these rites of passage also accompanied other forms of collective rituals, such as that of the harvest festival which thanked God for His providence and abundance.

Today, the concept of the life-cycle has been replaced by that of the life course. There are various reasons why the former has been jettisoned. One is to give a greater flexibility for cross-cultural and historical studies and to move away from an ethnocentric approach to the subject, one which produced broad and unwarranted generalizations. Another primary reason was to forge a framework in order to understand the life course in late modernity/postmodernity (Hunt 2005). In this regard there are various ways by which late-modernist or postmodernist writers have approached the subject of the life course. However, there is a general recognition that people do not pass through such clearly demarcated stages of life as they did in previous decades. For instance, it is now difficult to stipulate where childhood ends and adolescence begins, and whether age norms still hold, although it is apparent that to one degree or another some expectations remain. What is abundantly lacking is structural rigidity.

Writers such as Featherstone and Hepworth (1991) and Bauman (1992) see the postmodern life course as characterized by a number of overlapping, often disparate conditions associated with the blurring of traditional chronological boundaries and the integration of formally segregated periods of life. Fixed definitions of childhood, middle age and old age are eroding under pressure from two cultural directions that have accompanied the profound shifts in the political economy of labour: flexible retirement and traditionally structured forms of inequality such as social class. These developments have various repercussions. One is that, in contemporary culture, the prospect of an endless life has been revived through images of perpetual youth and a blurring of traditional life course boundaries. Now life in Western societies is reduced to a series of individual choices and projected plans for the future that have little community significance. Discontinuity and reversibility, and far-reaching disruptions such as redundancy and relationship breakdown, also complicate the life course. It follows that rites of passage in Western societies are mostly optional, not compulsory aspects of social existence, and are likely to disappear with the rise of individualism and the decline of the community setting where they once were an integral part of life and helped establish social identity. There may still be coming-of-age or retirement parties, but these are hardly of great social or religious significance.

Rites of passage are still observable in contemporary religious groups which display rituals marking some form of spiritual transition, such as baptism in Christian churches, while for ethico-religious collectives they remain important, as with the bar mitzvah among Jews that represents the transition from boyhood to adulthood. Yet, even in many religious spheres, such rites appear to have declined. Evidence of this is the near-disappearance of 'churching' – a tradition in some churches where women are prohibited from returning to the congregation until a month after giving birth.

Some religious rituals remain, albeit in the form of social conventions. The proportion of people coming to church to be married, baptized and buried remains higher than the number of members or regular attendees. These rites are, however, in observable decline. In 1880, practically all newborns were baptized (albeit after an appreciable length of time, beyond which their survival was perceived as likely). In England in the mid-1970s there were 428 baptisms per 1000 live births, compared to 554 in 1960. The basis on which baptism statistics are calculated altered after 1979, but the decline has continued. For the Church of England between 1885 and 1950 the number of baptisms fluctuated between 60 and 67 per cent. In 1922, it was 53 per cent. In 1993 it had declined to a mere 27 per cent.

At the same time there has been a discernible decline in the number of marriages conducted in church. In 1929, 56 per cent of marriages in England and Wales were performed in the Church of England compared with 37 per cent in 1979. It may well be that people may opt for baptisms or church weddings, but it is probably not for essentially religious reasons. Plausibly it is the ritual and ceremony that is important, not the 'religious' content. Hence, major life events may psychologically require markers of change but are increasingly stripped of their essentially 'religious' significance.

Arguably the steady reduction in such religious ceremonies is because, for various reasons, the great milestones of life are of less importance. The fall in infant mortality may mean that families are less inclined to give a religious significance to the arrival of newborns. Some social institutions, such as marriage, are less subject to social pressure and increasingly a matter of choice. Yet it is also true that this continuingly relatively popular social institution indicates levels of secularity, since it is frequently empty of its religious relevance. Indicative of this is the List of Approved Premises, produced by the Office for National Statistics in the UK, which encompasses a register of legitimate non-religious sites for weddings other than places of worship. They include zoos, soccer grounds, museums, nightclubs, golf clubs and restaurants. In the nineteenth century almost all weddings were religious ceremonies. In the case of England in 1971 this was down to 60 per cent. This was then followed by a fairly steadily decline – to 31 per cent in the year 2000.

Divorce statistics indicate that marriage is not necessarily a lifelong commitment. It is no longer perceived as being 'made in heaven' and witnessed in the sight of God. The religious sanctity of marriage is also undermined by increasing divorce rates, which have been interpreted as a symbol of growing rationalism and individualism (Gibson 1994). Just as individuals rationally choose to enter into marriage and select a partner in instrumental terms, divorce may be an equally pragmatic decision. This is also reflected in divorce legislation, where the philosophy of 'till death do us part' is replaced by a range of rational–secular legitimations for marriage annulment.

Of all life course events, coping with the death of kin or a loved one is perhaps the most difficult for those left behind. Malinowski's (1954) renowned anthropological work showed that religion was especially significant at specific times, in particular in situations of individual emotional stress which, in turn, threatened collective solidarity and sentiment. Anxiety and tension tended to disrupt social life. Malinowski noticed that in all pre-industrial societies life crises are surrounded with religious ritual. Death was the most disruptive of these events since it severed strong personal attachments and thwarted people's future plans. This is why he regarded the ability to deal with the problems associated with death as probably the main source of religious belief. Thus, through funeral ceremonies, belief in immortality can be expressed, in a sense denying the fact of death itself and thus comforting the bereaved. Indeed, bereavement signifies a particular type of discontinuity. Death means the cessation of someone's life and the end of the relationships that the deceased shared with others. Moreover, it brings a unique form of psychological challenge, since death is final.

Perceptions of death in Western society profoundly reflect social change – not least of all as a result of relentless secularity and its declining communal context. Today, death is not a public event. Rather, it is a private experience and, for the most part, will take place within an institutional setting (Aries 1974). Western culture is also age- and death-denying. Where there is an emphasis on prolonging life, of consuming strategies to retain youth, there is an inability to tolerate death in a culture oriented towards perpetual happiness (Featherstone 1982) which, in turn, undermines thoughts of the afterlife. Moreover, the way that society is organized, with its rationalization and emphasis on optimum performance, means that it cannot afford long periods of mourning. The standard funeral, which generally gives scant reference to the afterlife or religiosity, is often void of meaning and insufficiently deals with the mourning process – one where postmodernity gives insufficient guidelines (Walter 1999). This plausibly explains the rise of 'alternative' funerals underscored by the value of 'choice' and, increasingly, with little or no religious element apart from that concocted by relatives from a pick 'n' mix 'spirituality'.

SUMMARY

This chapter has primarily been concerned with the immediate context of religious life: institutional belonging, religious voluntarism, socialization and change in the life course in as much as it has impacted belief and practice. Important changes are discernible, many of which underscore the increasing individualization and privatization of religiosity. Institutional decline and decreasing religious socialization on the one hand, and increasing voluntarism on the other, would seem to enhance seekership and consumption in the religious marketplace. Yet, at the same time, they are not developments which lend themselves to the long-term vitality of religion. The institutions and processes of socialization which have historically transmitted belief and practice are in decline. Religiosity is thus the domain of the autonomous individual in the realm of religious consumption.

There is more to consider, however, in the broad context in which religion takes place. Other important demographic variables also impact on religious life. The most relevant are perhaps gender, ethnicity and social class (the subject of ethnicity will be considered in Chapter 7).

Each brings its unique range of overlapping influences which endure even if their importance continues to decline in the contemporary world. The significance of age is also to be noted, although its relevance is tied up with broader factors, not least of all the changing dynamics of the contemporary life course. These variables will be considered in the next chapter, with the emphasis placed on recent changes that have impacted on the everyday experience of religion.

5

DEMOGRAPHIC VARIABLES
CONTINUITY AND CHANGE

In the past, a great deal of sociological literature has explored the themes of gender, class and age as they are related to the 'phases' of the life course, in order to account for different levels of religiosity, but rarely how they add to the complexities of the secularization debate. However, at a time when social mobility and greater affluence have eroded class differences in Western societies, and increased opportunities for women have likewise eaten away at gender inequalities, it may be argued that differences in levels and expressions of religiosity have likewise been undermined and, according to various indices, suggest the future convergence of previous variations. Differences by way of attitudes towards religion may also have declined with the breaking down of stringent age categories at the present time, although the picture remains rather complicated. A consideration of all these demographic structures not only denotes a certain amount of convergence but a tendency towards convergence in a downward direction that would seem to point to religious decline, signifying that their erosion may have made religiosity at the everyday level less sustainable.

AGE AND THE 'PHASES' OF LIFE

Today there is an inclination in sociological theorizing to play down the significance of age categories. The meaning of being 'young', 'middle-aged' or 'retired' is open to interpretation and negotiation, by way of identity construction, throughout an increasingly varied life course. Furthermore, shifting age categories and lengthening life expectancy mean that these are no longer clearly defined 'stages' of life with accompanying norms of behaviour. Rather, such stages are more the subject of choice and negotiation as to how they are lived out in terms of lifestyle options, and are subject to aspects of commodification.

Such developments will prove important given the fact that the various stages of life were once frequently associated with fairly distinct and divergent religious values and beliefs. Now it is increasingly difficult to make generalizations regarding age categories and broad religious orientations. This is not to suggest that they are entirely redundant, since empirical studies continue to establish a link between religiosity and age. However, it is the larger picture which must be considered, one where religious socialization is of decreasing importance and a culture of choice has become more established across generational differences. Given cohort experiences, it is probably the younger generation that is more subject to preference in the spiritual marketplace and thereby breaks away from communal and kinship religious affiliation to be subsequently exposed to the freedom to choose some aspects of religiosity or none at all. Evidence suggests that it is the younger cohorts in an increasing socially and geographically mobile society where the decline of religious socialization will be felt most acutely compared to older generations. Here, a measure of comparative analysis is possible. Hence, we commence with a brief discussion of religiosity in later life.

Later life

Some evidence suggests that religion is of more central importance in the lives of older people compared to younger generations (Gray and Moberg 1977), while other studies have found that the association is inconclusive (Steinitz 1980). Christiano's (1987) survey of people of various church backgrounds indicates that older individuals, and older women in particular, are occupied with church activity, often by force of custom. At the same time, the involvement of the elderly in religious organizations may indicate increasing social marginalization. This is in stark contrast with pre-industrial societies, where old age may infer a greater social status. Retirement in contemporary society effectively means, for many older people, leaving the public sphere. Thus, for them, the bases of identity and self-worth must be derived from the private sphere – family, leisure, perhaps religion. Increased emphasis on the religious bases of individual identity, then, may represent for older people an attempt to transform the previous cultural emphasis on work and parenthood to a fresh self-valuation based on spiritual growth.

Belief in an after-life may possibly also be related to later stages in the life course. In so far as older people typically display higher levels of belief in a life after death, it is not clear whether this is because they have lived longer and are nearer death, or because they were brought up in a more religious era. Clearly this is a complex picture and, as Finney notes in his survey *Finding Faith Today*, bereavement and suffering are among the factors reported in finding faith at any time of life. It may well be that the ageing process and bereavement of family and peers is accentuated in old age, yet it could equally lead to a loss of faith (Finney 1995: 50). Cutting across these variables are wider cultural changes. While progressive old age may concentrate thoughts of the after-life and while chronic illnesses associated with later life undoubtedly constitute so-called mortality markers, the emergence of a Third Age of affluence before 'deep' old age, flexible retirement and lifestyle choice will invariably confuse the link between religious belief and older age categories. At the same time, the improving political and economic situation of the elderly, as a growing section of the population, may break the link between old age and religion as some kind of compensator for social marginalization.

There is more to consider by way of long-term developments. Brierley (2000), in a chapter entitled 'Bleeding to Death', indicates a pessimism about future levels of religiosity. For each of his earlier three English surveys he estimates the age profile structure of the various denominations and suggests that, with the exception of the Pentecostal churches that recruit mainly from the Afro-Caribbean population, churchgoers are considerably older than non-attenders. This has been even more the tendency over the last two decades. In 1999, 29 per cent of Anglican attenders were over the age of 65. The trend may vary in other Western countries, but it could be estimated that they are probably not that distinct from the UK given that overall cultural and structural changes are similar. The higher levels of religiosity may die out with the older generation, while the forms of religiosity expressed by the next generations in later life, as we shall see, will likely be very different. The legacy left to subsequent generations is indiscernible at this time.

The religion of the mid-lifers

Middle age may be a period of increasing church involvement for some. In the USA, in 1980, the overall pattern in adult church attendance showed a steady increase from the late teens to a peak in the late fifties to early sixties, followed by a slight decline in old age which can largely be put down to physical incapacitation (Atchley 1980: 330–40). These figures, however, do not necessarily reflect greater religious sentiment among middle-aged people, but could be viewed as changing patterns of involvement in voluntary associations, especially when their children leave home, or, alternatively, could reflect career patterns when work becomes less significant. Thus involvement in church life may increase as commitment to work-related, sport-related and school service associations reduces over the same period.

The time of middle age is often regarded as a period of 'identity crisis' not unlike the teenage years, one brought about by biological changes and altering social roles. While acknowledging that this 'crisis' may at least partly be a medicalized construct, belief and belonging could help establish a new sense of identity and status. Certainly, a long-standing rather commonsense view is that the attraction of religious belonging, particularly for women of this age, is plausibly linked to the loss of socially ascribed gender roles as well as natural changes in reproductive capacities. These assumptions, however, are not easily substantiated and have to be supplemented by the fact that women of all age groups tend to be over-represented in many expressions of religion.

These are obviously generalized observations concerning mid-life, and again cohort effects must be taken into account. Here, Wade Roof's influential survey of the USA (1994) is worth exploring at length. It is one which looks at the religious orientation of the 'Baby Boomers' – those born between 1945 and the 1960s, who were exposed to immense cultural upheavals of the permissive society, political idealism, the greater availability of higher education, new musical forms, and the rise of New Religious Movements. As a younger generation, 'dropping out' of church paralleled dropping out of practically everything else. Those affected by these value-shifts are, according to Roof, least likely to have returned to church-belonging (Roof 1994: 171). Thus Baby Boomers have a distinct generational outlook on life, moulded by the events of their late adolescence and early adulthood and including a distrust of authority figures and institutions. This means that the traditional Church, with its hierarchy, rules and regulations, holds few attractions.

In Roof's account, experience takes priority over beliefs for the Baby Boomers. In their formative years this generation jettisoned cultural and religious certainties in favour of authentically 'living in the present moment'. The Baby Boomers hankered for something that would suit them, rather than something to which they would be expected to conform. The search was therefore directed to the immediate, inward and present, self-actualizing spiritual experience, probably best described as 'mystical', whether it was 'knowing' God or 'getting in touch' with one's true self. It was important for this generation to free the human spirit from potentially stifling social institutions and conventions, from the hypocrisy and dullness of the Church, in order to discover liberty in new forms of religiosity.

The Baby Boom generation has now come of middle age. These are mid-lifers who have dropped out of traditional religious institutions and are now, according to Roof, looking for something meaningful – moving across religious boundaries, many combining elements from various traditions to create their own personal meaning systems. Such individuals claim not to be religious in the conventional sense, but 'spiritual'. Adler, in line with Roof, suggests that they are among the strongest adherents of the new Christian churches, although it is this generation which has primarily been responsible for rediscovering occultism and developing spirituality through the New Age movement (Adler 1986).

The 1960s were the beginning of the affluent society, of post-materialist values, the focus on the well-being of the self and the search for meaning. The virtue of self-denial thus gave way to the ethic of self-fulfillment. Hence, the Baby Boom mid-lifers may prefer churches with an emphasis on spiritual growth, but the stress is predominantly on fulfilling one's potential and the embrace of various kinds of psychological therapy. Diversity of choice has also been an important feature of the Baby Boomer generation in consumption, media viewing and especially lifestyle. Religion is a matter of preference and pluralism is highly valued. 'Pre-packaged' religion is often treated with suspicion. Hence pick 'n' mix spirituality has its attraction for the fluidity of Baby Boomers' allegiance and the way in which they select and combine aspects of various religious traditions – perhaps, for example, mixing Christianity with Celtic spirituality.

What are the attitudes of the Baby Boomers to the religious socialization of their children? Roof and Gesch (1995) suggest the evidence of their study proves that there are changing attitudes to religious socialization among the parents derived from the Baby Boom generation. They found that the principle of individual choice is now prevalent even inside the family, with nearly half the Baby Boomers surveyed saying that family members should choose for themselves about religious matters, rather than necessarily attending church as a family. Whether future generations, especially in the mid-life phase, will display such qualities of seekership remains to be seen. None the less, it is likely that the patterns laid down by the Baby Boomers result not just from the cultural vagaries of an historical cohort but are part of wider social developments over a protracted period of time.

Youth

Perhaps the most important reason behind studying the young is that it is they who will transmit religious beliefs and practices for future generations. There are perhaps two key considerations. First, decline in belief and practice in younger age groups would not bode well for the future of religion, rendering valid speculations as to its decline. Hence, an increasing lack of participation over generations would be a strong indication of secularizing trends. Second, and related, is the question as to what precisely the beliefs of the young are as compared to those of their parents and previous generations.

With reference to the UK, Grace Davie notes that opinion poll data over time indicate younger generations are less religious than older ones. Furthermore, Davie argues that not only are young people leaving the churches, they are also, it seems, rejecting even the nominal belief that may potentially allow them to grow into greater religiosity in old age (Davie 1994: 121–3). More widely, in Europe, evidence from the European Values Survey suggests that, while levels of religiosity increase up the age scale and cut across other variables such as class and gender, when it comes to mainline Christianity in particular, younger cohorts will not, in time, endorse a greater religiosity (Cook 2000).

The reasons behind the felt estrangement of the young from mainstream

Christianity have been open to speculation. Evidence suggests that the culture of church life contributes to the reduction of young people belonging to Christian denominations. Richter and Francis's sample interviews of those leaving churches in the UK more than indicate that they did so because churches were thought to be dominated by older people and displayed a culture that was 'old fashioned'. Moreover, the later years of young adulthood bring further distractions. Richter and Francis's study indicates that young people brought up in church life may leave as a result of other distractions the secular world has to offer, or be involved in work commitments and family responsibilities (Richter and Francis 1998: 12, 134). While Richter and Francis identify such commitments as often being temporary, and that return to church life is possible, the matter of priorities suggests itself. Squeezing church life into a lifestyle crammed with other options and responsibilities is seemingly not a prospect which younger adults relish.

Those young people who leave the more established denominations may gravitate towards churches which are described as 'more lively', 'exciting', 'creative', 'youth-oriented' and 'alternative' (Richter and Francis 1998: 124–5). Many of these are undoubtedly of an evangelical/charismatic persuasion with a distinctive form of theology and culture which may suggest the type of Christianity that will emerge as the twenty-first century unfolds. As we shall see in the next chapter, they are largely independent churches, ones which will probably replace the established denominations over time. Whether they will make up for the decline in denominational church attendance, especially with their attraction for the young, is unlikely however.

While the picture is gloomy regarding church attendance among the young, it is none the less difficult to make generalizations, and the USA again comes out in stark relief. Here, C. Smith (2002: 601) uncovered a number of interesting recent comparisons. In the case of the USA, adolescents would seem to exhibit a great deal of variation in their frequency of religious service attendance. Some 38 per cent attend weekly, while around 15 per cent do not attend at all. Between are those who attend infrequently or only on special occasions. Around 13 per cent of youth claim to have no religion whatsoever – roughly the same proportion as non-religious adults.

These are notable statistics compared to lower rates in Europe and suggest that the possible decline in church attendance in the USA in the future will be a very slow development. Yet it is the long-term picture which has to be taken into account. The conclusion by Smith (2002: 609–10), on considering the evidence, is that the majority of American youth, despite some important regional variations, are religious in so far as they affiliate with some religious group or tradition. Yet the number of American adolescents within the Christian tradition has been gradually declining; about half of America's youth regularly participate in religious organizations; on the other hand, the remainder are not religiously active. There are gender differences too. Girls tend to be somewhat more religious than boys, but perhaps the greatest determining factor in religious participation is differentiated by race and ethnicity. Smith found that Afro-American adolescents have the highest rates of church attendance, followed by whites, and then other racial and ethnic youths who display comparatively low attendance. This ethnicity effect is evident across all categories of frequency of attendance, from never attending to weekly. It is also evident in participation in religious youth groups. Such a tendency Smith puts down to the cultural expectations of religious participation and aspects of integration within the racial and ethnic communities to which they belong (C. Smith 2002: 610).

The same study also found an uneven distribution of youth affiliation according to Christian and non-Christian groupings in the USA. Between 1975 and 1996, one of the most significant changes was that the proportion of American youth of 'other' religions and those who are not religious grew by 5 per cent each, hence a twenty-year increase of declining affiliation with traditional Christianity and other faiths. As Christian socialization has broken down, according to Smith (2002), attendance also varies by affiliation when mainline churches are compared to quasi-Christian and non-Christian groups. The more conservative constituencies, and those with larger proportions of African-Americans such as the Jehovah's Witnesses, Mormons and Pentecostals, have high rates of attendance which might be expected of the more sectarian forms of religion where socialization remains strong. By contrast, youth in mainline religious groups seem to exhibit a more moderate attendance. The poorest attenders among this age group were Quakers, Utilitarians and Christian Scientists, and other similar sects. At the same time, rather surprisingly in terms of ethnic constituencies, Jewish, Buddhist, Hindu and Muslim affiliations were also in decline.

Despite divergences, the most recent generation would seem to express particular attitudes towards religiosity, attitudes which do more than hint at lower levels of belief and practice. The so-called 'Generation X', following Douglas Coupland's book (1992) of the same name, represents a cohort born between 1960 and 1980. This cohort has followed the previous generation of Baby Boomers in a quest for personal freedom and autonomy, but entertains few notions of changing the world, and is subject to discontinuities and the risk of 'being your own person' where self expression is given a high premium in a pick 'n' mix culture. This latter generation, however, are less concerned with rebellion and closer to their parents (a more rebellious generation in their time) than for many decades (Ritchie 1995: 151). It is a generation that is more conformist and embraces the values of the dominant commodity culture of today.

In a contemporary Western world, where traditional authorities such as the Church have been relativized and undermined, there is very little influence on the lives of the Generation X-ers in terms of structured beliefs and moralities (Wilkinson and Mulgan 1995: 29). At the same time, when compared to earlier generations, this cohort tends to be less idealistic and much more pragmatic. Many have seen their own family life break down and have been raised in a 'me' society – one of 'hype' and parody, visual media saturation, surrounded by a sensory culture. Generation X-ers recognize that there are no easy solutions and are pessimistic about what politics can do. As with their parents' generation, there is a suspicion of traditional religious institutions. What is common to the values of these generations is that they display a different mode of faith and less institutional affiliation in response to profound cultural shifts.

In the 1960s and 1970s commentators began to recognize that teenagers were not leaving the churches for the same reasons they had before. These were reasons less associated with adolescent rebellion and more to do with changing cultural values (Roof *et al.* 1995: 245). This is still the case, although the values of Generation X, as we have noted, have changed in many ways from those of their parents. Whatever the particular generation of youth, however, it is the period which represents a crucial developmental transition from childhood to adulthood and so can disclose significant insights into religious socialization and changing religiosity throughout the life course. Anticipating the future, it is likely that the religiosity of those born around the beginning of the twenty-first century, the so-called Millennium Generation, will follow the identifiable trends in religiosity over the last four decades.

GENDER AND RELIGIOSITY

As already noted, various factors cut across the importance of religious socialization, institutional belonging and religious belief and practice, particularly in how they are expressed throughout the life course. Gender appears to be more than a significant variable. Indeed, it is a well-known fact in the sociology of religion that according to various indices women display higher levels of religiosity than men. This does not just refer to adherence to mainline Christianity or the new religions but is true in broader, more abstract terms. For example, USA Gallup polls have for many years included items on religion and the paranormal and found that, compared to men, females were more likely to pray, to say religion was a very important part of their lives, and to read the Bible. Other indicators are that twice as many women as men say they believe in some kind of after-life (Davies 1997). They are more likely than men to believe in the devil, heaven, hell, creationism, in ghosts, communication with the dead, ESP and astrology, and more likely to report having paranormal experiences; but men are more likely to believe in UFOs and that aliens have visited Earth (Tobacyk and Milford 1983; Goode 2000).

Research has confirmed what is obvious to members of the main Christian denominations: that there are still wide gender differences in religious practice from infancy to adulthood. The disparity can be perhaps most obviously observed in terms of church attendance. The predominance of women in the churches is pretty much universal. In Germany, France, Norway and Ireland, women make up 60–5 per cent of active churchgoers, and in South Korea, India and the Philippines they constitute 65–70 per cent of congregations (Ruether 1994: 285). This trend does not stand just for adults, since, in the case of the USA at least, it also applies to adolescent girls compared to boys. In turn, this suggests that certain dynamics of socialization and social learning play their part. Smith *et al.* report that in the USA the number of male youths claiming to have no religion is higher than females. More girls attend weekly church services compared to boys; on the other hand, more boys than girls never attend church (Smith *et al.* 1998: 605–6). These divergences are not, however, of that great a significance and they are closing.

How might these gender differences in religiosity be accounted for? Besides such sociological explanations emphasizing wider gender roles and differences in socialization, there are psychological accounts and even speculation regarding physiological origins. Indeed, as Stark (2002) points out, there is a growing body of plausible evidence in support of the once-debunked physiological bases for gender differences in crime. It is plausible that, like criminal activity, irreligiousness may be an aspect of a general syndrome of short-sighted risky behaviour among males. In turn, conjectures Stark, this plausibly leads to the conclusion that irreligiousness could also have a physiological basis. Stark none the less counters psychological and physiological arguments by attempting to salvage the socializing explanation.

The variable of socialization is invariably linked to the matter of social roles. Perhaps the key argument is that female socialization is said to emphasize expressive emotional values which are congruent with religiosity. It seems that women with a family-centred role, rather than the economic role of the male, are expected to be more church-oriented because of the continuing bonds between church life and the family (Francis 1997). There is nothing essentially new in this relationship. Historians argue that religiosity became highly feminized in the late eighteenth and nineteenth centuries, as separate spheres emerged for men and women in the industrial society, with women 'placed at the fulcrum of family sanctity' (Brown 2001: 59). The supply side, like the Church of England in the UK, accepts and even legitimizes this long-term distinction by making it something of a priority to establish contact with young mothers through nurseries and primary schools (Levitt 1996).

It may be argued, however, that if religious gender socialization is an important variable then it is merely the *means* by which some important differences may be transmitted from one generation to another. The origins of a greater female religiosity may therefore be deeper. Here, deprivation theory has proved to be a popular generalized explanation as applied to gender. Certainly deprivation theory serves for a good deal of the basis for research in examining the social correlates of religion and paranormal beliefs. The general theory maintains that paranormal beliefs provide people with the means to cope with the psychological and physical strain of disadvantaged social and economic status (Stark and Bainbridge 1980). Thus, belief in the paranormal should be higher among marginal social groups, such as ethnic minorities and the poor. Indeed, studies examining the correlates of traditional religious beliefs present a fairly uniform set of conclusions which are, for the most part, consistent with deprivation theory. At a general level, as Goode shows, Americans who believe in religious paranormal phenomena tend to be disproportionately women, African-American, and less educated (Goode 2000).

In explaining the over-representation of women in Christian churches, Walter (1990) tentatively speculated a link with deprivation in that a good deal can be accounted for in terms of a search for solutions to a number of negative social and psychological experiences in everyday life. Feelings of anxiety, a range of emotional difficulties generated by domestic roles, and dependency on the male sex, are frequent concerns of women which need to be psychologically addressed. In addition, argued Walter, compensators might also be sought for such deprivations as poverty, low status and lack of opportunity, again linked to the limitations of female social roles and child-rearing in particular.

However, in later work with Grace Davie, Walter cast doubts on the deprivation explanation in the link between females and high levels of religiosity. Davie and Walter overview social deprivation theories which look at the socially induced vulnerability of women, particularly their more direct involvement in birth, death and their caring roles (Walter and Davie 1998: 647–8). They suggest that the findings do not always match up or are often contradictory when looking at mainstream Christian churches. For example, women attendees are frequently older, middle-class females, while members of deprived groups and urban working-class white males are least likely to participate in religious activities. Deprivation may be the reason for participation for some, but the theory does not explain why women respond in different ways. If response depends on what is culturally defined, then what is this defined aspect appreciably and quantifiably offering women? Walter and Davie conclude that a review of the reasons for women's greater religiosity leaves more questions than it provides answers.

In contrast to females, a number of studies have shown that men participate in religious ritual and worship less often, espouse different religious motivations for their participation, profess less devout beliefs, testify that religious faith is not always relevant to their everyday activities and identify less with 'being religious' than do women (Batson *et al.* 1993). The way in which masculinity has been conceptualized in mainline religion may alienate some men. Psychologists have argued that men are expected to internalize sex-appropriate gender orientation and live with masculine expectations to avoid all things feminine, which includes being religious (Brannon 1976). Similarly, earlier sociological studies proposed than men's lesser religiousness was guided by the gendered division of labour. In short, that because men were to take on the provider role, they encountered a socialization track that placed them on a non-religious path (de Vaus and McAllister 1987). Participation in church activities was hence socially viewed as incongruent with workforce participation and men's everyday provider roles (Roof 1987). A later discussion exemplifying these traditions was offered by Miller and Hoffman (1995). Men's irreligiousness was defined as another type of masculine risk-taking behaviour and would seem to enforce the above-mentioned speculation of Rodney Stark, since the blueprint of a traditional masculinity is one which urges men to avoid 'sissy stuff' and 'give 'em hell' when necessary.

Another part of the picture of religiosity is that boys are much less likely to follow in their parents' footsteps. Girls are generally brought up to be more conformist than boys. As Nelson points out, young females tend to have closer contact with their mothers, are encouraged to be obedient and to exhibit responsibility, while boys are allowed greater autonomy. Given that in Western society religious participation and responsibility for religious nurture tend to be associated with women, rather than men, attempts to inspire religious participation in their offspring are inclined to be somewhat biased towards girls. This helps produce what is referred to by Nelson as 'a basic discontinuity in the familial transmission of religiosity' (Nelson 1981: 639), making male children much more likely to drop out of church. The situation is, however, rather more complicated than this simple depiction implies. Nelson suggests that later-born children, especially males, tend to be more influenced by their peers and less by their parents. Thus 'birth order' has some impact on the transmission of religion to children.

Kay and Francis's (1996: 4) assessment of research into sex differences leads them to conclude that a psychological account should be preferred to a sociological one, in particular that men are alienated by religion because it is interpreted as feminine and this is reflected in the decline in the proportion of men in the mainstream Christian churches. Despite such evidence, there is some indication that gender is of less and less significance in influencing levels and expressions of religiosity.

Thompson and Remmes (2002) found that some males are now increasingly prepared to break through the constraints of traditional masculinity and are beginning spiritual quests in earnest. They report that previous work, especially based in the USA, has shown a significant relationship between gender outlook and being religious in samples of college-age and adult men. In essence, before entering later life, men who question traditional masculine roles display greater religious involvement than other men.

It is hard, despite such evidence, to discern whether the feminized, so-called 'New Man' is widespread or what his religious preferences are: whether they are traditional or new forms (a theme further discussed in an overview of the new spiritualities in Chapter 9). There are other speculations too. Levitt (2003) anticipates that the patterns of church attendance could alter if women's roles at home changed to match their increased participation in the workforce, leading to a decline in church attendance. The implication is that women increasingly have an economic role, and the socialization of boys and girls will be more similar than in the past. Hertel (1995) anticipates that women who work full-time are less religiously active than those who do not. This will have consequences given that more and more women are entering the workforce. The reason is not so much time and involvement, in that women who spend more time at home and with children are more likely to identify with church life, but that many churches idealize traditional family life. The churches – the supply side – then, may be out of line with what religious consumers desire.

CLASS

In the past a great deal of sociological ink has been spilt on the link between religion and social class, and rightly so. In Europe, post-Reformation, historical evidence shows that the fragmentation of a religious culture was often along class and localized fissures and, in each location and period, sects and denominations tended to have a distinctive social identity which not uncommonly displayed the social standing or dilemmas of their membership. Empirical evidence from the early studies substantiated this in terms of sect development. Most of the innovating work evidenced a direct causal link between the type of religion and something intrinsic about the group. Indeed, examples

more than hint that the oppressed and disinherited are attracted by mil-
lenarianism, emotionalism and orthodoxy, or that sects provide compensators for a range of shared deficiencies. Even recent writings of the
rational choice school, such as that of Stark and Finke, suggest sectarian
groups 'are remarkably heterogeneous in terms of social status' (Stark
and Finke 2000: 198).

In understanding the significance of class we may range wider. Roof
and McKinney's (1985) research in the USA showed class profile to be
relative to other variables. For example, evangelical Protestantism may
be seen as a sectarian religious tradition with a constituency which has
lower educational attainment, less wealth and greater rural and southern
residence. Additionally, evangelical adherents are more likely to be old,
female, married and have higher birth rates (Hunter 1983). None the
less, more contemporary evidence has challenged this link between forms
of deprivation and sectarianism. Using a strategy of self-identification
with specific religious traditions, Smith *et al.* argue that evangelical
Protestants are not disproportionately poor, nor particularly uneducated,
rural, female or old (Smith *et al.* 1998).

Park and Reimer (2002) attempt to explain these recent discernible
changes. Class and regional differences are declining, while the characteristics which distinguished the sect-like from the church-like, namely
lower class and southern rural residence, are slowly converging with the
other major church traditions in the USA. However, black
Pentecostalism is the most demographically distanced on gender distribution, marriage and birth rates. Given these patterns, the classical theories which link certain religious groups to demographic characteristics
must be brought into question, with the variable of ethnicity now out-
weighing class and additional demographic factors.

Other studies suggest that those of different social classes express
their beliefs as well as institutional belonging in different ways. In the
USA, a series of studies have found that even in a more 'religious' society the lower classes were less likely to attend church, more likely to
pray in private, to believe in the doctrines of their faith, and to have
intense religious experiences (Demerath 1965). There is also a discernible difference in the kind of church attended as evidenced in the
USA with, for example, Episcopalians tending to be better off than
Baptists (Gallop and Castelli 1989: 103, 110). Even within the
Christian faith different social classes appear to be attracted to different

variations of the faith – those which are congruent with their status and worldviews. For example, upwardly mobile people may seek more liberal variants which stress equality of opportunity and social issues. Alternatively, more conservative forms of religion might be supported by those who have a stake in society as it is – a reactionary or fundamentalist constituency with a fear of losing status; while those at the bottom of the social order and alienated from it might seek sectarian forms as a source of compensation (Schoenfeld 1992).

Outside of the Christian churches, it is clear that the middle classes are the carriers of the new therapeutic-oriented religions. The New Age, for example, is for the most part open to those who have sufficient time and means to pay for a narcissistic journey of self-discovery. Hence, it is specifically appealing to the university-educated middle classes working in the 'expressive' professions: social workers, counsellors, writers and artists – the bottom layer of the privileged classes. By contrast, less educated lower-class people, particularly from poorer rural areas, are unlikely to be interested, although arguably they may be equally attracted to occultist practices and superstition. The evidence is, however, complicated. Occultist practitioners have been found to have a wide range of occupational backgrounds (McHugh and Swain 1999), but although pagans have been discovered to be more highly educated, with some two-thirds claiming a college degree, they did not enjoy particularly high incomes. Research also shows that better educated people are less likely to believe in ghosts, astrology and reincarnation, but that they are more likely to believe in telepathy, ESP and *déjà vu* (Kirkpatrick *et al.* 1986).

SUMMARY

In Western societies there has long been a relationship between demographics and adherence to certain religious traditions since they were first observed in Niebuhr's *Social Sources of Denominationalism* (1957). Niebuhr demonstrated that certain sect-like denominations drew constituents from lower classes and immigrant groups, while church-like denominations were derived from the upper classes. One aspect of this approach was to establish a colour line within American Christianity. Since Niebuhr, research has emphasized both the stability of the demographic characteristics of certain religious groups and their changing contours (Greeley 1975; Lensky 1961; Roof and McKinney 1987). However, much of the recent evidence explored above indicates a slow convergence on certain demographics highlighted by age, class, gender, as well as marital status and number of children per family.

This is certainly so with forms of Christianity. Contrary to previous research, evangelical Protestantism is not now very distinct demographically speaking, at least in the USA. The only aspect which remains is black Protestantism, and this marks the continuing importance of ethnicity. Using data from the General Social Surveys from 1972 to 1998, Park and Reimer (2002) considered recent developments. They found that, among Christian traditions, slow convergence is occurring with those demographics that have been historically viewed as distinguishing religious groups. Other demographic characteristics such as age, gender, marriage and birth rate are slowly diverging among the major Christian traditions. Similarly, Roof and McKinney (1987: 145) suggest that the demographic distinctions between denominations are weakening. Increased social status of many groups, changing socio-religious boundaries, and greater voluntarism have broken down earlier denominational divisions. At the same time, it has become less fashionable to speak of social class as a useful category. Rather, lifestyle and consumer preferences are said to be dependent on income and wealth in an infinitely fragmented culture which drives the dynamics of the spiritual marketplace.

How might we conclude? Park and Reimer's findings regarding the USA are speculatively relevant to other Western societies. Globalizing forces weaken the effect of some demographic distinction, and to a limited extent have homogenized a large part of the American population. The increase in transience and mobility, the spread and availability of information technology, the ubiquity of the mass media, the increasing availability and participation in higher education, and greater ethnic and religious pluralism, all these tend to erode previous group demographic characteristics. The ethnic link, however, continues and can be ascribed to the isolation of African-Americans in self-contained realms of poverty that are fairly removed from the globalizing forces which have brought homogenization to the predominantly white religious traditions (Park and Reimer 2002: 442–3). As much may be said of a number of other enthic minority groupings.

6

FROM 'CHURCH' TO 'CHOICE'

TRANSFORMATIONS IN CONTEMPORARY CHRISTIANITY

THE POST-CHRISTIAN SOCIETY

The decline in historical Christianity in Western societies is discernibly a central discussion of both modernist and postmodernist accounts of developments in the religious sphere. In the renditioning of the former, the secularization thesis, rooted in modernity, frequently meant that when many sociologists referred to secularization as 'the decline of religion', they largely had in mind the fate of the Christian faith. Postmodernist writings also observe this decline but tend to account for it in terms of the fragmentation of culture and the eclipse of all-embracing mega-narratives.

From the modernist viewpoint there was a time when it was possible to speak of the 'Christian society'. Over previous centuries Christianity provided important political, educational and social functions, and claimed, nominally at least, the allegiance of a great mass of the population. Many people 'went to church' as the foundation of religious and social affiliation. Village and small-town life was often dominated by the local church which, in many instances, was situated, geographically speaking, at the centre of community life. Infants were baptized there, while the inscriptions on the graves in the churchyard were a constant reminder of those who had 'passed on' into 'the Lord's keeping'. Today, however, much has changed, and this is demonstrated by the decline of the Christian Sabbath. Sunday is no longer 'the Lord's Day'. The demands of the consumer, not just large capitalist concerns, have ensured that it is a day like most others: people may go to work and most certainly will engage in aspects of consumption and leisure. Now, even Christians undertake shopping on the day of rest without too many scruples.

The postmodernist account of the health of contemporary Christianity has not departed significantly from many of the earlier 'hard' secularization depictions of the decline of the faith, although there is a greater emphasis on its relation to cultural change than the modernist concern with functional marginalization that grows out of the inescapable processes of social differentiation. The orientation of the former is exemplified by Jean Baudrillard's pronouncement that 'God has departed' (Baudrillard 1990: 6). This God is the Christian God that was once the centre of the European world and provided the historical grounding and symbols of several centuries, marking a distinct culture for the ruled and their rulers. God has departed from the foundations of a civilization and everyday life since Christianity has been challenged by pluralism, relativism, choice and the vagaries of the spiritual marketplace.

That the post-Christian society has indeed arrived in earnest is not just the claim of the sociological fraternity. Many church leaders and theologians have been seduced by the postmodernist paradigm in identifying the decline of Christianity. For instance, Don Cupitt (1998), the liberal theologian, maintains that Western culture is no longer identified by the conviction that progress is inevitable, and the optimistic view of history that once characterized modernity no longer prevails. Thus a cultural acceptance of the 'truths' and future promise of Christianity become a casualty of the general disappearance of meganarratives. Thus, too, the progressive views of the world shared by the Christian faith and secular ideologies, converging on the notion of progress, have suffered a terminal decline.

Indices of decline

Signs of a progressive decline in ritual aspects of Christianity such as baptisms and church weddings, as already noted, are evident in many Western societies. Church attendance and affiliation are, however, perhaps the most important measurement of participation, although attendance varies considerably from one country to another. In some Scandinavian nations, such as Sweden, the proportion of those attending church on a Sunday may be as low as 5 per cent. The statistics in the UK are slightly higher at closer to 7 per cent, while church attendance remains impressive in Northern Ireland (nearing 50 per cent) for largely historical reasons. In Holland, according to the latest European Values Survey, the percentage of people who are not affiliated with one of the Christian churches increased from 24 per cent in 1958 to about 60 per cent in 2002. As a result, in 1999, only 18 per cent of the Dutch population considered itself Roman Catholic, and only 15 per cent claimed affiliation with either of the two principal Protestant churches in the Netherlands (8 per cent Dutch Reformed and 7 per cent Neo-Calvinist).

Analysts have spoken of the 'unchurching of Europe' as practically equalling secularization (Ashford and Timms 1992), yet in many countries the decline of Christianity has not been a straightforward or equal one, with the Catholic faith in countries such as Spain and Italy fighting a more rigorous battle against the ravages of modernity than Protestantism. This unequal development questioned some modernist accounts regarding structural differentiation. The problem was that differentiation as a universal process in industrialized countries proved not to be evenly spread across North America and Western Europe. From the nineteenth century, in particular, it appeared to be the case that Protestant countries were secularizing far more speedily than Catholic ones.

The 1999 European Values survey indicated that, from a denominational point of view, it is possible to classify the different countries into three groups: Catholic, Protestant and 'mixed' (Lambert 1996). If these countries are arranged according to the level of Christian religiosity, almost the same patterns emerge: Catholic countries, such as Ireland, Italy and Spain, are more religious than the 'mixed' variant such as Germany, UK and the Netherlands. Finally come the predominant Protestant (Lutheran) countries of Finland, Denmark and Sweden (Lambert 2004).

In recent history, Catholicism viewed the modern world with much more suspicion and, as a result, managed to keep up its cognitive defences against modernity more effectively and until a more recent date. Throughout the nineteenth and early twentieth centuries there was no Catholic counterpart to Protestant liberalism. Vatican II marked an attempt to come to terms with the modern world, or at least reinterpret and restate Catholic beliefs. Peter Berger predicted that this was the 'opening of the dykes' (Berger 1970: 26–31): it constituted the slippery slope to accommodation and compromise. As a result of inward change and external pressures in many European countries, the Catholic monopoly has been broken at different levels. In Catholic nations such as Spain and Italy the political power of the Church, especially in terms of political institutions, has been undermined, while church attendance in these nations and other Catholic ones continues to decline. The fact that in some such countries the birth rates are among the lowest in Europe suggests the Papal ruling on the use of contraceptives is being largely ignored by the Catholic population. In many respects, then, the Catholic countries of Europe are moving towards the model of the secular state and culture of those nations once identified as 'Protestant'. Moreover, while the Catholic Church may uphold its traditional norms, among young Catholics individual conscience has displaced external authority in the matter of social and personal ethics. Such developments do not necessarily uphold the 'hard' secularization thesis, but at the very least they indicate the on-going decline of religion in the broad social sphere as part of a continuing process of differentiation and, beyond that, a further reduction of religion to the individual and privatized realm.

US exclusivism

Outside of these developments in Europe, the fate of the Christian faith in the USA appears to be an anomaly of considerable proportions. The country of high church attendance, the phenomenon of the 'Bible belt', and a politicized form of fundamentalism, would seem to resist the more simplified secularization thesis. Yet the USA was always different as a result of a separation of religion and state, an emphasis on religious liberties, where the denomination was the institutionalized basis of Christian life, and where a civil religion created myths borrowed from the major tenets of the Judaeo–Christian tradition.

Rational choice theorists have explained these developments in terms of identifying a vibrant spiritual marketplace in the USA, and in doing so have by-passed the secularization thesis altogether. Hence, Finke (1992) points out that the evidence of church attendance during the nineteenth century in the USA, at the very time it was modernizing, suggests it does not fit into the secularization paradigm. Furthermore, those churches which are now growing are the more conservative ones. The difference is the lack of religious regulation. A similar conclusion is reached by Stark and Iannaccone (1994), who explain that the USA was always unimpeded by an established state (monopoly) religion, in contrast with the case of the Anglican church in England and the Roman Catholic church elsewhere. The USA permitted a level playing-field for religious groups to compete, and hence it has always generated a greater degree of religious activity. From this perspective, the USA may be seen as historically engendering a religious supermarket where relatively low levels of regulation allow religious pluralism to flourish.

The reality, however, is that in the USA there may be considerable religious over-reporting across various indices (Demerath 2000). Certainly, if the claim of a greater religiosity is largely based on participation through church attendance and membership, then the statistics are very much open to interpretation. However, while there are undoubtedly difficulties of interpretation, these are probably no greater for religious data than for any other subjects when it comes to historical accounts. As far as the situation today is concerned, areas of apparent unreliability can also be checked. For instance, the Catholic Church issues annual attendance rates which may be set against total community size and thus confirmed by way of their true level of accuracy.

According to survey statistics published in 1987 by Roof and McKinney, 46 per cent of the American population attended church at least once a week, while a further 21 per cent were occasional attendees. Although this still marks a decline from the 61 per cent supposedly attending in the late 1950s (according to the *Yearbook of American Churches* for 1957), Hadaway *et al.* (1993) argue there is much to suggest that such statistics are misleading. This is not because of the way they are calculated but the way they are collected. The attendance figures among Roman Catholic and Protestant churches may be only 50 per cent of what they are commonly held to be. This is largely because of the way people exaggerate their frequency of church-going, leading to statistics notably higher than those recorded by church organizations.

If Hadaway *et al.* are correct, then this is further evidence that church attendance in the USA may be closer to the figures displayed in some European countries. As far as Christian belief is concerned, there remains evidence to suggest that the major tenets of the faith are weakening. There is indication of this even in Roof and McKinney's 1987 account, where they record 7 per cent of the American population claiming no religious preference, and in an earlier work of theirs in which they record an increase in the percentage of the population who indicate a faith outside of the three main traditions from 1 to 9 per cent (Roof and McKinney 1985). Other evidence in the USA shows some signs of religious weakening. According to the 1991 and 1998 ISSP surveys the USA is moving slowly towards the long-term developments found in Western Europe.

American views of religion may also be changing from one where opinion polls show some 75 per cent of the USA 'believe in God', to weaker occultist beliefs. Rice's nationwide random-sample survey of the general US population suggests that millions of Americans are doubters when it comes to traditional Christian paranormal dogma, but have no problem believing in 'classic' paranormal phenomena. At the same time, roughly 90 per cent of the respondents provided evidence of believing in at least one of the two types of paranormal phenomena, leaving very few sceptics. None the less, Rice points out that opinion polls show people have not lost their faith in science, and thus they accord science and the paranormal their own separate realms (Rice 2003: 104).

Another part of the equation is that the meaning and significance behind the act of church-going in the USA may have little to do with levels of religiosity or the felt need to express collective devotion. Church attendance may have historically been associated with 'belonging' in a very broad sense, as explored in Herberg's (1956) seminal work. In short, Herberg argued that in the USA, from an early stage in the nation's development, religious affiliation had more to do with belonging to Protestant, Catholic or Jewish communities, and it enhanced a feeling of what it was to be 'American'. This may still be the case, although measuring the motivation for church attendance remains an arduous task. In Europe, by contrast, church membership is far less likely to denote membership of the community, adherence to the values of society and nation or markers of social belonging (Wilson 1966, 1982). Perhaps equally valid is Berger's contention that Christian church-going, American-style, amounts to a search for respectability. Writing in the late 1960s, after a decade of increasing adult church attendance, Berger maintained that this was more out of the citizen's desire for moral instruction for their children and the direction of family life, or just because it is part of the lifestyle of their particular neighbourhood (Berger 1970: 17). Thus, in the mid-twentieth century at least, this brought the USA closer to nineteenth-century England where church attendance may have had much do with social convention and respectability.

The orientation of at least the mainstream churches must also be taken into account when considering higher levels of Christian allegiance, USA-style. In the late 1960s Luckmann argued that in the USA many of the churches had been subject to an 'internal secularization'. In short, they had become this-worldly in their orientation, rather than focusing on the fundamentals of the faith with their emphasis on directing belief and practice towards the next life (Luckmann 1967: 36). The difference between European and American patterns was aptly characterized by Luckmann as that between, respectively, 'secularization from without' and 'secularization from within'. Hence the apparent high level of religiosity in the USA, at least in terms of the number of churches and historically high levels of church attendance, may plausibly be explained by its world-accommodating nature and by conformity to American culture. Indeed, this may well have been a long-term development. Yet there has apparently been a reaction to these tendencies, one, as observed below, primarily reflected in the growth of conservative churches.

Pick 'n' mix Christianity

It may well be that in the larger picture of secularization, the global context, it is Europe which is the exception, not the USA. Peter Berger has recently underlined what he terms the 'European exception' by way of religious, specifically Christian, decline in contrast to the rest of the world (Berger 1999). An alternative view is that, given some measure of evidence, Europe is moving closer to the USA in terms of beliefs, and a convergence is perhaps taking place. Despite church attendance decline there may exist a widespread belief in the basic tenets of the faith, which is important at the individual, personalized, albeit generalized level – a Christian belief without belonging. The 1981 and 1990 European Values surveys largely supported the earlier evidence of an increasing secularization of Western Europe. Almost all the variables showed a retreat from historical Christianity which was even deeper among young people. However, in the last European Values survey of 1999 there appeared to be some significant changes. The downward trend is now counterbalanced by the development of a seemingly greater religiosity without belonging, especially among young people.

The EVS on several occasions has more than hinted that in Europe conventional Christianity is being undermined by people's selective adherence to Christian beliefs, and these may be supplemented by non-Christian ones in a kind of pick 'n' mix way, one which shows belief increasingly being uncoupled from a conventional system of morality and teachings of divine punishment, alongside more ambiguous conceptions of God (Gerard 1985; Harding *et al.* 1986; Cook 2000). The 1999 survey showed that, across countries of different religious traditions, two indices (along with after-life beliefs) were on the rise: that churches bring answers 'to the spiritual needs of individuals' (from 44 per cent to 52 per cent); and that there is a 'personal God' (30 per cent to 38 per cent).

On the decrease were self-appraisals related to being a 'religious person'; feelings that 'religion brings strength and comfort'; a sense of belonging to a religion (from 85 per cent to 75 per cent); global belief in God (from 74 per cent to 68 per cent); and belief in sin (57 per cent to 47 per cent). Admittedly, the rates of change in all these indices have slowed down from 1990 to 1999, except in the case of belief in sin – a sign of the decrease in the feeling of religious guilt. Moreover, the EVS conducted between the 1980s and 2000 indicate that under 33 per cent of Europeans believed in the 'personal God' associated with Christianity. While 40 per cent believed in heaven, only 23 per cent believed in a hell as conventionally taught in the churches. Around 50 per cent claimed that God was significant in their lives. Again, there were variations. In Sweden, perhaps the most secular country in Europe, only around 7 per cent professed to be 'confessing Christians' (Sjodin 2002). All such statistics, of course, are open to interpretation. Not least of all, what is meant by 'significant' or 'confessing' and the problem of how can such claims be measured. The signs of the decline in conventional Christian beliefs are none the less evident.

Perhaps most indicative of change has been the area of after-life beliefs. The EVS of 1981 and 1990 asked respondents whether they believed in life after death, and found those answering 'yes' constituted around 40 per cent of the sample: this figure had changed little over the decades. However, the surveys also contained more specific questions about what the after-life was supposed actually to entail. For example, it showed that, whereas belief in heaven remained fairly buoyant (at around 30–50 per cent), belief in hell had definitely gone out of fashion.

Lambert (2004), in a discussion of the most recent EVS, argues that the development of this autonomous and diffused religiosity in Europe is apparent and illustrated mainly through variables which are less typically

Christian, such as 'taking a moment of prayer, meditation, contemplation or something like that' (54 per cent of the 'religion-less' Dutch); belief in 'a life after death' which included belief in reincarnation; belief in God as 'some sort of spirit or life force'; and being led to 'explore different religious traditions' rather than 'stick to a particular faith'. These variables need to be partially distinguished from the more specifically Christian ones, like 'a personal God' or 'confidence in the church'. Also, belief in 'life after death' or in a 'Higher Power' is to be partially distinguished from specifically Christian beliefs. These accounts suggest a level of New Age sensibility in the wider sense of the term. Many of the recent EVS respondents preferred to talk about spirituality rather than religion when defining themselves. A fair few respondents also believed in what may be termed 'parallel beliefs' (astrology, divination, lucky charms and telepathy), although these beliefs are also shared by many Christians, especially those who practise less.

Lambert concludes that, in contrast to the rather homogeneous evolution which was observable until the 1980s, the situation now is one of more and more diversity according to country. However, the general pattern is still of decline in conventional Christian beliefs. While this was observable in all the nine countries surveyed, they can be found in different proportions, with some indication of resurgence in others. Lambert concludes that Europe still has less religious activity than most parts of the Christian world. However, the new tendencies seem to tone down the exceptionalism thesis. Europe is experiencing a distinctive and significant mutation. To some extent, suggests Lambert, this marks a de-sacrilization, but only at the level of individuals, the level at which surveys operate.

INSTITUTIONAL TRANSFORMATION

At the same time that Christendom has experienced decline in terms of church attendance and decline or dilution of conventional beliefs, most quarters have also been subject to institutional change of not inconsiderable significance. Many of these changes bring Christianity in line with the demands of the spiritual marketplace, although other processes are also discernible which mark a departure from earlier forms of institutional representation.

The last 200 years have seen the gradual evolution of churches and sects into denominations as the most common form of Christian organization, especially in the USA. In turn, such forms have also experienced a long-term decline. The pertinent explanation for this initial expansion of denominationalism is that it often seemed designed to dovetail with the pluralist nature of modernity and marked an expression of the religious needs of particular social groups (Wilson 1976). Baptists, Methodists, Congregationalists, and many more besides, increasingly came to represent the mainstream of Christianity and were characterized by free and voluntary member-ship, and a less centralized hierarchy than the church, and were void of a claim to embrace a monopoly of the 'truth' (Roof and McKinney 1987). This slow transformation of Christianity from church to denomination in most Western societies, however, marked more than a response to the growth of cultural pluralism. It also indicated the decline of the social power of Christianity, at least in relation to the separation of Church and state, even if the process has varied consider-ably in tempo from one country to another.

In the latter half of the twentieth century certain developments, such as the charismatic renewal movement, appeared to strengthen denominational allegiance. However, the great majority of denomina-tions have experienced membership decline, while the boundaries between them have broken down and their world-accommodating inclinations have become more discernible. Denominations were once typically bureaucratic organizations sometimes linked to occupational or cultural groups, and they provided a guide to ethnic belonging or class identification over generations. Today, it is increasingly common for people to leave behind their family allegiances and theological preferences and change denomination at will as part of an apparent spiritual voyaging.

It may well be the case that in the spiritual marketplace, as Ammerman and Roof (1995: 5) argue, greater choice need not under-mine religious loyalties. Indeed, it can actually enhance clarity of com-mitment. As a result of increased choice, parishes and congregations may take on distinctive identities as they come to reflect the preferences of their members. Denominational labels, then, may mean less in iden-tifying a church than the particular worship styles, programmes and mission activities created by those who have chosen it. On the other hand, there may be problems with the denominational supply side, especially where churches do not meet the demands of 'customers'. In this respect, Marler (1995) maintains that in the USA many Protestant churches have not moved with the times. In particular, they remain wedded to nostalgia for a traditional family structure which is no longer socially dominant. Marler documents that churches are getting their 'market share' of traditional families and older singles, but are losing younger singles and other non-traditional households. 'Other family' and 'non-family' are two of the fastest-growing household types in the USA, but are under-represented in church memberships.

While denominational structures constituted the institutional norm of Christianity in modernity, in the contemporary setting it is progressively difficult to delimit what falls under the remit of 'mainstream Christianity', given many of the changes that denominations have undergone in organizational, cultural and theological terms. Indeed, changes in institutionalized Christianity over recent decades have brought into question not only long-standing sociological typologies of religious organization but also their relevance to contemporary religiosity. Such changes have a bearing on notions of a spiritual marketplace. The institutional and organized expressions of Christianity constitute its supply side. However, this organizational basis is undergoing transformation and even disintegration. These organizational changes, while displaying a certain flexibility, are indicative of a response of Christianity to new socio-cultural conditions, and they also mark an accommodation to the world not, as in the past, to the political status quo but to the demands of choice and commodification at the individual level and strategies for survival in the spiritual marketplace.

Although established Christian churches and organizations may still be designated 'mainstream religions', it is less and less realistic to argue that they have a monopoly of religious life. Indeed, the institutional basis of religious life may have irreversibly declined. Alongside the reduction of church attendance and membership there has been a general decline in and increasing fragmentation of traditional Christian institutions. While a widespread 'belief without belonging' has yet to be forcefully demonstrated, there is little doubting that the institutional arrangement in which Christianity has been expressed, and belief and practice organized, has changed considerably, and these developments may be tied up with some of the major characteristics of contemporary culture, dynamics which have perhaps allowed particular forms of Christianity to stave off some aspects of decline.

The conservative constituency

There are implications here for stricter forms of Christianity, including the typology of the sect. At one extreme the sectarian option maintained, for some two centuries, a supernaturalist position in the teeth of a cognitively antagonistic world which would only be possible in a counter-community with considerable strength and sense of solidarity. The problem with sectarianism, however, as Berger observed, is that the circumstances that began the sect are not likely to recur (Berger 1970: 32–3). Social mobility and worldly integration would probably increase, not recede, over a protracted period of time. Neither, it might be added, is the spiritual marketplace the natural home of the sect. Yet, there appear to be a fair few sects that still flourish.

Many of those of the nineteenth century initially materialized in the USA and subsequently spread globally over the next 150 years. Some, such as Jehovah's Witnesses and the Church of Jesus Christ of Latter-day Saints (Mormons) continue to grow because they constitute what Bryan Wilson (1970) calls the 'adventist sect', those that are driven by eschatological longings to proselytization. There are now allegedly some 4 million Jehovah's Witnesses in over 200 countries across the world. In 1997 Mormons claimed to have nearly 10 million members with a little under half of them in the USA.

The view of rational choice theorists is that such sects arose to satisfy a religious demand in the nineteenth century and still have their attractions well over a century later. However, as Bruce (2001) relates, their relative growth has not replaced the membership lost to the more conventional churches. Bruce notes that the total membership of non-Trinitarian churches (Christadelphians, Christian Scientists, Mormons and Jehovah's Witnesses) has risen in the UK, for instance, from 71,000 in 1900 to 537,000 in 2000. The Mormons and Jehovah's Witnesses account for more than half such growth. Yet that figure amounts to only one sixth of that lost to the Trinitarian churches. Moreover, the reason why they may be at least holding their own in the spiritual marketplace may be more to do with proselytizing endeavours and retaining membership throughout the generations.

As much may be true of the conservative Trinitarian churches, although some literature sees their expansion as a notable aspect of a growing religious marketplace where the wares of conservative Christians have considerable attraction (Marty and Appleby 1992). Many accounts fall back on some of the observations made by Dean Kelley in his seminal work, *Why Conservative Churches Are Growing* (1972), which attributed the numerical growth of conservative churches, and the decline of more liberal denominations, to the fact that belonging to conservative churches 'costs something in money ... time, effort, anguish, involvement or sacrifice' (Kelley 1978: 168). Mainstream churches were declining because, Kelley claimed, they asked too little of their members. 'Strong organizations are strict ... the stricter the stronger' (Kelley 1972: 95). Kelley's findings have a relevance that extends beyond conservative churches. In fact his 1972 book's title, *Why Conservative Churches Are Growing*, is somewhat misleading. He later clarified its meaning, suggesting a more applicable title: *Why Strict Churches Are Strong* – whether 'liberal' or 'conservative' (Kelley 1978: 167). Growing churches, of whatever background, were, he claimed, 'serious' about their essential task and hence attractive to those seeking religious satisfaction.

It may well be that, in an affluent and materialistic society, there is still a need for strict faith and a supernatural view of the world. Thus conservative churches may fill some of the 'gaps' in the spiritual marketplace as the mainstream churches decline. However, Bruce claims that very little of the growth of the Trinitarian conservative churches can be explained by them attracting either disappointed long-term members of liberal or mainstream churches, or those with previously no faith at all. Bruce suggests this kind of church-switching is fairly minimal (Bruce 1995: 69). Thus the growth of conservative churches owes much to their success in retaining their own children within the church. Children raised in liberal churches, by contrast, are much more likely to go their own way and give up their church allegiance altogether. However, the evidence would suggest that Bruce is only partly correct. There is a growing tendency for a sizable number of people in the USA to move from liberal to more conservative churches if they do not drop out of church life altogether, although this may only occur after a time of prolonged searching in the more conservative constituency by those who may have begun in the liberal church sector (Mauss and Perrin 1992) – a variation of what Bibby calls the 'circulation of the saints' thesis (Bibby 1978).

Herieu-Leger (1986) has argued that successful churches use both strategies of accepting and resisting modernity in adequate measure. It is possible that this is the direction in which many so-called conservative churches are heading, with the effect, as Bruce (1996) notes, of producing a series of new schisms with congregations breaking away from what were once conservative organizations, with each turn of the wheel creating ever smaller sectarian forms.

Mauss and Perrin (1992) come to a similar conclusion to Herieu-Leger as a result of their survey of Vineyard churches – a successful (if now waning) confederation of charismatic congregations that are particularly attractive to middle-class people. The thrust of Mauss and Perrin's account results from a debate with the work of Kelley. They argue Kelley was broadly correct, in that 'seekers' in the spiritual marketplace are looking for 'the essential functions of religion', that is, 'making life meaningful in ultimate terms' (Kelley 1978: 166), but that he was wrong in that successful churches necessarily demand personal commitment and self-sacrifice through a change in lifestyle.

Kelley insisted that conservative religion makes demands on members in terms of belief and commitment. Many conservative churches, according to Mauss and Perrin (1992), offer a convincing belief system, a sense of being caught up in a successful movement of revival, but are not strict about lifestyles or commitment. There are the additional attractions of emotional healing, contemporary music and a middle-class cultural milieu which allows the opportunity for like to be with like. In short, middle-class people will be attracted to churches with members of a similar background to themselves. If Mauss and Perrin are correct, then successful churches are often world-accommodating and open-minded, and do not demand a great deal of conformity. Moreover, on many issues their theology cannot easily be distinguished from alternative secular ideas. Miller (1997) substantiates this tendency. What he designates as 'New Paradigm Churches' – his description of the independent, so-called 'mega-churches' and 'post-denominational churches' – combine a biblical literalism with a more self-centred spirituality. The attraction of those such as Vineyard, as well as Calvary Chapel and Hope Chapel in the USA, is the emphasis on personal conviction, spiritual experience and variations of 'Christianized' therapeutic techniques. Miller believes that these new churches, while offering a satisfying spirituality, help people feel 'comfortable' with church life. Indeed, there are success stories with the 16,000-strong Willow Creek Community church in Chicago which, with its annual revenue of millions of dollars, signifies the high-technology mega-churches and their embrace of some aspects of American culture. The church holds four weekend services plus a midweek service for 6,000 people, and has shopping malls for the convenience of its worshippers. The church appeals mostly to a younger generation and holds seminars to teach other churches how to market themselves effectively. For an increasing number of churches in the USA, this constitutes conservative Christianity in the religious marketplace. Others remain more dogmatically 'fundamentalist' in orientation, a declining if still vibrant constituency which sets its face against the new incursions of world accommodation.

New forms of organization

Stackhouse (1994) conjectures that new kinds of religious connectedness are emerging which have transformed Christian denominational allegiances. The tendency is now more towards loose affiliations and networks rather than specific identifiable settings. This weakened affiliation may be found within mainstream denominations, but is also integral to new charismatic-oriented groups and fellowships. Stackhouse points out that old categories simply do not work any more in response to wider socio-cultural change. Hence, many of the new emerging Christian collectives fit only loosely into old typologies: they are best thought of as 'sectish' or 'churchish' but not in the style of 'sects' or 'church'.

Another fairly recent development is the proliferation of the totally independent church which has no, or few, associations outside of its own geographical context (although such churches did flourish for a period during the nineteenth century). These churches are now the fastest-growing segment of Christianity in both many Western countries and the developing world. They constitute, in the case of the UK, some 14 per cent of all Christian churches (Brierley 1991). Frequently included in their titles are the designations 'Community Church', 'Family Church' or 'Christian Fellowship'. They tend to be commonly of a charismatic persuasion. In the USA, there are somewhere in the region of 60,000 such independent charismatic churches. Many have established networks with others so that they constitute loose, overlapping ministerial associations without the bureaucratic encumbrances of traditional churches and denominations. The Vineyard church alone (which has origins in the Jesus Movement of the late 1960s), based in Anaheim, California, claims over 280 local assemblies.

There are other alternative expressions of Christianity appearing, now that the mainline denominations seem to be in fatal decline, but these are also in stark contrast to the 'mega' churches and ministries. In other contexts the iconic and the communal, the temporary and the flexible, may be sought within non-traditional settings and with no institutional basis at all – for instance, those churches which meet in bars or other informal environments. Sometimes embraced by varieties of evangelism, it is an expression of Christianity which is suspicious of bureaucracy and hierarchy, one which stresses the spiritual dimension of everyday life rather than institutional belonging. Hence, like other forms of religion, contemporary Christianity may be losing its organizational significance and is now focusing around limited objectives such as educational alternatives or relief programmes, or what Wuthnow (1994) calls 'moral communities' or 'networks of mutual obligation and shared beliefs'.

The preference for these non-institutional settings has partly resulted from internal critiques of organized Christianity, including the conservative sector. Dave Tomlinson's much celebrated (in some circles, at least) work, *The Post-Evangelical* (1995), is critical of an authoritarian style of Christianity, a form which has proved effective in bringing people to faith, but which finds it difficult in helping them progress. It is an environment that is dogmatic, and with high expectations of conformity in thought and behaviour. Tomlinson argues that authoritarianism does not sit well with postmodernity. The relativizing of Christian faith and other grand narratives is difficult to reconcile with a claimed monopoly of the truth. Religious seekers are suspicious of pre-packaged grand theological schemes. Postmodern post-evangelicals are not impressed, Tomlinson claims, by the 'personality jostling, political maneuverings, and empire-building' of 'bigger', 'better' and 'more powerful' churches (Tomlinson 1995: 144–5). Rather, post-evangelical Christians long for a fresh sense of spirituality and are turning to the more symbolic and contemplative traditions of Christianity or, in the case of Tomlinson's own practical mission, the 'alternative church' of Holy Joe's which meets each night in a London bar, where there are no sermons or hymns and where the assembled gathering decides what it is going to discuss.

The breakdown of traditional Christian institutions also has to be seen in terms of the lifestyle and choice that contemporary society would seem to offer. The postmodernists are probably correct in their argument that tracing individual paths of biographical identity construction may be achieved by looking at the practices which are adopted to make sense of life. In the everyday context people bring together their ethnic and religious backgrounds, alongside their particular needs and interests at different times of their life. This is evident, says Ammerman (1997), in that Christian believers may use the services of a number of churches and religious organizations, without necessarily offering primary allegiance to any. Contemporary Christians, in line with non-Christian consumers, tend to choose to construct religious identity in an ongoing, dynamic way, from the different offerings now available.

'BEING RELEVANT': CHALLENGES TO CONTEMPORARY CHRISTIANITY

From the nineteenth century, in particular, the traditionalist–modernist division throughout Christianity was often observed via conservative–liberal theological disputes and sectarian schisms within the churches. For the liberal churchmen the issue was the very survival of the faith, especially with the separation of church and state in many Western European countries. To retain social, if not political influence, liberal Christianity endorsed a process of accommodation. Churchmen of this persuasion attempted to construct a faith 'relevant to modern man' in his everyday life. Once this meant issues of social reform, dealing with poverty and unemployment, advancing the cause of mass education and the establishment of a 'social gospel'. More recently, this has entailed taking up issues such as environmentalism, women's and gay rights, opposition to racism, the needs of ethnic minorities, and the negative consequences of globalization including Third World exploitation. Today, then, the liberal Christians cannot avoid certain key debates forced on them by the outside world, especially those related to political liberties.

Indicative of the liberal ideal has also been the cause of ecumenism, where churches of this disposition have sought each other out to find common ground and common cause. This might suggest the weaknesses of organized Christianity. As Bryan Wilson once contended (1966), in previous centuries Christianity held sway in the allegiance of the great bulk of Western societies, thus the churches and denominations could bicker over the often minute doctrinal and ecclesiastical differences which hitherto separated them. Under the challenges of modernity they were increasing forced to huddle together for protection. More recently, this has meant churches accepting the legitimacy of other Christian traditions, even exploring what other faiths and, in recent years, the attractions of the New Age have to offer.

The evidence regarding the impact and appeal of the liberal wing of Christianity is mixed. It may well be that the liberal cause is self-defeating and has few attractions beyond single-cause groups which campaign for social issues out of religious humanitarian conviction. In short, it has had the unintended consequence of alienating those in the churches. Sihvo (1988) presents evidence from Finland where many people deem that the Lutheran church has become too secularized. Thus, it fails to offer a rigorous set of beliefs, and has little to say about religious conviction and how people should lead their lives. As a result, those leaving the churches may adopt more fundamentalist forms of religion as an alternative to giving up religious faith altogether. On the other hand, evidence from elsewhere in Europe suggests that people may change churches or leave them altogether if they are perceived as too reactionary on social issues, often taking an uncompromising and authoritarian approach (Goddijn 1983). Indeed, despite the wealth of sociological works, particularly in America, indicating that the conservatives are seemingly thriving, there is a case for suggesting that liberal Christianity has carved out its own segment, albeit not a particularly large one, in the religious marketplace. At the very least, perhaps the liberal variant of Christianity should not be overestimated. Indeed, Peter Gee (1992) makes a case for suggesting that the liberal wing should not be written off and maintains that liberal beliefs and causes provide the basis of life for many churches in the UK and elsewhere, and the means by which those at the grass roots can become involved in the issues which impact their lives and communities on a global scale. However, Gee probably overstates the argument, and even the more vociferous single-cause groups within the liberal wing remain small and marginalized constituencies.

The proliferation of such groups as the Lesbian and Gay Christian Movement in the UK has arisen from the grass roots and parallels the secular gay movement. Here, the justification of a lifestyle, not just a sexual orientation, is based on a reinterpretation of scriptures – especially those which designate homosexuality as a 'sin'. The debate around the gay issue now constitutes probably the most controversial issue in many churches (Hunt 2002). In the UK there is a membership of around 2,000. Thus the LGCM is a cause group which cannot claim a great numerical strength despite establishing a niche in the spiritual marketplace. Gay movements within the churches are opposed by the conservatives, who cleave to their interpretation of the scriptures but are, none the less, forced to frame their cause in the secular language of 'rights' rather than moral absolutes; the right to safeguard the family or the right of Christians not to be offended.

While the liberal Christian cause may be relatively strong in Europe, its counterpart on the other side of the Atlantic rarely gets a mention. That America is a deeply religious conservative country may, however, again be brought into question. Adams's account of the reaction of conservatives to the issue of gay marriages includes the observation on the one hand that it constitutes a moral panic, which obscures the relatively small size of conservative numbers, and on the other, that liberal Christians (and not only Quakers and Unitarians) have been relatively well organized and successful. For instance, they have proved to be influential in the US Supreme Court in seeking equality for gays and lesbians (Adams 2002).

SUMMARY

At a broader level the pluralism, relativism and fragmentation of the cultural life of contemporary society have taken their toll on the grounding once given to Christian socialization. The USA should not be seen as an exception. The USA is often painted as a religious society, as being in some ways exclusive. However, Reiff (1995) refers to the Christian churches in the USA as a cognitive minority. For this minority, passing on the faith to the next generation is proving increasingly problematic compared to the past. Quoting Michael Warren (1987), Reiff suggests that children in the USA are bombarded with a plethora of images, ideas and alternative ways of life as they gaze through the 'enormous picture window' of popular culture. Extending the metaphor, Warren calls the influence of religious education a 'peephole' by comparison. The problem for Reiff is the ability of the Christian churches to establish a clear vision and role in the midst of the cultural complexities of a pluralist society.

In this pluralist context the marketing of the faith becomes an attraction. In the USA, such marketing is not new and may explain higher levels of participation. In his work *Selling God*, Moore (1994) demonstrates that, in America, religion, especially Protestantism, grew up with a commercial basis. It learned from an early stage to make strategic concessions to cultural developments, and has adapted itself well to contemporary conditions, satisfying many 'customers'. There is now a more intense market. To be sure, evidence from the USA suggests that some 'switchers' who move from one denomination to another frequently do so on the basis of spiritual and moral choice rather than for more cynical reasons (Warner 1993: 1077). However, there is no doubting the attraction of certain wares. In Canada, Bibby similarly describes an increasing movement from religious commitment to religious consumption (Bibby 1987). Churches display their wares, compete in the field of advertising and marketing, and allow their potential customers to browse among an ever more exotic array of religious possibilities. Not only is this marketable Christianity but it is often thoroughly world-accommodating. Attractions range from the razzmatazz of faith healers to the nostalgia of liturgical traditionalists. This tendency has been otherwise put by the theologian Henry Maier, who comments that while a personal relationship with God is sought, people want 'an easier, faster, no fuss, microwavable God', one where Jesus Christ comes dressed up in the clothes of their own culture (quoted in Lyon 2000: 136–7).

Some Christian segments of the spiritual marketplace can claim an element of success but in doing so have made major concessions to today's culture. Contemporary dress and music, state-of-the-art church buildings, alongside aspects of commercialization, now constitute what has rapidly become part of a Christian consumer subculture. Particularly successful are the mega-churches which increasingly inspire other Christian constituencies. In terms of marketability, it is also evident that many contemporary evangelical churches in the West have been transformed into what Harvey Cox calls 'designer churches' which wish to be judged by the speed of growth of their congregations, funds available, attractive buildings, prestigious leaders and other hallmarks of success reflecting the wider enterprise culture (Cox 1994: 272). Such churches have become increasingly world-accommodating, displaying a willingness to employ marketing techniques to evangelize and appeal to their members. Whether the glitz and glamour can provide a form of Christianity that will thrive over generations remains to be seen.

7

FAITHS OF CERTAINTY

FUNDAMENTALISM AND THE RELIGIONS
OF ETHNIC MINORITIES

THE AGE OF FUNDAMENTALISM?

On 11 September 2001, the world witnessed harrowing images of a terrorist attack on the twin towers of the World Trade Center building in New York. The scale of the horrifying event was portrayed in vivid instant pictures on the television sets of millions of viewers across the world. As a result of this gross act of violence several thousands died, while the pride of the USA, the world's foremost political and economic power, was gravely damaged. This man-made disaster had various repercussions: an impact on the global economy; war in Afghanistan wrought by the USA; and a warning to the West that not all of the world accepted the alleged virtues of the free market and Western-style secular democracy. The act was attributed to Bin Laden and his terrorist organization, Al Qaeda, an Islamic fundamentalist movement which proclaimed itself vehemently opposed to these core values and institutions.

The harm inflicted on the city of New York was matched by the undermining of the credibility of the Muslim community, whether fundamentalists or moderates, who explicitly wished to distance themselves from terrorist acts. At the same time, Muslim minorities in Western societies were forced to cope with instances of reprisal at worst, or ridicule and suspicion at least, as the public and the media began to generalize about an 'Islamic peril'. September 11 became a date to remember as the events etched themselves on the minds of ordinary people. A large number of political commentators claimed that the world would never be the same again. This may prove to be an exaggeration. None the less, at the very least, negotiating the possibility of terrorist attacks when engaging in international travel has become one of the 'risks' of contemporary life and a consequence of living in the emerging global order.

Not all fundamentalist terrorists who offer a threat to the West are 'external' foes. In May 1998, a radical right-wing Christian fundamentalist sect, calling itself The Militia, reduced the Federal Building in Oklahoma City to rubble in what was stated to be an act of revenge against the federal government. The conviction of The Militia was that the government, the gun control lobby, genetic mutations and UFO activity constitute part of a vast conspiracy to overthrow the United States constitution, undermine the nation's traditional way of life and establish a communist-style state. The Militia is believed to be one of dozens, or even hundreds, of such groups across the USA. While not condoning such terrorist acts, opinion polls suggest that tens of thousands of American citizens would subscribe to at least part of the political agenda of these factions, endorsing a right-wing ideology which, above all, condemns what is perceived as the growing power of federal government and its incursions into the lives of its citizens.

The movements described so far mark the violent and extreme edge of fundamentalism. However, the great majority of fundamentalists, whatever their religious persuasion, are not terrorists, nor for that matter are they necessarily extremists. Simplistic and sensationalist media coverage frequently equates fundamentalism with terrorism. This has the unfortunate consequence of obscuring the range and true significance of fundamentalism as both a religious and a socio-political phenomenon, since Christian and Islamic terrorist organizations are, in reality, merely polarized expressions of a distinct religious manifestation. Neither is fundamentalism something new and innovative, as the media also tend to portray it. Among the major world religions – whether Islamic, Christian, Judaic, Hindu or Sikh – fundamentalist movements, often designated by many other names, have periodically arisen throughout the centuries, commonly in response to unique socio-economic and political circumstances. It follows that their recent global appearance since the 1970s says something about a changing cultural and international order. Once these movements seemed to be simultaneously a product of and a response to modernity and its economic, political and social changes.

Now they are frequently deemed to be an intrinsic part of the contemporary world which has enhanced some of these features of modernity while bringing a new range of challenges to the realm of religion, subsequently touching the lives of millions across the world.

Clearly, 'fundamentalism' is not a neutral term and most fundamentalists receive 'bad press'. This is not merely because of the terrorist outrages conducted by the extremists – acts which most self-styled fundamentalist activists in the various faiths would condemn. Rather, public and government perceptions are those that focus upon perceived negative attributes of fundamentalism, namely religious bigotry, fanaticism and an anti-modernist outlook. By contrast, for some adherents at least, to be designated in this way may be a matter of pride. For others, 'fundamentalist' is just a term, indeed a label applied by the outside world to those who would earnestly seek to uphold the beliefs and practices of their faith as they see fit.

'Fundamentalism', then, is a slippery concept and, if manifest in religious movements, a complex phenomenon. It can enshrine ethnic and national aspirations, initiate moral and political campaigns, and, at the same time, offer a stringent set of beliefs and a way of life to individuals in a world of uncertainty. In the West, fundamentalism has for over a century frequently expressed itself as a social movement focusing on moral and political issues. The scale, if not the impact, of some of these campaigns in recent years initially took the sociological world by surprise and seemingly challenged the view that religion was becoming increasingly marginalized and withdrawn from the political arena. This was witnessed in acrimonious disputes, especially in the USA, related to such controversies as abortion, the teaching of religion in public schools, and the mixing of politics with religion in many areas of civil life. Christian fundamentalism, therefore, continues to impact upon the political scene and constitutes a way of life for hundreds of thousands people. In Europe, by contrast, cultural and historical factors have rendered fundamentalism, certainly in its Christian variety, less potent. None the less, a fair number of ethnic minorities in countries such as the UK, France and Germany contain constituencies where religious fundamentalism has frequently arisen as a response to local and global events. For some, in the context of diaspora, it constitutes part of everyday life and experience. Fundamentalism in its various manifestations thus merits a consideration in some depth and an attempt at balanced appraisal.

Fundamentalism defined

'Fundamentalism', as already noted, is not an easy term to come to grips with by way of definition. To a degree, contrasting designations are intrinsically linked to sociological explanations as to their historical manifestations. Earlier academic writings preferred a narrow definition and located fundamentalism within the conservative Protestant tradition. This is perhaps understandable given that Christianity was the first religion compelled to respond to the challenges of modernity. James Barr (1978), for example, regards fundamentalism, within the Protestant sense at least, as a formal belief system predicated on the assumption that the Bible is without error and its 'truths' can never be brought into question. This definition, which equates fundamentalism with a scriptural literalism, may be partly justified in that the self-designated term 'fundamentalist' was first proudly proclaimed by a faction of conservative Protestants who published a series of pamphlets at the beginning of the twentieth century entitled *The Fundamentals*. These were writings which sought to preserve what were believed to be the core teachings of the Christian faith and its literal scriptural interpretation.

Given the stress on scriptural literalism, it follows that those churches or sects that claim such a theological allegiance have often been designated by sociologists of religion as 'fundamentalist', even if they disagreed with each other and perhaps even though they might reject the label. For instance, with reference to the USA, Roof and McKinney (1987) bring under the remit of 'fundamentalist' those churches or movements such as Adventist churches, Conservative Evangelicals, Pentecostals and Southern Baptists. What they almost certainly have in common is an emphasis on the literalism and authority of a sacred text. At the same time, this tendency is by no means limited to conservative-minded Christians, since most forms of fundamentalism from the different world faiths display a good measure of reliance on their scriptural references, which help establish boundaries with the outside world and enhance a sense of collective identity. The fact remains, none the less, that describing fundamentalists by their emphasis on scriptural infallibility is too restrictive an account and would perhaps be more appropriate to the 'religions of the book', namely, Christianity, Islam and Judaism. Clearly fundamentalism entails more than this criterion and may broadly be understood as a self-conscious attempt to represent or reassert what are perceived to be authentic religious traditions and beliefs, even if these are reconstructed and fall back on myths and subjective interpretations of religious texts (Percy 1995).

In attempting to defend or recreate the past, fundamentalism, especially in the form of socio-political movements, has frequently represented an organized protest against modernity. Perhaps most obviously, the modern order has challenged the core of religious beliefs and practices. Science and rationalism offered an alternative worldview and presented different explanations of 'ultimate questions' as to the meaning of life and the nature of the universe. Modernity also engendered the growth of diversity and pluralism which undermined a cohesive and unified community and collective way of seeing the world. This demise of community life and its attendant value system – typically underpinned by religious faith – was, according to the sociological accounts of those such as Peter Berger (1967), at the very heart of the secularizing process. Religious worldviews in a secular age became the preserve of what Berger famously referred to as a 'cognitive minority'. Fundamentalism seeks to preserve such a distinct worldview.

Other issues which concern fundamentalists clearly indicate a reaction to changing moral values. In the past, Protestant fundamentalists have organized themselves against what they saw as the corrupting effects of changes in family life, permissiveness and secular education. Campaigns have also aimed at technological innovations, especially those linked to mass communication: the radio, television, the cinema and much else that was new and innovating and could be seen as corrupting public morals. Some of these threats to morals are now more acceptable but, from the 1970s, another set of 'evils' become the subject of political campaigns.

Many such campaigns are related to the family and sexuality, and, as David Lyon (2000: 47) has pointed out, to issues related to the body and discernibly impacting upon aspects of everyday life – with smoking and alcohol consumption, genetic engineering, abortion and a range of similar issues to the fore. These controversies, Lyon suggests, exemplify developments within postmodernity and to some extent reflect the scope of technology in intervening and altering the body, while consumption attempts to perfect it in terms of identity and lifestyle. The connection of 'body' politics with the religious sphere, according to Lyon, points not only to questions of legitimacy and identity in postmodernity but also to other boundaries such as that between the private and public spheres. Ironically it is to the private that religion is supposedly limited in its reach, but in postmodernity it steps into the public arena through far-reaching moral and political debates.

Whether responding to the ravages of modernity or postmodernity, in the USA it is clearly the fundamentalist lobby, frequently designated the Christian Right or the Moral Majority, which has become active and vociferous. However, it would be wrong to believe that all fundamentalists have resorted to political activism as a result of their religious convictions. Some, notably many traditional Pentecostals and Conservative Evangelicals, have turned their backs on the world and left it to its own moral mire and destruction. These constituencies typically see the world as irretrievably lost. Thus, political campaigns to change what is regarded as a satanically dominated world system are deemed to be irrelevant. However, towards the end of the twentieth century more conservative-minded Christians appeared to be prepared to enter stridently into the political arena, and became part of a movement whose rise, in the first instance, confounded many commentators.

Fundamentalism as a lifestyle choice

Despite the attractions of the liberal and seemingly more socially relevant forms of religiosity that have made an appearance in recent years, there is little doubt that fundamentalism has a great deal to offer individuals and communities within the context of the contemporary spiritual marketplace. For those seeking a religious persuasion it provides one possible route through the emerging cultural order. Fundamentalism, then, may have become a matter of lifestyle choice, offering attractions at the individual, everyday level. Quite what the attractions are has been discussed in the sociological literature long before notions of religious consumption developed, and largely connected to the matter of relative deprivation.

The work of Marty (1978) would suggest that, historically speaking, fundamentalists have not necessarily been inspired by religious conviction. Marty argues that those who advocate fundamentalism do so largely as a smokescreen, since they are, in reality, a product of social forces and historical events which encourage a certain psychological disposition. In short, they have some motivation other than the stated conviction of changing the world in religious terms. Marty's assertion is that Christian fundamentalism attracts those people who are relatively deprived and goaded by their situation. This would appear to be plausible given the evidence of various forms of sectarianism and their social composition. At the very least it could be said that the rise of fundamentalism is not merely concerned with religion but provides a vehicle for expressing conservative views of the world. In this sense fundamentalism could be construed as a religious 'resource' in contemporary pluralist societies, upholding traditional images such as that of the family and conventional gender roles within it (Himmelstein 1986).

One way of attempting to prove such speculation is to identify precisely who is involved in fundamentalist political activism. Early work on sectarian membership stressed the notion of status discontent, which seemed to make sense in relation to the question of who joins such religious collectives, membership of which did not necessarily have to be limited to the poorest sections of society. Relative deprivation may impact the middle classes as well. Studies in the USA of Christian fundamentalism and the issue of deprivation have tended to focus on the declining middle classes who are driven by the problem of status discontent. Much work has been inspired by Gusfield's (1963) assertion that those involved in the USA temperance movement in the 1920s were experiencing a decline in social group status which was only upheld through a symbolic crusade seeking public affirmation of their group's values over those of the rising social classes. In short, those whose status is threatened by changing cultural norms may attempt to assert their values politically in order to re-establish the ideological basis of their social position and prestige. Such theorizing has also been more recently applied to the New Christian Right and its moral campaigns over abortion and pornography (Zurcher and Kirkpatrick 1976).

The problem with these approaches is that they tend to ignore the actor's point of view. They consequently neglect the possibility that the motivation for moral campaigns may, in fact, be purely religious. This conviction upholds the need of Christian fundamentalism constantly to reaffirm the worldview of its adherents. Hence, sociological theories of the 'hidden' motivations behind fundamentalist activity fail to appreciate the potential and powerful force and appeal of independent religious beliefs (Thompson 1997). Indeed, detailed empirical research has tended to endorse this direct link between personal beliefs and attitudes towards certain issues, particularly those related to aspects of morality. For example, Laythe *et al.* (2002) found in their sample that fundamentalist inclinations among those surveyed were a significant positive predictor of an individual's prejudice against gay people over a protracted period of time.

Fundamentalism appraised

Another explanation advanced for the rise of the Christian fundamentalists in the USA focuses on the parallel decline of civil religion. As we have noted, some American commentators have charted the decline of civil religion through the latter half of the twentieth century, especially with reference to increasing pluralism and social and ethnic divisions. Anthony and Robbins (1990) speculate that, in response to its decline, conservative Christians have attempted to reinvigorate the nation's civil religion by recourse to a stringent cultural and moral system. This explains why fundamentalism appears to be infused with American cultural values. It is 'American fundamentalism' as much as Christian fundamentalism.

Such an endeavour is observably an integral part of the so-called 'cultural wars' which relate cultural lifestyle issues to the political arena (Johnson and Tamney 1984). In this regard, Hunter (1991) describes the culture wars in the USA as the struggle to define America, detailing that recent major cultural clashes over homosexuality, abortion and the content of education are not mere differences of opinion but are fundamentally different conceptions of moral authority and amount to a conflict over contrasting ideas and beliefs about 'truth', obligation and the very nature of the community. In the USA, this means a struggle for identity and a battle to redefine the nation. These cultural wars have touched many individual lives and institutions, not least of all the family, in so far as they relate to abortion, sexuality, gender roles, child-raising and even definitions of the family itself. The cultural wars have impacted upon what happens in public education and the media, and constitute a struggle often cast in the language of 'rights'. Hunter (1996) concludes that these opposing moral visions have become political chasms which threaten to further fragment the common culture of the USA. As these issues are increasingly polarized it becomes less and less possible to adopt ambivalent or mediating stances.

The telling question is undoubtedly: has Christian fundamentalism in the USA won the 'war', or even significant battles? More broadly, is Christian fundamentalism registering a success and impacting in any meaningful way on social and cultural life? To be sure, there are different ways by which its relevance can be gauged. One, as explored in the previous chapter, is that it is possibly the more conservative Christian churches which have been growing, most notably in the USA, and since 1950 this growth has been linked to the declining membership of the liberal churches and the marked demobilization of long-established denominations (Bibby 1978). Evidence of this came when, in 1967, the conservative Southern Baptist Convention overtook the Methodists as the largest Protestant denomination. Churches within the Convention have increasingly displayed all the characteristics associated with sectarian fundamentalism (Ammerman 1987). Survey data in the USA also estimate that conservative Protestants make up nearly 19 per cent of the American population, while up to one-third of Americans claim to be 'born-again' Christians – the self-assigned badge of fundamentalist–evangelical Christianity (Hunter 1987).

By way of its broader social impact, conservative Protestants have, according to Hunter (1987), succeeded in widely publicizing and presenting their agenda in the USA. In the early 1980s they had founded 450 colleges and 18,000 schools, set up 275 periodicals, established 70 evangelical publishing houses and 3,300 Christian bookshops. None the less, Hunter asserts that the expansion of conservative Protestantism does not disprove the fact that there is a general decline of Christianity in the USA, but merely that the process is complicated by discernible cycles of secularity and religious revival.

In terms of moral campaigning, other evidence suggests that religious fundamentalism in the USA has proved to be something of a liability in its chosen political home, the Republican Party. Green *et al.* (2001) have explored the uneasy relationship between social movements and major political parties by considering the case of the Christian Right and the Republican Party in elections. They looked at a number of states where the movement was active in party politics and the Republican Party's fortunes varied. The survey found that the degree of intra-party divisions generated by the Christian Right seemed to damage the party at the precise time its involvement plausibly aided it. The majority of those controversies frequently associated with support for the Christian Right, such as the family, abortion and the gay issue, did not help account for electoral outcomes.

So, at what level does Christian fundamentalism truly impact? As Ammerman (1987) points out, there exists in the USA a fundamentalist subculture which is propped up by the appropriate religious audio recordings and reading matter, even to the point of cooking with a Christian handbook. Fundamentalist activity may, therefore, do little more than convince its followers of their distinct lifestyle in the spiritual marketplace. The fact that fundamentalists appear to be cocooned in their own worldview is undoubtedly saying something significant. To put it simply, it suggests that fundamentalism offers one lifestyle among many – one that must be continuously bolstered by cultural and media environments and by political lobbying which reaffirms a subjective worldview.

In the USA in the 1980s, over 34 million houses viewed the 'electric church' Christian television programmes featuring popular fundamentalist preachers of different persuasions (Hadden and Shupe 1987). The question is, however, whether in the USA in particular, with its alleged high levels of religiosity, fundamentalism is *that* widespread. While statistics suggest high viewing figures, studies indicate those who *frequently* watch are almost exclusively already committed conservative Christians and that the programmes probably do little else than simply affirm their existing beliefs (Stacey and Shupe 1982). Indeed, this tendency proves the need of Christian fundamentalism to constantly reaffirm the worldview and way of life of a cognitive minority in a secular society.

THE RELIGIONS OF THE ETHNIC COMMUNITIES

As we have noted above, fundamentalism may be linked to ethnicity and nationalism, but not necessarily so. Hence the equation of fundamentalism with ethnicity in a rigid and deterministic way is misleading. Fundamentalism may be evident as a component of ethnic religiosity, but for many reasons they are worth keeping separate. What they both have in common, however, is not just that they are seemingly fairly stable and enduring areas of contemporary religion, but that they constitute religions of certainty, enforcing boundaries of communities, providing badges of identity, and linking individuals and their experiences of everyday life to a wider community through a sentiment of belonging.

In diasporic and globalizing conditions, religions produce examples of transnational constituencies which can provide individuals as well as diverse ethnic groups with a sense of community that is capable of making connections between local and international contexts. These ethnic constituencies are, in short, transnational 'imagined communities'. As particular groups begin to define themselves in terms of personal and community ethnic and religious identity, at least alongside and sometimes in place of other identity markers, the wider host society may respond either by recognition or rejection of such self-identification. While the connection between faith and ethnicity comes into clear relief, the level of controversy generated is related to several variables: the attitude of the population, state policy, the faith of the ethnic grouping itself, and significant global events. All these factors may impinge upon the everyday life experiences of the individuals who comprise the numerous ethnic minorities in the West.

Like religious fundamentalism in all its guises, the religions of ethnic minorities are increasingly making news in Western societies. In part this is because, as noted above, there is a link between some forms of religious fundamentalism and ethnic communities at the localized or global level. But there is more besides. There is the association between ethnicity and religion and the heated political debate about whether cultural assimilation is a desirable goal or, alternatively, a truly pluralist society, which allows for the full range of ethnic and religious diversity, should be encouraged. With regard to the attitude of Western states towards ethnic religions, it is evident that policies vary considerably. They range from state neutrality in religious affairs, or overt secularism, as in Belgium, Holland and Sweden, to the upholding of a state religion as in Denmark. This is supplemented by policies towards ethnic minorities. Most Western nations espouse the virtues of a multicultural society, although others such as France have strong assimilation policies. Additionally, there are varying attitudes regarding citizenship which may encourage different levels of political activity by religious–ethnic groups. Thus political activity has tended to emerge more quickly in those countries, such as the UK and France, where immigrants have in the past acquired citizenship relatively easily.

The valuation of ethnic religion is very much bound up with the culture of ethnic minorities which may be designated as social 'outgroups', while the visibility of their faiths is enhanced in the increasingly secular societies of the West. It follows that the secular nature of Western societies may generate controversy in the perceived clash between these faiths on the one hand and the values of a secular culture on the other.

More widely in the West, problems have often displayed themselves in a clash of cultures, particularly in the case of hostility to liberal attitudes about sexuality and in the desire for the education of children in accordance with religious principles. Other difficulties have included dietary requirements and specific needs related to death and burial. Such clashes of culture may spill over into ethnic tensions. In France, local conflict over the right of Muslim schoolgirls to wear hair-coverings in class has became a controversy made use of by hostile local native French elements to arouse fears of the Muslim population as an 'internal Islamic threat'. In response, the migrants may use it as part of the construct of a contrary worldview, or what Bloul (1996) terms an 'alternative universalism'.

Ethnicity, boundaries and identity

The relationship between religion and ethnicity is complicated by divergences within the major faiths and, perhaps simultaneously, divisions within ethnic communities. Migrants from various parts of the world may belong to different Islamic traditions, perhaps upholding sectarian forms of religion at a time when mainstream Christianity is on the decline. Those from the Indian subcontinent may be Hindu, Sikh, Muslim or Buddhist, while Caribbeans are frequently divided by their loyalties to various Christian traditions. Conversely, black Caribbean Christians may associate more with the faithful from the white host population, while Islam is capable of banding together those of varying ethnic and national roots.

Irrespective of these variants, it is clear that religious faith constitutes a primary aspect of life for many ethnic minorities. This is particularly so for those migrants from the Third World where religious belief and practice are an essential element of community and culture. The significance of religiosity could nevertheless be magnified by the upheavals of migration itself, not to mention the challenges faced in the transition from one society to another. This is most clearly relevant for the first generation of migrants for whom religion commonly provides a source of identity, continuity and value orientation. Thus religion performs one of its erstwhile functions in permitting social and psychological certainty for those experiencing upheaval and adaptation to a challenging, perhaps belligerent environment. Religion may not, however, be just an integrating force for ethnic communities but may form part of the process of boundary maintenance which confirms the integrity and solidarity of the community. This it does by firmly establishing the cultural differences from wider society, and for the early generations of migrants this might be an imperative irrespective of their aspirations to succeed in a new country. Thus the strengthening of boundaries is frequently how ethnic groups survive in the face of even the most overwhelming adversity. The relevance of religion is that it brings a clearer delineation of the culture of a community and enhances internal solidarity even where it was not particularly strong beforehand.

Markers of cultural identity may be internally imposed, yet they are frequently fostered by experiences of discrimination or perceived discrimination. In the UK, the state's strengthening of immigration controls brought the creation of Asian community support groups and enhanced cultural bonds which encouraged dedication to Islam and the proliferation of the construction of mosques as centres of community life from the 1960s (Barton 1986). It is also worth noting that ethnic relations in a fair few European countries appeared to degenerate from the 1980s – creating a higher profile for ethnic faiths. Much has been linked to the high levels of prejudice which emerged against a background of economic problems, alongside the increase in applications for entrance into Western societies from political refugees facing persecution in their homelands, or the so-called 'economic refugees' from the former Soviet Empire and Third World countries who came in search of a better standard of living. Thus ethnic groups, whether Turkish Muslim *gastarbeiten* in Germany, North African immigrants in France and Italy, or Vietnamese refugees in Scandinavia, have experienced not just violence from right-wing racist movements but not uncommonly overt racism from local organized community groups.

The response of the ethnic communities who find themselves experiencing insecurities and threats in the new surroundings of the West has been to strengthen their cultural boundaries, and this has become a fairly predictable pattern. This was, for example, the case in Germany where Turkish Muslims came to understand themselves to be in the land of the 'infidel', in an environment that was profane and *haram* (Mandel 1996). In this context they sought to create a realm for themselves – forming barriers of distinctiveness ranging from dietary habits to language, from dress to domestic arrangements, which provided meaningful expressions of Turkish Muslim identity.

Ethnic groups are also affected by global developments. A recent example is the events influencing Islam. There have been the consequences of the Gulf Wars of 1991 and 2003 during which there was evidence of at least some support among scattered localized European Muslim populations for Saddam Hussein's war effort. The Gulf Wars, between the nations of the West and Iraq, once more showed that the former still had considerable global economic and political interests in the region. Such global events have sometimes led to unpredictable consequences. In the USA, the Black Muslim movement founded by Elijah Muhammad and made famous by Malcolm X and Louis Farrakhan, was a model for many groups in Europe from the 1990s. This movement sought to construct a new morality which fought against drug peddlers and addiction, and to break with dominant Western norms in order to mark out a strong community identity and protect those living in ghettoes. At one time the Black Muslim movement was profoundly intolerant of non-black races and religions. Their beliefs and Koranic references were interpreted as forming a protest against the values and attitudes of the dominant white United States culture, and a dualist ideology of some Black Muslims identified the 'evil' nature of Western materialistic societies and the white oppressors (Lincoln 1989). The movement was also relatively unconnected with Islam as a world religion. The spread of global fundamentalism began to change a great deal. Thus, some strands of the movement have embraced a wider vision and embarked on an intense study of world Islam, becoming part of the Sunni branch of the international faith and linking with Muslims in other countries.

Assimilation and 'internal secularization'

Issues concerning the desirability or otherwise of assimilation are among the central debates, not just within the various ethnic minorities but within the institutions of the political states of the West. Sociological conjecture is perhaps more interested in the social dynamics which may lead to inevitable assimilation, and this would invariably include a reduction in the religiosity of ethnic minorities. Although there is a vast difference in terms of assimilation to be found among ethnic minorities, the general pattern may well be one of assimilation.

Some of the ethnic faiths lend themselves more readily to assimilation than others. Sikhism, for example, has an ethos that is democratic and egalitarian, with keen social awareness and a spirit of reconciliation, and has consequently not experienced as many difficulties as rival faiths in being transplanted to an alien soil (Thomas 1993). By contrast, Muslims have rarely found it easy to respond to the challenges of living within Western cultures. The broad picture can be said to be a paradoxical mixture of achievement and frustration, acceptance and alienation, polarities of assimilation and isolation. None the less, in many respects Muslim communities have been more stringent in sustaining religious beliefs and practices than other faiths (Anwar 1981).

Perhaps the ethnic–religious community which gives the greatest clue to future developments is that of the Jews, who have been settled in many Western societies far longer than many other groupings. While it is difficult to draw conclusions given the range of social and political environments in which the Jewish community is located, there are discernible trends or, more precisely, responses to the forces of modernity including social and geographical mobility which have eroded the sense of belonging. This is important not just for the Jews since, as Wade Roof (1987) has argued, the highly differentiated societies of the West have undermined local and tradition-based religious perspectives shared by persons who interact freely, thus providing mutual support for belief and practice – processes integral to the dynamics of ethnic communities.

If the young can be regarded as providing an indication of the strength of Judaism, the future does not appear promising. In the 1980s, up to two-thirds of young Jews in the UK did not marry in a synagogue, preferring instead the simple ceremony of a secular registry office. Another indication is the findings of Kosmin and Levy's (1983) study of religious ritual practice in Jewish schools compared to non-Jewish schools in the UK. Although the former scored higher, once home background was taken into account there was virtually no difference between the two groups in terms of the religious socialization of young people. According to this study, the next generation is not being rigorously inculcated with traditional religious values.

Political and moral change, increasing pluralism, a culture of disbelief and doubt, these are the essential 'external' challenges that organized religion has had to confront in Western societies. In historical terms, the challenge has been primarily to the Christian churches. More recently different world faiths have been forced to face what they frequently see as threats undermining a traditional worldview from 'within', threats which mark a reaction to the challenges of modernity. In Judaism, both its ecclesiastical and its community expressions have responded to the rigours of modern society through strategies of adaptation, largely by transforming and reinterpreting beliefs via Reformed or Liberal Judaism, a response which has inevitably brought conflict with the Orthodoxy. The attraction of the former is conceivably greater to those Jews alienated by what they feel is outmoded tradition, and who might otherwise abandon the faith altogether.

What of the future for other ethnic faiths? Historically, Islam, despite its resilience on some fronts, is capable of adapting itself to local conditions and has frequently proved to be tolerant of other faiths. There are also signs of assimilation. As Abdullah points out in the case of Germany, only slightly over half of the 1.7 million Muslims living there actually practise Islam (Abdullah 1995: 77). Evidence in the UK shows that members of the younger generation of Muslims with a Western education have been inquisitive about their roots and seek an earnest understanding of their cultural identity. At the same time, however, they have come to question some of the cultural and religious postulates of their parents. Indeed, given such evidence in the UK, Gill (2001) predicts that over the course of future generations the strength of Islam (and other traditions) is likely to wither.

Although deserving to be treated differently from rival forms of religion in Western society, those of the ethnic minorities are none the less subject to the dynamics of the spiritual marketplace. In this respect, Hammond and Warner (1995) believe that assimilation is advanced by the transformation of religion into more private expressions. They argue that, at least in the USA, the evidence suggests that the relationship between religion and ethnicity may be on the decline (although this noticeably varies from one ethnic group to another) – even at a time when communities in the USA are claiming their ethnic distinctiveness. Hammond and Warner speculate that neither religion nor ethnicity will entirely disappear in the near future, but the linkage between the two is almost certain to be weakened. Above all, religious allegiance becomes increasingly a matter of individual choice for members of ethnic minorities, as it does for the host population. According to Hammond and Warner, ethnicity, along with other social background characteristics, will have a diminishing effect in determining religious identity because of the incursions made by rival religions into ethnic enclaves. A sign of this is that Pentecostal Protestantism has made considerable inroads into Hispanic Catholicism, as has black Islam into African-American Protestantism. Such a weakening of the relationship between ethnicity and religion does not mean that religion fades in importance for expressing ethnic concerns. Neither does it suggest that, because religion is becoming a matter of individual choice, it is of lesser importance. Indeed, it may actually be of greater psychological significance even as its social and ethnic consequences diminish. However, the declining link between religion and ethnicity continues as a long-term trend.

SUMMARY

This chapter has been concerned with the religions of 'certainty', an apparent growth area in the religious marketplace. Perhaps it is inappropriate to bring fundamentalism and the religion of the ethnic minorities under the same rubric. Yet they deal with overlapping issues. Both, to some degree or other, are concerned with aspects of boundary maintenance as a response to the challenges of social change, providing an anchorage against the relativizing nature of contemporary culture. There is a globalizing aspect too. Thus Castells (1997: 355) sees fundamentalism as a means of constructing 'resistance identities' in the face of the globalized dissolution of traditional identities and the social institutions which have historically shaped them. In terms of its ethnic dimension, the 'evil' is capitalism and its accompanying culture. Global capitalism breaks down communities and instils an ethos of individualism and materialism.

There is a danger, however, in generalizing about ethnic religion in terms of fundamentalism and seeing the present global order ushering in deterministic trends. Too often there is a dichotomy stressed, as in Barber's *Jihad versus McWorld* (1995), which tends to oversimplify complex issues. Moreover, in today's social setting, fundamentalism can be seen as a response to relativity and cultural flows by presenting absolutes and fixity, but they are dependent upon complex currents where 'glocalization', or local context, plays a part. Much else separates the fundamentalist movements of the world faiths. Some Sikh, Judaic and to some extent Islamic movements, interpreted as fundamentalist, are merely territorial and identified with ethnic minorities under particular conditions. Christian fundamentalism in the USA is different again. While rejecting what are understood to be moral evils, it also frequently upholds what is perceived to be the American way of life, including its unshakable faith in individual responsibility and the entrepreneurial spirit.

In the USA, fundamentalism seems to add to its religious exclusivism. Indeed, it would seem to vindicate Casanova's (1994) claim that some religions are now re-entering the public sphere, not just to defend their traditional rights and influence but to participate in the very struggle to define and set the modern boundaries between public and private; between family, civil society and the state. Part of this re-entry process, Casanova claims, is made possible by changes and even crises within the public sphere itself because globalizing tendencies by no means guarantee the securities of the nation-state. Much again, however, is open to interpretation. The attempt to re-enter the public sphere may merely denote the beleaguered nature of religion in the face of secularity and regulation. The key question is whether religion, particularly in its fundamentalist and indeed its ethnic forms, is exercising its social power or merely fighting a rearguard action in response to the incursions of secularity.

How might we conclude on the subject of the religions of certainty? In many respects the theorizing of the postmodernists and exponents of rational choice is correct. As with other forms of religion they are forced to compete in a spiritual marketplace. Yet, it is a relativizing one, suggesting to adherents that their belief and practice is one among many in a pluralist society. To be sure, in such a marketplace, individuals may still be part of a traditional, well-integrated society. Ethnic religions will always be a haven for some, while fundamentalism offers a self-enforcing lifestyle for others. Collectively they continue to provide an alternative way of life, but are forms of faith that are relentlessly chipped away by secularity. Moreover, such religions are not 'alternatives' in the spiritual marketplace in the sense that, while they do win converts outside of their ethnic confines, subscribing to one or other of them is more to do with being socialized into a culture rather than choosing freely as part of a spiritual seekership.

8

THE RISE AND FALL OF THE
NEW RELIGIOUS MOVEMENTS

THE WORLD OF THE NEW RELIGIONS

Over the last forty years or so a formidable volume of sociological writings has been directed towards describing, analysing and accounting for the rise of the so-called New Religious Movements (NRMs). The near-preoccupation results not merely from a fascination with innovating forms of religion, but because their proliferation seemed to argue against the broad secularization thesis. This was particularly so since they emerged at a time when mainline Christianity was continuing its decline, at least by way of institutional affiliation. However, the observable recent reduction in literature about the NRMs suggests that not only has the fascination with the subject reached saturation point, in that they have been studied from just about every conceivable sociological angle, but that such religions may well have had their day.

The changing fortunes of the NRMs need to be put into perspective. While many of the NRMs have come to have a global influence, their impact in the USA has proved to be especially significant. Indeed, many arose in the North American context. Exemplifying the larger movements, The Family (formerly the Children of God) emerged in California and then spread to Europe and beyond. Others, perhaps most notably the Unification Church (the 'Moonies'), started outside of the Western context, but have grown to win converts in the USA and Europe. A fair few other movements were manifest in the form of

Eastern mysticism or occultism imported via the arrival of immigrants from the Far East, and in some cases deliberate proselytization. Alternatively they marked a continuation of derivative forms carried by the intellectual middle classes who had developed a taste for exotic spiritualities since the nineteenth century.

Whatever their origins or means of dissimilation, the NRMs added to the religious pluralism and increasing diversity of the USA and Western Europe. Especially in the USA such religions have proved to be a consistent part of religious life, have frequently proliferated during periods of religious enthusiasm almost since the time of the founding of the nation, and have been interpreted as a source of collective belonging, as well as offering an alternative belief system for those attracted to Christian revivalism or new forms of spirituality (Melton 1987). Bromley and Shupe (1981) largely argue along these lines by insisting that NRMs may be seen as part of a normal cycle of religious movements identified with the USA since the nineteenth century, in which periods of social flux were followed by a time of religious revitalization that in the long run brought a greater social stability and integration. While this may be so, the NRMs which emerged from the 1960s onwards appeared to display more social significance than those movements that went before by way of the scale of some of them and the controversies that surrounded a good number. A minority, such as those mentioned above, have endured into the twenty-first century as sizeable movements. Yet, as broadly cultist forms of religiosity, most of the new religions are highly precarious types of organization. Their characteristic pluralist doctrines, their members' general individualistic mode of adherence, alongside problems of authority, frequently render many of them more unstable than other types of religious collectivity.

New Religious Movements: some typologies

The designation of NRMs as 'sects' or 'cults' has proved attractive largely because they enhance a categorization based on their orientation towards the world, whether embracing or rejecting it. In this regard Bruce makes a distinction between the world-rejecting forms that are closer to sects, and world-affirming movements that are akin to cults – a typology originally established by Wallis (1984). The world-rejecting movements, according to Bruce, are demanding of the time, energy and commitment of their adherents, and joining the movement is regarded as 'conversion'. Bruce notes that such movements typically accord a very low value to the 'human self'. As in traditional Christianity, a fair few see the self as essentially sinful – a condition which can be overcome only by being subordinated to some higher supernatural authority. By contrast, world-affirming movements see the individual as not so much evil as *restricted*. Bruce's approach to these typologies in relation to the self is a useful one because it identifies the more 'religious' movements as compared to those that are principally concerned with this-worldly self-improvement. The self, in the renditioning of world-affirming movements, is designated as extremely powerful but muted by igno-rance of its true capabilities and potential. It follows that human beings need to be taught to free themselves from the internal constraints which are the legacy of the way society has forged them.

There are, according to Bruce, two very different sorts of world-affirming movements: those, such as Scientology, which add a spiritual dimension to a Western preoccupation with secular psychotherapy; and those which, like Transcendental Meditation, tailor an initially oriental product to modern sensibilities. Both types do not renounce the world, which, in principle, is understood to be essentially good and full of potential. What is not good is that more people cannot enjoy the potential that the world offers because the self has not fulfilled its latent capabilities. All such movements differ to some extent in their recognition of some power other than the self, something which, if it is not sufficiently personal to be worshipped, can at least merge with an ecstatic experience. However, Bruce observes that those movements which have endured managed to be flexible about what counts as success in the lives of those who subscribe to them. He gives the example of Gakkai Buddhists who believe that chant-ing produces results in terms of specific, often material goals. However, when they fail to attain these, the results can be reinterpreted in a way other than was initially sought. For example, if a marriage does not work out, separation is seen in retrospect as an opportunity to realize the greater potential of the self (Bruce 1995: 101).

World-affirming movements are at the opposite pole to world-rejecting movements. The latter, as noted above, play down notions of self and play up the emphasis on the divine and relationships with supernatural entities. In terms of their sectarian characteristics they make consider-able demands on the lives of their members and are in tension with the outside world. It may be these characteristics which have led to the decline of these forms of NRMs. Such movements display a clearly defined perception of the supernatural, a strong system of morally ascribed rules, and often a puritanical range of beliefs. The teachings will be critical of wider society and its value systems. This type of movement will earnestly seek to change the world and usher in a new spiritual order, for which the membership will prepare by proselytizing the world while at the same time separating themselves from it.

Another aspect of Wallis's typology is that there appears to be a link between the membership of NRMs and various forms of deprivation. Plausibly, those not sufficiently affluent to be engrossed by the world-affirming movements will be attracted to an alternative. Wallis (1984) touches upon this in his account of recruitment to a third, intermediate category, world-accommodating movements. These movements neither completely embrace nor reject the world, but they can display elements of both. Those like Subud (which claims origins within Islam but has observably modified its principal beliefs and practices) often tolerate other faiths and are more pluralist in outlook and closer to denominations in the Christian sense. Their beliefs and practices are rarely totally unorthodox. Wallis believes that this means they have come to acquire a certain social respectability. For such a reason they seem to appeal to particular types of people, while there is the tendency for these movements to separate the religious and worldly in a distinctive way so as to serve the spiritual needs of their membership. These are people who generally have some stake in the world but are attracted to the movements because they help them cope with their everyday experiences and, above all, alienating social roles. In this capacity they offer the safe haven of a subculture that members can turn to in a world which they see as too materialistic, lonely, impersonal and void of spirituality.

NRMs and the spiritual marketplace

One estimate is that there are now some 2,500 new religions in the Western world (Barker 1999: 16). Despite this impressive array, few are of any great numerical importance at the beginning of the twenty-first century. This raises the questions as to why they arose when they did and why they began to decline at a particular time. Given the diverse nature of the NRMs emerging from the 1960s, their appearance may be explained primarily in terms of religions of the 'gaps'. Considering what the new religions have had to offer in the spiritual marketplace, they would seem to epitomize the sentiment of choice. This observation brings us close to Stark and Bainbridge's (1980, 1985) account of new cult movements (a term which largely covers the vast range of NRMs). The emphasis here is on the growth of a free market of religiosity and consumption that is synonymous with highly developed economies and pluralist societies. The new religions, whatever their origins, are generally free of the deficiencies of the older religious faiths since they deal with the needs of individuals in the contemporary West. From this perspective, the NRMs can be discerned as a major growth area in religiosity at a particular time and place.

According to rational choice theory, the 'needs' of those who subscribe to NRMs could be social or psychological but are not limited to these concerns since individuals have very real spiritual requirements. Hence, the rational choice model developed by Stark and Bainbridge suggests that the new religions fill the 'gaps' left by more traditional forms. In this regard they can offer a more convincing, faster, direct path to satisfying a range of needs or may simply provide a meaning to life in religious terms and deal with practically any negative experience.

For commentators such as Stark and Bainbridge, the growth of the new religions is additionally enhanced by the breakdown of religious 'monopolies', that is traditional Christianity, and the proliferation of a spiritual marketplace in North America and Europe. In many respects this suggests the emergence of a more sincere form of religiosity since people opt for the new religions out of 'true' conviction rather than social obligation, tradition, or because religion was imposed on them by the state or Church. The fact that many are in decline does not disprove the theory, but shows that at the beginning of the twenty-first century, they are not fulfilling their original functions and those which do survive are, in many cases, evolving so they now offer their market wares in a different cultural environment.

NRMs, the counter-culture and beyond

A major concern of the early sociological accounts of the NRMs was in explaining why they arose when they did and what their true social significance amounted to. These themes led to a number of subsidiary questions, such as what were the attractions of these religions, who joined their ranks, and what were the processes involved in 'conversion'. The general argument was that they were a product of the profound social and cultural changes wrought by modernity, or a response to its more damaging consequences. Quite what the most important social factors were in generating these innovating forms of religion led to a great deal of sociological debate throughout the 1970s.

Some commentators saw the new religions as symbolizing a rejection of modernity through the counter-culture revolution of the 1960s – offering an alternative lifestyle to an increasingly materialistic, rationalist and individualistic society and a corrupt morality – a rebellious denunciation fuelled by protests against the Vietnam War (Bellah 1976; Wuthnow 1976). Bruce goes further and, while arguing that many NRMs appealed to the counter-culture and marked a response to the dehumanization of the public world, he suggests they came to realize that human effort was not enough to change the world (Bruce 1995: 111). Hence, many of the world-rejecting movements claimed that some divine agency or power was poised to intervene in the world, and the millennium would be ushered in by supernatural means if people would commit themselves zealously to the endeavour of bringing it about.

Typical of many of these observable tendencies of counter-cultural expression was The Family, one of the larger NRMs with communities in many parts of the world. Yet, while rejecting modernity, The Family never entirely escaped from it. Bainbridge suggests that, except for the deep religiosity of its performers, the songs of The Family today might be purely interpreted as the counter-culture music of the 1960s, laced with white folk and pop from earlier decades. Born in a dramatic exodus from 'the system', The Family was thus originally part of a larger cultural milieu (including a level of sexual permissiveness) which has also adapted itself to the present day, or, in Bainbridge's words, 'The Family forces Christianity to confront the technological and sexual realities of modern society' (Bainbridge 1997: 239). In this way the movement is obliged to deal with contemporary issues in much the same way as conventional Christianity, but does so particularly effectively by making significant concessions to the modern world while retaining eschatological longings.

As plausible as these theories of the emergence of NRMs appeared to be at the time, they seemed to have less relevance as the counter-culture largely fizzled out in the late 1970s. A later set of writings came to suggest that the new religions were not so much a product of the counterculture but rather helped people deal with its negative consequences and excesses: the drug abuse, sexual permissiveness and, perhaps above all, its failure to construct a viable alternative way of life. A range of NRMs, such as the Divine Light Mission and ISKCON (better known as Hare Krishna), have been interpreted as partly embodying retention of certain counter-culture values but subsequently translated into a new idiom that rejected the counter-culture's anarchic, ill-disciplined and frequently destructive lifestyle. This was Steve Tipton's assertion in his suitably entitled volume *Getting Saved from the Sixties* (1982). Tipton designated the largely young and middle class membership of such movements as 'survivors' from the 1960s belonging to a counter-culture that was an inadequate basis for an alternative way of living but one which these new religions could however provide.

NRMS AND IDENTITY CONSTRUCTS

The broad set of theories discussed above that interpret the rise of NRMs as related to one 'crisis' or another of modernity, crises which precipitated social and/or individual psychological malfunctioning, have their limitations. Above all, it must be noted that some of the social changes considered significant at the time are long-term processes in the West and do not fully explain the proliferation of NRMs from the 1960s. There is also a problem of generalizing about *who* joined such movements. If a number of NRMs did recruit heavily among ex-participants in the counter-culture, this was not true of all (Barker 1984), and while early adherents to movements such as ISKCON *had* been involved, those who joined them at a later stage had not (Rochford 1985).

Given the failings of these explanations, some commentators, predating theories of postmodernity, established a link between the new religions and a search for self-identity that was exacerbated by a contemporary world dominated by bureaucratic structures and fragmented social roles. NRMs were said to address this need by promoting a holistic conception of self, especially through therapeutic movements and mystical cults (Westley 1978). The more cult-like groups seemed to offer the ability to control and change the individual's social identity and self. In contrast, the more sect-like groups appeared to address the search for self-identity and plausibly included those rising out of the Jesus Movement of California in the post-Woodstock years. These movements allegedly provided such a function by consolidating all of an individual's fragmented social identities into a single, central, religiously-defined self which was strengthened by the strict control of an authoritarian structured movement (Bird 1978; Dreitzel 1981). Put succinctly, they provided a harbour of self-identity in a society that found it hard to provide one. In offering this function many of the cultist NRMs seemed to look forward to the New Age movement which emerged in the 1980s. Indeed, at least some of those that have endured put forward beliefs and techniques which overlap with a number of the major appeals of many of the strands of the New Age. At the same time, the more authoritarian sect-like groups seemed to tender attractions now primarily associated with postmodernist and rational-choice accounts of fundamentalism.

More recently the function of the new religions in providing identity constructs has perhaps befallen the more world-affirming groups and may at least partly explain their endurance under contemporary conditions. Some individuals plausibly come to feel that, while they have become more affluent, they have done so at the price of repressing their 'true selves', creating a restrictive lifestyle that pushes out emotional dimensions of their existence. Hence, a fair number of the world-affirming movements provide the context and method for liberating spontaneity, for expressing and finding the real self. At the same time, the world-affirming religions display aspects of the very rationality they may seek sanctuary from. Thus the world-affirming new religions offer a promise to enhance the individual's capacity for rational action by so-called spiritual means. They establish the strategies, techniques or knowledge required to reduce the gap between aspiration and actuality. Hence, those such as Transcendental Meditation or Scientology would attempt to increase members' abilities so as to be able to achieve their life goals. Moreover, there is a further sense in which the world-affirming new religions are a product of the rationalizing impulse and can be observed in their view of the self as an appropriate site for corrective action. These are thus the new religions of the educated and affluent middle classes who have little time for constricting moral codes or salvationist religions, and for whom fulfilling human potential is more important than petitioning a deity.

There may be a strong link between at least some NRMs, gender and constructs of identity. The over-representation of females in some NRMs is well-documented. A fair few seem to endow females with more liberating roles and pathways to self-transformation and image construction, and furnish an alternative source of authority and power through distinctive beliefs, rituals and symbols. Such NRMs are consciously articulating alternative spiritual beliefs and practices which envisage and celebrate positive images of females, including homage to a female deity, rituals of female empowerment and moral norms which do not promote female submissiveness (Palmer 1994). Recent developments in some NRMs seem not so much to deal with the deprivation felt by females but with their self-realization, and in doing so come in line with broader developments in the sphere of religion and the ascendancy of world-affirming movements. Puttick (1999) suggests that many attract women who have achieved secular and professional success and are now looking for a spiritual dimension to their lives. As a whole, the beliefs and practices of these movements are more fluid and flexible, sometimes with a focus on androgyny, and usually include women in the leadership positions that they also enjoy in secular life. NRMs such as the Osho, the Brahma Kumaris and many Buddhist and pagan groups offer equal opportunities, without a 'glass ceiling' to bring limits to promotion, and enhance the possibility for women to combine work, marriage and motherhood with the pursuit of spiritual growth.

THE TRIUMPH OF WORLD-AFFIRMING NRMS

More recently, there has been good evidence that many of the New Religious Movements are heading in the world-affirming direction. To be sure, these relatively new forms of religion are very much a mixed bag by way of beliefs and practices. Nevertheless, they must be thrown into the secularization equation since what they have to offer today can be appreciated by way of their long-term developments towards world affirmation. In short, the new forms of religion or spirituality may well have to adapt themselves to this world in order to survive, in much the same way as have the more liberal Christian churches, despite being oriented to the more narrow concerns of the well-heeled middle classes.

On the other hand, there is a discernible decline of the more all-embracing, authoritarian and community-based NRMs. This should not be surprising in a culture of atomized individuality, self-absorption and crass materialism, while the sustainability of those movements which reject such values and cultural attributes is increasingly difficult. It was the latter that had attracted most of the early attention from sociologists of religion and, as we have also explored, appeared to deal with the problems generated by socio-cultural changes at the time. By the beginning of the twenty-first century these NRMs no longer seemed to have the same appeal and at least some had begun to experience a decline in membership. Other NRMs, those which did not demand such a rigid lifestyle, have continued, although hardly flourishing in any great measure.

Today, there are good grounds for arguing that in the spiritual marketplace it is the world-affirming forms of NRM which are increasing in popularity, at the expense of the world-rejecting and world-accommodating types. It is the former which are more compatible with the emerging conditions of Western society and the prevailing cultural ethos. While many of the social origins that helped establish the world-rejecting movements have declined or may now be deemed as not particularly appealing to religious 'seekers', world-accommodating movements have also experienced the same development plausibly because of the general decline of organized religion and of denominationalism in particular. By contrast, world-affirming types of movement demand a much lower level of commitment than the other expressions and are less stigmatized. In addition, as Marx and Ellison (1975) suggested as early as the mid-1970s, they may offer strategies related to human potential and a sense of community and belonging on a part-time basis without the less attractive full-time, more utopian and demanding aspects of the authoritarian movements. Wallis (1984) also recognized such a tendency. What he referred to as 'epistemological individualism' was increasingly articulating itself in religious terms in a consumer society where there are ever-changing tastes and fashion. It follows that world-affirming groups become more popular at the expense of world-rejecting movements, since they offer immediate gratification for those who take part.

Evidence to support the increasing domination of world-affirming groups has been presented by Khasala's (1986) survey of the 3HO Foundation and Vajradhatu (a Tibetan Buddhist church whose members are mostly well-educated, middle class white Americans). These constituencies have become less world-rejecting and have subsequently developed an ideological orientation that supports material success as a spiritually relevant enterprise, and thereby identify no dilemma in embracing both the spiritual and the earthly realms. It is not, however, necessarily a matter of a sectarian type of religion becoming more worldly as a result of an inevitable process. Rather, the evidence suggests that the transformation is brought about by a pragmatic leadership decision in response to changing social and economic conditions in an attempt to promote the survival of the movement. The opting for worldly success establishes a firm basis on which the religion can grow. At the same time, it provides otherwise-deviant groups with a strong image of legitimacy, and this is enhanced by the emphasis on individualism, enterprise and success.

There are other examples too. While Buddhist groups remain firmly traditional in the Far East, in the Western context the faith is often transformed. In the case of the USA, even those factions that have kept organizational continuity with their original sects in Asia have adapted to North American conditions. In the form of NRMs, those such as Soka Gakkai International, with its origins in Japan in the 1930s, have in the post-war years sought to extend their membership globally. By the movement's own reckoning there are tens of thousands of members internationally. There are no monasteries, monks, distinctive robes, no breathing techniques of meditation or images of Buddha. There are few references to the teachings of the founder of Buddhism, his Four Noble Truths or the Eightfold Path to Enlightenment. Rather, the emphasis is on chanting mantras which are held to have intrinsic power and believed to provide practical results in this world. Hence, the members of Soka Gakkai International usually chant with specific benefits in mind, both spiritual and material.

While world-affirming NRMs appear to be those that endure because of their compatibility with contemporary culture, those world-rejecting movements that survive today have done so for perhaps three broad reasons. First, those which have continued may be referred to, using Nelson's (1968) concept, as 'established cults'. These are not unlike Spiritualism and similar movements which endured for nearly 150 years. Most that do survive typically undergo transformation from cult to sect, and this is typified by Scientology, the Unification Church, and many factions derived from the Jesus Movement. Hierarchical control, charismatic leadership, discipline and a rigid belief system have served these movements particularly well.

A second reason for the endurance of a number of NRMs is their search for a greater respectability. Some have adapted themselves accordingly. The reputation of an NRM may be enhanced if it can demonstrate its ties to an ethnic community and/or a major world religion. For instance, to improve its image, ISKCON has emphasized its relationship to the wider Hindu community (Carey 1987). It claims to have a priestly function derived from its roots in the ancient tradition of Vausnava Hinduism, which cultivates worship of the god Vishnu and his *avatars* (incarnations) Krishna and Rama. This had the affect of moving the cult towards the structure of a type of denomination – hence it was an attempt to court a greater respectability in the eyes of the outside world. Scientology (with its origins from before the 1960s), by way of another example, seeks respectability in combating drug abuse through its organization Narconon. By this strategy it attempts to project a good public impression in an attempt to throw off the rather stigmatized image which it had acquired.

A third explanation for the endurance of some of the earlier world-rejecting movements is that they have become more user-friendly. As David Martin (1991) notes, movements of this type are increasingly inclined to accommodate themselves with the world in order to survive and sustain their membership. It is a recognition that few people seek full commitment and immersion in a radically different and totally religious way of life. To be sure, as Heelas (1988) maintains, world-rejecting forms will undoubtedly continue to endure because they still provide for the needs of some people and resist the tendency towards weak commitment and marketable strategies. They have their place, albeit not a significant one in the spiritual marketplace. However, it is such low levels of commitment and involvement which prevent full-blooded immersion.

There is good evidence that some world-rejecting movements have made concessions to weaker membership, and that it is these which have assured their survival. In 1995, The Family produced the *Love Charter*, which it claims is based on biblical principals as well as on the writings of its founder David Berg (*Introducing the Family*, nd: 2). Each full-time Family member believes they have been called by God to serve Him within the movement in some capacity. To this end the movement is divided into three general groupings: first, the Charter members, who live in community, tithe 10 per cent of their income, and abide by the Charter and family rules; second, the Fellows, who do not live in community, or contribute a tithe, and do not abide by the full extent of Charter or Family rules; finally, those individuals associated with The Family in some way, perhaps regularly receiving literature and working in a missionary capacity or on social welfare projects. This membership flexibility will probably ensure the survival of The Family, at least in the short term.

NRMs: into the twenty-first century

The new religions attract a broader public interest, largely because of the controversy and notoriety that surrounds the more world-rejecting expressions or those movements misleadingly referred to as 'cultist'. Those such as the Solar Temple in France in 1994, of whose membership some 70 committed suicide following the exposure of cases of abuse, and the Aum Shinri Kyo movement with its infamous attack on the Tokyo subway system in 1995 which led to thousands of people being hospitalized, helped shape perception of NRMs in the public mind and may ultimately alienate the prospective potential members of hundreds of other less conventional religious groups. In this sense the notoriety surrounding several movements is a substantial 'cost' in terms of social stigma when weighed against all the possible 'rewards' of joining up. Hence, less notorious movements such as the Unification Church and The Family are not only injured by their own past, and by often media-amplified misdemeanours, they are strained by general public perception and by state response to NRMs as a broad phenomenon.

What of the broad current relevance of the new religions? Numerical strength says a great deal about their dwindling appeal in the spiritual marketplace. On the most generous estimates, Brierley (1999) could only account for 14,515 members of the major organizations in the UK. Of the larger ones, in 1989 the Unification Church could claim merely 350 full-time members, the Emissaries of Divine Light 150 members, and Hare Krishna 300 full-time members. Bruce puts the situation succinctly when he suggests that '[s]et against the shrinkage of the Christian denominations and sects, such figures are trivial' (Bruce 1995: 101). Few people in the UK, including the thousands who leave the churches, have taken the opportunity to explore alternative forms of spirituality offered by the NRMs, which, according to Bruce, are 'numerically all but irrelevant' (Bruce 1995: 8).

In respect of the possible future of NRMs, an important consideration is the 'problem' of the second generation that Niebuhr (1957) identified with sect development. As NRMs become older, and as the years
pass, the proportion of first-generation converts declines. This has
already happened in the case of the Mormons and Jehovah's Witnesses,
and can be observed in the dynamics of the Unification Church and
ISKCON, where members try to ensure their children are brought up
within these movements and remain in them as they mature. When this
occurs, such movements are less likely to be viewed as 'threatening to
society', since they can no longer be accused of splitting up families to
the same degree. On the contrary, membership is more likely to be a
contributory factor to family coherence and stability, as is the case in the
established Christian denominations (Chryssides 1996: 21).

Eileen Barker (1999) has also commented on such developments,
pointing out that one important characteristic of the new religions is
the first-generation converts. What they lack, in contrast to the older
religions, are family traditions of belonging: because NRMs are new,
members belong by choice rather than from habit. Even in the case of
NRMs that do not actively proselytize, belonging has come about by
converting to the movement, rather than because of a long-standing
family tradition. Members of the second generation, the children of the
initial converts, are thus under less compulsion to remain in the movement and, in a culture of choice and alternative lifestyles, are more
likely to opt out.

Those world-rejecting movements typified by the Unification
Church and the Jesus Movement which emerged in the 1960s and
1970s are dwindling, and it is unlikely that they will stand the test of
time. Indeed, Barker suggests that, despite the large number of NRMs
and the present sizeable membership of some of them, there is no indication that any one movement will become a major religious tradition
in the future (Barker 1999: 15). Those that do remain are also, as we
have noted, undergoing significant transformations.

The world-affirming movements, as suggested, are perhaps doing better, but they demand a lower level of commitment and are less tied-in to
organizational structures. Because such movements tend to reconcile
adherents to their place in the world or help them perform better in their
present roles, the impact is limited to the requirements of the few people
practically participating. This orientation has not reversed its decline,

even when compared to world-rejecting forms. Yet it is not all about numbers and the scope of membership. Measuring the significance of world-affirming NRMs must also be in terms of a comparison with more conventional expressions of religiosity and measured by way of substantive definitions of religion: reference to the supernatural, divinely-given moral systems, high levels of belief, practice and commitment. By these criteria such NRMs would seem to hardly constitute religions at all.

SUMMARY

For several decades it sometimes appeared that sociologists spent more time writing about the new religions than about mainstream religion. To some extent this was understandable given their numerous forms, scale and rapid rise. The internal dynamics, experiences of members, and relationships with the outside world were sources of endless interest and speculation. However, it may be that the NRMs have reached their apogee, although it is difficult to draw conclusions and anticipate future developments. It might glibly be stated that there will be sectors both of decline and of consolidation. Many of those that survive have degenerated further to become psychotherapeutic cults of self-indulgence. Moreover, it is clear that a fair few world-rejecting NRMs have accommodated themselves to the world, and this may at one level suggest further indices of secularization and a dwindling transcendence for many. A number may continue to exist for some time and offer an alternative for seekers in the spiritual marketplace. Yet, in a culture of choice, membership may be fleeting since the freedom permissible in that marketplace allows seekership, joining and leaving, and potentially endless searching for a spiritual home – a flexibility which can only mean supply-side instability to the detriment of the long-term survival of the new religions.

The new religions of 'the gaps' were those which appealed to the young, at least in the late 1960s and 1970s. There was much to suggest that a fair number of the NRMs also displayed discernible attractive attributes, while avoiding a good deal of the negative aspects of traditional Christian churches. In the dawning of the Age of Aquarius, the decade of the 1960s, such movements offered a sense of belonging and identity and a safe haven from the ravages of modernity. The Age of Aquarius has, however, now arrived in earnest with all things New Ageist, but it is an era which, for the most part at least, dispenses with collectivism, the hope of an imminent supernatural intervention, and much of the counter-cultural baggage of many NRMs. The new religions of the post-Woodstock era have thus given way to the new spiritualities disseminated in the New Age, although frequently furnishing it with their beliefs and practices and ensuring a compatibility with the demands and aspirations of the everyday life of the early twenty-first century.

9

THE NEW AGE, SELF-SPIRITUALITIES AND QUASI-RELIGIONS

It is perhaps with a good deal of conceptual contortion that this final chapter attempts to bring together for discussion a diverse range of contemporary expressions of religion and spirituality which have only been discussed in a number of the earlier chapters in passing. Hence, included here are those as diverse as the various strands of the New Age, neo-Paganism, Wicca, and the numerous so-called self-spiritualities and implicit or quasi-religions that seem to have grown in popularity in recent times. What they have in common, none the less, is that they are manifestly new, newly discovered or invented forms of religiosity which are frequently said to be of increasing significance in the spiritual marketplace at the beginning of the twenty-first century. The fact that there is an overlap between many in terms of beliefs and practices arguably adds to their appeal for the religious 'consumer' by providing a mix 'n' match religiosity that is frequently manufactured for contemporary requirements.

Many of these new and emerging expressions of religion – or, if preferred, spiritualities – have mystical and occultist elements, involve little by way of belonging and association, and allow differing levels of dedication. Some of them embrace fairly clear perceptions of the supernatural. Many others do not, and those frequently termed implicit or quasi-religions rarely have such conceptions. Despite the diversity of religious forms, one of the common denominators of this broad rubric is the inherent individual focus of orientation – a tendency which undoubtedly further ushers in the demise of conventional religiosity by way of its broader collective importance.

Most such new spiritualities, but by no means all, offer something in the lives of their adherents through various techniques of human potential with a spiritual gloss, and constitute quasi-therapeutic cultist expressions which appear to be in many respects highly secularized forms of religiosity. In that way, a good number of the emerging forms of religion mark a continuity with earlier developments in a fair few of the world-affirming New Religious Movements, and are thus consistent with the culture of choice, consumption, self-absorption and exploration, albeit within freshly contrived holistic and universal frames of reference. Despite these commonalities, the new spiritualities are multi-faceted and syncretic, rendering their categorization and analysis an arduous task. This is certainly the case with the New Age movement. Although the extraordinarily diverse belief system and ethos has some overlap with a number of aspects of a range of the NRMs which came out of the late 1960s, many strands of the New Age call on diverse forms of religiosity which are significant resources in the spiritual marketplace and would seem to be simultaneously modern, pre-modern, anti-modern and post-modern, according to differing sociological accounts.

THE NEW AGE DEFINED

Given the range of attractions offered by the New Age, we may legitimately ask whether its emergence has meant a reversal in the fortunes of religion in the West to the extent of further undermining the 'hard' interpretations of secularization in terms of the number of its adherents and wider social impact. This is no easy question to answer given the amorphous nature of the movement. Neither can broad generalizations be made concerning what kind of people subscribe to the New Age and their reasons for doing so. Nevertheless, despite the difficulties in coming to terms with what the movement amounts to, and while acknowledging a number of its apparent inherent contradictions, some broad generalizations can be made.

In seeking to discover the roots of the New Age, the first observation is that many of its origins can be found in the esoteric culture of the mid-to-late nineteenth century when Spiritualism and occultist practices were relatively popular in Western Europe and North America. Yet there are sufficient departures by way of belief, practice and cultural orientation to justify interpreting the New Age as a distinct form of spirituality in its own right and not merely a continuation of older expressions. Indeed, in many respects, the New Age epitomizes the mix 'n' match culture of today. With its eclecticism which ranges from alchemy to pendulum dowsing, from Quabalah to Zen, comes a diffuseness that means there are few clear divisions and boundaries, and few representative organizations. Instead there is what might be termed a New Age milieu in which people acquire and absorb a variety of beliefs and practices which they combine into their own pockets of culture and lifestyle preferences to which they attend with differing degrees of seriousness. There is a strong mystical element, too, which would seem to fly in the face of science and rationalism. In this regard, Lee and Akerman suggest that a re-enchantment of the world has occurred at a time when the realm of science is no longer considered as adjudicating all meaning of reality (Lee and Akerman 2002: 120). Much here, of course, mirrors the classic postmodernist statement of the nature of contemporary culture with its relativizing tendencies and all this implies.

Despite the complexities, it might be generalized that the New Age desire for spiritual experience directs a quest for the inner life and exploration of the self. Hence, in the spiritual marketplace, what it has to offer is not only 'consumed', but internalized. In this context, the voice of ancient tradition or divine revelation is of less relevance, or ignored altogether, in favour of the inner 'voice' or intuition which is taken to be thoroughly authoritative in the spiritual pursuit. Belief is thus demoted, experience promoted. What is perceived as divisive doctrine is diminished, while a unifying stress on spirituality is magnified.

On the other hand, in countering the perceived excesses of conventional religion, there is a rediscovery in the New Age of 'lost' secrets which legitimate this new spirituality. Much is evident in the broad assertion that earlier 'simple' communities understood essential 'truths' about healing power, gender and the environment which modern industrialized societies have apparently lost. Thus, there is an observable tendency to borrow myths, legends, rituals and symbols from ancient Celtic, Polynesian, Tibetan, Eskimo, Aborigine and Native American culture. It is from many of these that the New Age has taken ideas of Mother Earth, Gaia, as a religious system which initially developed from a desire to be close to nature (Johnstone 1996).

Organizational elements

If, as Bruce suggests, the organization of religion has moved through those of Church, denomination and sect to the 'movements' and cults associated with the spiritual marketplace since the 1960s, the New Age perhaps constitutes the end of organized religion and, in many respects, we might also note that it erodes the coherent institutionalized aspect of the supply side of such a marketplace since it takes individualized and privatized forms of religion to their furthest conclusion. This does not mean, however, that organizational expressions are totally absent from the New Age, but that they are loosely structured. Bruce (1995: 103) points out that some of the new religions which originated in the 1960s – primarily those of the world-affirming type – were at the cultic end of the continuum, but the most prominent were the sectarian forms. In the New Age, the balance is reversed; most of the principal strands are cultist in nature and even to call them movements is to imply a degree of cohesion and structure which they do not possess.

The most common way in which activity in this cultic milieu is expressed is through client and audience cults – typologies originally developed by Stark and Bainbridge (1985). The client cult is focused on the individual relationship between a customer and a purveyor. Typical are the alternative therapists who advertise their services in an appropriate magazine or on the notice board of a health-food shop, and who provide individual consultations for a fee. Audience cults are generally structured around the mass distribution of a message, spoken and printed. Hence, the core of the New Age is constituted by specialized books, magazines, audio cassettes and public lectures. If there is personal contact, it is usually in the form of a lecture-and-workshop circuit. Promoters of particular revelations or techniques advertise their meetings, present their spiritualized philosophies and therapies, and then take them elsewhere. In this way the supply side of the new spiritualities may be as temporary as the fleeting interest of the religious 'seekers'.

Similarly, many forms of the new spiritualities akin to the New Age do not insist on high levels of involvement. Much is exemplified by so-called neo-Paganism. For the more dedicated neo-Pagans, there may be household altars and shrines, and day-to-day activities such as meditation, communication with the gods, rituals and celebrations. Yet, because of its vast diversity, there is a lack of any central organization.

This prevents the movement becoming dogmatic and authoritarian but it also makes it impossible to estimate how many people are involved. While Pagan organizations such as the Universal Federation of Pagans in the USA are representative, many adherents will affiliate with loosely organized local groups. The consequence is that the varied forms of neo-Paganism have been faced with the dilemma of finding the desirable balance between relaxed spontaneity and practical organization. Over the decades, neo-Pagan groups have tended to disintegrate because they have refused to become more institutionalized, thus rendering the movement highly amorphous and volatile.

Commitment and voluntarism

Without specifically naming the New Age, Fenn (1990) argues that it is the more mystical forms of religion which are most compatible with today's world because they permit a restricted scope to the sacred and advance a low degree of integration between corporate and individual value systems. It is occult and esoteric religion which best exemplify this type of religious culture. Since they can be practised without coming into conflict with everyday occupational roles and secular demands, such forms of religion confine themselves to very particular times, places, objects and issues. They provide an ecstatic and magical form of activity and an opportunity for the individual to indulge in the irrational against the enforced rationality of formal and bureaucratically structured organizations and roles of everyday life. While the New Age is sufficiently more than a range of mystical and occultist activities, and links individuals to a broader global and cosmic order, there is much in Fenn's analysis that effectively accounts for the movement's growth and direction.

Clearly, the lack of organizational structure in the New Age and associated strands of spirituality lends itself to different levels of commitment, which is in line with a culture of choice, personal preferences and voluntarism, and is clearly dependent on the more mundane demands of everyday life. Different levels of commitment also have the added advantage of avoiding ridicule from the secular world towards the more structured cultist group. Choosing what amounts to a part-time form of religiosity for many adherents, as a result of competing pressures and possible stigma, must in turn be interpreted as a further sign of secularity. This is not to suggest that some adherents do not take their spirituality appreciably more seriously, yet the freedom to choose levels of involvement further undermines the cohesion of the movement.

All this is more than mere speculation. The findings of studies related to levels of belonging such as that of Paul Heelas are important because they shed light on the nature and extent of commitment in the New Age movement. Heelas distinguishes three levels of commitment (1996: 117–19). First, there are those who are 'fully engaged'. These people are deeply committed and have given up conventional lifestyles for a spiritual quest, and are often practitioners providing services to clients, or they are organizers of New Age events. Second, 'serious part-timers' are individuals whose spirituality is compartmentalized as part of their everyday life, albeit a relatively serious one. New Age activities do not prevent adherents from living conforming lives and following conventional careers. Third, 'casual part-timers' includes people who are interested in exotic and esoteric things as consumers, but fail to become seriously involved. This constituency is the smallest but fastest-growing, and, for Heelas, threatens the movement with an inherent superficiality through its crass commercialization.

The cult of the individual

At the same time, the diffuse nature of membership and organization dovetails well with the individualized orientation of the New Age, since it is the individual who is the locus of concern. In this respect Bruce discusses its nature with reference to *modernity*, maintaining that if we have to make one element of modernization central to understanding the New Age, then in religious terms the movement constitutes the 'zenith of individualism' (Bruce 1996: 122). The New Age would seem to exemplify cultural assumptions and point towards the central features of modernity, not least of all consumer products with the individual as the locus of consumption. Individualism, continues Bruce, used to mean the right to act as one wished provided that it did not harm others, and the right to hold views radically at odds with the consensus. However, individuality has subsequently shifted up in abstraction from a behavioural and ethical principle to an epistemological claim. It now falls to the individual to decide what is and is not true, a decision enhanced by widespread literacy and effective ways of communicating alternative ideas.

The individualistic nature of the New Age is also discussed by Kubbiak (1999), but from a postmodernist rather than modernist perspective. Kubbiak contends that the New Age can only be accounted for in terms of postmodern culture. The main features of the movement can be viewed in this way because of its clear lack of definition and its spatio-temporal contexts, a loose network structure, holistic themes, and the transformation and autonomy of the different elements which comprise it. Individualism is at the heart of the network of ideas and the identification of New Age spirituality. Through personal experience of the mystical, such individual forms of spirituality necessarily circumvent belonging and undermine rigid belief systems.

Many of the strands of the New Age are aimed at establishing what adherents claim to be 'a new spirituality' and the rediscovery of a lost sacredness in the world and human society. As one advocate puts it: 'A new spiritual awakening is occurring in human culture [that] represents the creation of a new, more complete worldview [that] is opening up to us the real purpose of human life' (Redford 1995: xv, xviii). Hence the global and universal concerns of the New Age suggest that its representation as an extreme form of individualism is perhaps one which needs to be tempered. Indeed, Ammerman and Roof (1995: 3–4) argue that from the early 1990s there has been a trend away from the more extreme expressive individualism of previous decades. One major reason is that many of the Baby-Boom generation who comprise a major component of subscribers to the New Age are now rearing children and are thus confronted with the responsibilities which come with parenthood over and above mere hedonistic concerns. There is considerable awareness, too, that preoccupation with the self has its limits: genuine personal fulfilment lies in the discovery of a vital balance between self and concern for others. That is, through attachments to other people and commitment to worthy causes such as environmental welfare, New Agers attempt to find meaning and satisfaction in their everyday lives.

If the concern with the wider social and natural order suggests those such as Bruce and Kubbiak have overstated their case, it remains true that the individualized nature of the New Age surpasses other forms of religion in the concern for the self and the related matter of identity. Indeed, much sociological ink has been spilt in exploring the link between the New Age and its role in identity constructs. For instance, Paul Heelas (2000) has taken up this theme with reference to the New Age and postmodern culture. Effectively Heelas argues that the disintegration of the certainties of modernity has left a situation in which postmodern religion – particularly mystical or New Age spirituality and what he terms 'self-religion' – has emerged to fill a spiritual vacuum and satisfy the need for meaning in a society which finds it extremely difficult to provide one.

The New Age emphasis on self in this context is particularly significant. Contemporary culture brings a utilitarian selfhood – an expressive form of being, an emphasis on 'experience' and an 'off-the shelf' image. It establishes the freedom for individuals to create and sustain the self-image of their choice. Hence, traditional forms of religion give way to those congruent with contemporary culture, above all, consumerism. Neither are these tendencies limited to benevolent spiritualized aspects of the New Age. The increasing attraction of all things Satanic for some, largely derived from certain strands of popular culture rather than works such as those of Vivian Crowley, provide the opportunity to discover one's true identity, a 'dark side', and the 'reality' of human nature,

Culture-resisting or accommodating?

So far we have touched upon certain aspects of the central debate related to the correlation between the New Age and contemporary culture. The key question is whether the New Age is essentially culture-resisting or culture-conforming. The simple answer is that aspects of both can be discerned, although the general tendency is towards cultural conformity. Like world-rejecting cult movements, the New Age would seem to display a certain tension with society and could be said to be continuing from the counter-culture of the 1960s in its opposition to modernity and its display of hostility to the destructive tendencies of rationalism and rampant materialism, without the emphasis on community or belonging which would seem incongruous with postmodernity. In fact, Heelas (1996) regards it as partly counter-cultural but not on the same scale and with the same intensity – a shadow of the rebellious movement of the 1960s and now more subject to consumerist trends.

Irrespective of the divergence of belief and practice, there are common themes running through the New Age movement which make it this-worldly accommodating in orientation. Exemplifying this direction is the New Age's preoccupation with human potential techniques and related forms of healing. At first glance much would seem to be at odds with this tendency. Although healing is generated from within, for the New Age it constitutes the utilization of internal healing as stimulated by external forces, or what is often termed 'Universal Energy'. The emphasis is directed to providing a means of empowering the patient and allowing his/her natural internal systems of healing to be 'switched on' so that the healing process begins within the individual. This may not be a conscious decision, since the body, mind or spirit can be driving the patient, but it is s/he who actually undertakes the first healing process. Sickness is often perceived as a result of subjecting the mind, body and spirit to such harmful things as stress, poor diet and artificial chemicals.

Despite this orientation, one of the interesting facts about alternative therapies and medicines utilized by the New Age is that, like orthodox practices, they are focused on the level of the individual rather than that of the community. It is the individual who is treated and restored. To be sure, New Age healing includes healing the earth and the damages inflicted by industrial capitalism, yet there is far less emphasis on the effects of the wider natural and social environment which may be the most important consideration in underlining the causes of ill-health. Indeed, in treating the individual rather than the wider consequences, the New Age is in line with the rationalized medical profession. Featherstone (1982) sees this development in alternative medical systems as partly a result of the process of medicalization, since it is the individual who is the subject and orientation of medical science. So it is with New Age techniques of healing which also assume a projection through the life course, and even into re-birth for a better reincarnation the 'next time around'. Moreover, the demand for these forms of healing has its own supply side. In fact, as Bowman (1999) notes, the New Age's perceived 'need for healing' at individual and global levels has given rise to a range of new professions within the spiritual marketplace with distinct attitudes to money, the provision of training and the growth of an accredited sector of the spiritual service industry, where both clients and practitioners regard healing as an important element of their religious quest.

At the same time that healing activities are primarily focused on the spiritual, guided meditations often contain references to material rewards, prosperity and abundance, and all this is often interpreted in some New Age circles as related to 'wholeness'. Thus, not only is the New Age rampantly individualistic in many respects, it is also highly secular in some of its trajectories, and marks an essentially inward-looking endeavour. For this reason Hanegraff (1999) suggests that the New Age movement represents the historically innovative phenomenon of a secular religion based upon a radically private symbolism. Secularization in this context is not due to a decline or disappearance of religion but to its thorough transformation under new and far-reaching cultural developments. The essence of this process lies in New Age spirituality not embodied in the symbolism of an existing religion, but in a symbolism directly embedded in secular culture. From a historical point of view this development is unprecedented through the emphasis on self and fulfilling self-potential.

Evidence of such tendencies in healing techniques is the different interpretation of ancient practices. Shamanism is a case in point. It constitutes part of many Wiccan and Druidic circles and marks one of the clearest overlaps between neo-Paganism and New Age spiritualities. While it is an individual – even solitary – path, contemporary shamans attempt to adapt ancient practices to personal everyday needs. In the hands of New Agers, shamanism is more about effecting new dimensions of consciousness rather than believing in and visiting other worlds, hence more related to voyages of self-discovery and discerning areas which need to be healed, physically, psychologically and emotionally. Astral travelling, New Age-style, is now interpreted in much the same way. In its contemporary expression – as suggested by the popular book entitled *Astral Projection for Beginners* (McCoy 1999) – it precipitates an actual physiological change which can be measured by medicine through alternations in brain activity levels. This and similar literature is often couched with a rhetoric of concern focusing on reaching individual potential, such as finding out the purpose of one's current incarnation, any past-life issues yet unresolved, and the state of spiritual progress and personal relationships.

Who are the New Agers?

The question of who subscribes to the New Age is an important one because its social composition may tell us more about its nature and orientation. The little evidence available on who adheres to the New Age shows an over-representation of certain social categories as defined by age, class and gender, each of which indicates a specific cultural milieu, requirements in the spiritual marketplace, and generational preferences.

While it is easy to fit New Agers into simple social categories, the amorphous nature of the movement none the less makes it difficult to draw conclusions.

The New Age movement, and variations of neo-Paganism and Wicca for that matter, have proved more attractive to females than to males. A fairly precise indication is presented by the New Age Spirituality Survey which indicated that nearly three-quarters of those subscribing to the New Age are female (York 1995: 187–8). This over-representation would seem to be more obvious in certain strands of the movement. Those strands which have recently rediscovered witchcraft and paganism, as well as what has come to be known as spiritual eco-feminism, have embraced the cause and requirements of women. In such movements the teachings and practices might be loosely defined, but they seemingly express an aversion to hierarchy and the regulations of male-dominated institutions, with a few even inverting male–female and status roles. Wicca exemplifies a good deal, as does the veneration of Greek female deities including Athene, Isis and Mithras, who figure in feminized paganism which particularly affirms the female body and provides rituals for celebrating women's 'mysteries' such as menstruation, lactation and childbirth. Culpepper (1978) maintains that this is perhaps the most conventionally organized form of neo-Paganism in the sense of having initiation procedures and a hierarchical membership of feminine spiritual interest. Indeed, the common theme which unites most practitioners of the craft is the veneration of matriarchal forms of social organization. However, in terms of re-inventing religion, it can be pointed out that there is actually no evidence whatsoever for a religion of one goddess: early pagan religions were pantheist rather than female monotheistic. This is indicative of how pagan myths have been reconstructed, a process that is also evident in the current preoccupation with all things Celtic (Bowman 1993).

Despite the attraction of the New Age and related spiritualities to females, these feminized groups hardly constitute a large and burgeoning expression of religiosity, and, like the neo-Pagan organizations, tend to be rather small and little more than house groups. Typical of such contemporary homespun religion in the UK is the much-quoted example of the House of the Goddess, a Dianic temple. It is based in a wooden 'hut' in the garden of a suburban terraced house in London, where the small circle of initiates conduct 'alternative' weddings, divorces and funerals (York 1995: 116–17). By nature such forms of female spirituality tend to be clandestine and remain largely insignificant outside of the circles which embrace them.

If the feminist groups tend to be small, there is little to substantiate that the male equivalent is any different, despite its novelty. Some men have developed their own spiritual factions and these also appear to be linked, to one degree or another, with identity construction. The contemporary so-called men's spirituality movement does not seem to have any particular grass roots basis. Many of those that have endured are more like the 1970s therapy support groups which rejected the approach of the later movement towards articulating a ritualized spiritual expression of a new masculinity in the attempt to 'get in touch with their feminine side'. For the most part, the male movement appears to be largely an entrepreneurial effort in which, for the cost of subscription, men are brought together in a group setting for an orchestrated spiritual experience.

These groups, which include the Brothers of the Earth and the Radical Faeries, are premised on the basis that, although men's status and roles are possibly acceptable, individual males are not functioning well psychologically – indeed, some may be emotionally and socially crippled because they have been inadequately socialized into masculine social roles. Also proving more attractive to men are the various Druid groups which can be seen as the counterpart to the female-dominated Wiccan movement. There are, in addition, the more overtly masculine and conspicuously racist-oriented 'survival cults' and back-to-nature quasi-religious groupings which indulge in weekend retreats as the centre of their activities.

It would be easy to generalize that the New Age, like the new religions of the 1970s, remains popular in the more affluent and cosmopolitan constituencies of contemporary society. The personal voyages of self-discovery, the various therapies and accompanying paraphernalia that the New Age offers, have to be paid for and almost certainly appeal primarily to those who enjoy the vocabulary and the confidence to think and talk about their 'selves'. At the same time Ingelhart's (1997) view of the nature of contemporary religion, outlined in Chapter 2, would seem to be justified in that the preference for spiritual satisfaction over material satisfaction has greater attraction for those sufficiently affluent to indulge – those whose more pressing material needs have been satisfied. By contrast, the New Age holds few interests for the less well-off, whose daily struggle offers little room for such aesthetic concerns.

While the New Age may incorporate forms of occultism and super-stition, Bruce (1995: 117) suggests that as far as the working classes are concerned, those outside the churches interested in the supernatural prefer older forms: fortune-telling, horoscopes, superstition and charms. They see themselves as passive and, as a result of social experiences, pushed by obscure and deterministic forces which are beyond their control and which, in turn, reflect a social situation of alienation. Hence, unlike the New Agers, they are unlikely to regard themselves as empowered or to embrace a preoccupation with the 'self' as having practically endless potential.

This is a reasonable appraisal, although Bruce's account is clearly more applicable to those who avail themselves of the client and audience cults of the New Age. The movement is sufficiently broad, however, to embrace all-comers. Hence, there are the so-called 'New Age travellers' who have dropped out of mainstream society and live 'on the road', engrossed by an alternative culture with its hostility to the urban environment and materialist society as well as by the appeal of distinctive music and pilgrimage to such ancient pagan sites as Glastonbury in the UK. This is the flotsam of the younger urban underclass – a very different constituency to the subscribers of New Age audience and client cults with their expensive techniques of human potential that may appeal to an older and more affluent clientele. None the less, the latter remain the core of the New Age spiritualities

The social impact of the New Age

How might we measure the impact of the New Age movement? Does it add to the more popular expressions of contemporary religion which collectively would seem to undermine the conventional secularization thesis? Given that the movement circumvents institutional forms, it cannot be viably measured in terms of its organizational strength. Hence, measurements are largely two-dimensional: its social impact and where it seems to be strongest is at the individual, privatized level.

The argument advanced by some sociologists of religion is that the apparent mix 'n' match form of religiosity which constitutes the New Age has proved to be highly attractive to people as an alternative to mainline religion, while a number of its key ideas have discernibly permeated various aspects of social, political and economic life. At the individual, everyday level we are obliged to ask the question to what extent people are influenced by the New Age, rather than how many New Agers there are, since the amorphous nature of the movement makes the notion of membership redundant. There have been few attempts to use surveys to do this, and those which do suffer from all the obvious problems of clearly identifying and measuring the extent and depth of New Age belief and behaviour. Bruce (1995: 104), using evidence from Brierley's work (1993: 80), points out that it involves participation in occultist practices such as ouija, astrology and tarot. Bruce acknowledges that there are difficulties with using such statistics, because being 'involved' does not say very much, while to regard them as New Age is to ignore the fact that they have had popular appeal for over a century. Others, such as reflexology, channelling, and I Ching, are largely foreign imports and may only tell us of the popularity of all things oriental. However, Bruce acknowledges that a sign of the times is that, in well-known bookshops, volumes related to New Age themes are frequently given greater space on the shelves than Christian books.

Although the new spiritualities such as the New Age appear to have deeply private dimensions, it is possible to suggest that they impinge, in many discernible and perhaps less discernible ways, upon the public arena, with a distinct social and political agenda. Beckford (1992) admits that the number of activists and true believers deliberately pursuing or cultivating the principal ideas of the New Age may be relatively small. However, he contends that the movement's holistic consciousness has already made incisive inroads into public thinking about such issues as ecology, peace, gender and health. It has made its way into mainline religion and other social spheres: medicine, sport, leisure, education, dying and grieving, self-help, animal welfare and social work. Success can also be measured by the growth of green politics – taking the movement from the alienated fringes of public life to the centre. In this way the scope of the New Age means that it can no longer be regarded as a marginal phenomenon at the fringe of contemporary culture (Moerland and Van Otterloo 1996).

The danger, none the less, is in pushing these speculations too far. While gender politics, alternative ways of being born and dying, and growing public interest in such areas as sport and leisure, may buy into some New Age ideas and symbols, these areas of life concern were expanding long before the arrival of the New Age and result from pluralist and consumerist dynamics rather than from abstract philosophies and new-found spirituality. Similarly, politicians have increasingly paid lip service to environmental safeguards which may constitute a political vote-winner as long as they do not undermine a rampantly materialist consumer society and the enduring popular theme of a higher standard of living.

DEFINING IMPLICIT AND QUASI-RELIGIONS

There is an unnerving tendency for some sociologists to find aspects of religiosity in just about every area of social life. By using broad definitions of religion, a sleight of hand thus occurs in challenging the secularization thesis. This is the world of quasi-religions which increasingly feature in the vocabulary of sociologists of religion. I am not suggesting that the conception of quasi-religions or their study should not be of sociological concern. Indeed, their apparent rise at the same time that more conventional forms of religion are on the decline says something about contemporary culture and levels of secularity. Quasi-religions, however, should surely not be seen as some form of substitute for the traditional expressions of religiosity or used to justify the statement that religion still exists but has merely changed form and direction.

Quasi-religions, or as they are sometimes called 'implicit religions', include such a wide scope of social life that practically anything can be termed 'religious' according to several criteria. Put succinctly, quasi-religions amount to a range of social phenomena which appear to be religious when certain criteria are applied. At the very least these so-called expressions of religiosity seem to have some qualities in common with more traditional forms, although much depends, once more, on how religion is defined in the first place. Among the social phenomena which have been designated as quasi-religions by sociological studies are sporting activities, environmentalism, rock music, television, and the vast variety of therapeutic and healing cults often associated with the New Age movement. Given this range of so-called 'religions', the spiritual marketplace suddenly becomes very large and ever-expanding.

In contrast to quasi-religion, Bailey describes 'implicit religion' as a convergence of 'commitment, integrating foci, and intensive concerns with extensive effects' (Bailey 1997: 22). To complicate matters even more, Greil also speaks of 'para-religions' (Greil 1993). For Greil, 'quasi-religions' are recognizably 'religious' to outsiders though ambiguously so to insiders, while 'para-religions' have the normal religious characteristics save for any reference to the supernatural. For the sake of simplicity the term quasi-religion will be preferred here as an all-embracing concept. Whatever their precise designation, these forms of religion are the focus of sociologists who frequently 'discover' more 'hidden' forms and, in doing so, are obviously using very wide definitions which are largely derived from functional, phenomenological and postmodernist perspectives.

Functionalist and phenomenological interpretations

One theory is that some forms of quasi-religion may help integrate individuals to the collective through a new set of symbols and values and via new channels of expression. Calling upon functional definitions of religion, sometimes integrating functionalist and phenomenological approaches, contemporary theoretical frameworks have looked at 'mass' activities and the shared beliefs, symbols and rituals in certain forms of quasi-religion. As we have seen in Chapter 1, substantive definitions of religion tend to focus on a belief in spiritual beings or the supernatural. Functionalist definitions, by contrast, centre upon what religion does, particularly in terms of reference to sacred practices. It is this latter approach which allows a far broader range of activities and beliefs to be described as religion. Here, Durkheim's functional definition of religion has proved to be a starting point since it involves a common set of beliefs and practices which unite a shared collective system of morality. There is in Durkheim's definition, as earlier noted, no mention of the supernatural. Thus contemporary forms of collective religion may be without this component. For example, as Featherstone notes, a Durkheimian perspective would lead us to see the sacred in many layers of consumer culture. If, as Durkheim insisted, anything can become sacred, then this includes commodities that are at the basis of the consumer culture (Featherstone 1982: 119).

It is hardly surprising that a more functional approach has often been utilized in order to discuss such secular concerns as sporting activities to the extent that there is said to be a clear parallel between religion and sport because they share beliefs, symbols and rituals in common (Prebish 1984: 312). Greil and Robbins believe that, at least in the USA, quasi-religions are advancing in the space left by the decline of more traditional forms. They maintain that American 'folk' religion, with its emphasis on the one God, is losing its appeal. Primarily expressed through Christianity, folk religion is no longer satisfying or meaningful to large sections of the population. Simultaneously, the link between the religious and the non-religious is more difficult to discern as profound cultural changes continue to take place which blur the distinction between the two in an increasingly secular and materialist world (Greil and Robbins 1994: 16).

Sport may constitute an important example of a quasi-religion since it impacts the lives of millions, either as a spectator sport or an active leisure pursuit. Loy *et al.* (1978) conclude that sport in the USA has helped fill the gap left by the decline of civil religion, and reinforces the American way of life. It does this by restructuring myths and values and bringing a sense of history and tradition that subsequently enhances social integration. Alternatively, sport may provide forms of 'folk' religion for certain sections of society, and constitutes, especially for males, a distinct way of life and subcultural lifestyle (Demerath and Williams 1985: 166). Some sports even appear to display aspects of religiosity which make reference to superhuman or perhaps supernatural entities and elevate leading personalities to near-divine status.

A more phenomenological approach to quasi-religion is one which frequently sees it as fulfilling a so-called spiritual requirement and the need for meaning which some people possibly require. Traditional religion may be declining but the requirement remains. Hence, there is the necessity to sustain one form or another of religious belief and to have meaning in the world. The expressions of spirituality, however, are slowly being transformed. Luckmann puts this succinctly when he reiterates his long-term view that contemporary societies are witnessing a profound change in the relocation of religion away from the 'great transcendences' concerned with other-worldly matters, life and death, and the tendency towards the 'little transcendences' of earthly life, especially those which are concerned with self-realization, self-expression and this-worldly interests (Luckmann 1990). Quasi-religions, then, much like the new spiritualities, should not be viewed as curiosities or as being somehow 'outside' of society. In fact, they follow its cultural contours and embrace the core values of secularity.

Postmodernist accounts

While quasi-religions may have clear communal expressions, many parallel the New Age in their preoccupation with the self where contemporary cultural parameters, frequently understood as postmodern, lead on to the worship of the self through self-exploration or the indulgence of therapeutic techniques of human potential. Certainly quasi-religions would seem to be an area in which a preoccupation with the self, identity and lifestyle may flourish. It is evident that many of the quasi-religions considered above stretch definitions of religion to their furthest extent. However, in terms of lifestyle a preoccupation with health, fitness and diet may be interpreted as a form of religion that is linked to human potential. In the West today dietary practices can be said to have developed a form of religiosity all of their own. The tendency of dietary regimes to express an implicit religiosity is perhaps most notable with the increasing popularity of whole foods, health foods, organically produced foods and vegetarian diets. Consumers of these foods, according to some commentators, perceive them as having magical and mystical orientations even if dressed up in scientific discourse (Delamont 1984). More broadly, there appears to be a deeper dimension which goes beyond the desire for good health or, in fact, for any clear material goal. It may then be understood, in a consumerist way, as expressing to some extent a desire for a spiritual dimension in daily existence. Much may be evident in what Sellerberg (1991) terms 'ethical eating'. Concerns about processing, adulteration, denutrification and contamination of food often go hand-in-hand with opposition to nuclear power and even to science and technology. Such preoccupations frequently link with New Age philosophy, although they have their own implied religiosity.

What is it about postmodernity which lends itself to such themes? In attempting to answer this question Nesti sees quasi-religions arising from the inability of the contemporary Western world to provide a unified system of meaning. Today, people are fragmented by their own life experiences. There is a weakening of social identity and an ignorance of history which means the past loses its significance (Nesti 1990: 424–5). Implicit religion includes the search for meaning and identity in a world which finds it increasingly difficult to provide them. This search originates in the individual's life experience, expressing itself by means of a complex system of symbols and practices. These religions allow the unconditional relevance of a person's existence in the here and now. Hence, social forms and experiences are translated into spiritual metaphors – giving secular phenomena spiritual powers. They may also entail notions of a personal voyage or articulate themselves in the form of escapism, hence freeing individuals from social and psychological restrictions.

SUMMARY

The themes discussed above weave through an analysis of a range of contemporary forms of religion and self-spiritualities. What most of these new expressions tend to emphasize is a dwindling supernatural frame of reference and a reduction of religion to the more individualized, privatized and everyday sphere. This they do in several ways. One is to establish forms of religion which are not all-embracing, need little commitment, and are entirely voluntaristic in a consumer society of choice. Many are part-time religions, world-affirming, and typified by 'little transcendences'. To be sure, there are those which make a greater reference to the supernatural and a transcendental world, but a good number, as in the case of neo-Paganism, are reinterpreted and reinvented for contemporary needs. This *is* secularized religion.

In a discussion of world-affirming NRMs, Wallis (1984) points out that one of their principal teachings involves the attempt to unlock spiritual powers dormant in the individual which can be used for his or her potential by way of personal growth and healing. Much appears to have been taken to its final conclusion by New Age groups that tend to associate themselves with optimistic philosophies about the body, health and nature. The human frame is not viewed as essentially degenerate, or inevitably subject to the natural impulses which lower man. For many strands of the New Age, it is within the body itself that the latent cure lies, especially when mind, body and spirit are aligned with one another in attempting to reach the higher self. The link between this focus on the health of the individual and today's religion therefore comes into stark relief: personal health and healing is congruent with the more privatized and instrumental forms of religion which lend themselves so well to enculturation and marketability.

Durkheim spoke of the 'cult of man' as almost a 'divine' recognition of human progress and faith in what man was capable of (Durkheim 1915: 336). Westley (1978) believes that this prophecy has been fulfilled and is encapsulated in the contemporary human potential movement. Much is now exemplified in the New Age where spirituality has not only the individual as its locus, but the emphasis on the worship of the individual through spiritualized therapies. This is an expression of self-spirituality and perhaps takes it to its logical conclusion. Some of the new religions focus on the demands and problems of living in the modern world. Others satisfy the needs of people to more dynamically create a change in their self-image and self-perception. Many quasi-religions take this further still in attempting to give lifestyle preferences a sacred quality that is all but cultist in nature. By focusing upon aspects of religion related to the self and this world the concern moves away from substantive forms of religion and thus has no scope for God, gods, spirits and the supernatural and externally imposed systems of morality linked to reward and retribution, all of which are the reference points of conventional religiosity.

CONCLUSION

THE RELIGIOUS AND THE SACRED IN EVERYDAY LIFE

In a discussion of everyday contemporary religion in Western societies the theme of secularization offers itself as a convenient off-the-peg theoretical framework. The possible decline of religion, its stability or resurgence, constitute a continuing starting point by which to offer an understanding of religion in terms of belief, practice and other indices of religiosity at a popular level. But more than that, debates around secularization allow an engagement with current paradigms, especially those related to rational choice and postmodernity in their respective accounts of religious life. It is these contrasting approaches which largely constitute a revisionist line to the secularization debate. According to their accounts, despite their contrasting theoretical underpinnings, religion is not departing from the contemporary world even if it has undergone considerable transformations. Ultimately, however, these speculations rest not so much upon the evidence that can be mustered about the vitality of religious life, but upon the enduring question of what do we mean by religion?

In a Presidential Address to the USA-based Society for the Scientific Study of Religion, N.J. Demerath (1999) presented a paper on possible conceptions of contemporary religion as a new millennium dawned. It was a timely contribution. Demerath essentially argued that the sociological study of religion has laboured for too long under the constraint and misleading premise of 'religion', and has not sufficiently dwelt on the 'sacred'. He argued that defining religion 'substantively' but the sacred 'functionally' helps to resolve a long-standing tension in the field by broadening conceptions of the sacred and of 'sacralization'.

According to Demerath, such a categorization helps to diffuse the conflict between the two very different versions of the secularization theory: the 'all-or-nothing' versus the 'middle-range'. The all-or-nothing variety, which is derived from classical sociological theorizing, contends that religion is experiencing an inevitable and linear decline and is destined to disappear. The middle-range is more a product of the late twentieth century and sits between the poles of religious omnipotence and religious disappearance. The latter develops scenarios of secularization that are non-linear in that they are subject to reversals and circles. Although not pinpointed by Demerath, the rational choice and postmodernist paradigms would fall under this latter rubric or even abandon the secularization thesis altogether. The dichotomy established by the 'religious' and the 'sacred' allows us to understand their true contribution to the debate.

Demerath sees the secular–sacred distinction as poles of a continuum. If religion is kept distinct from the sacred, then it is possible to argue there are religious phenomena that have lost their power and are no longer sacred. Just as surely there are sacred entities and symbols which have a compelling power without being religious. For Demerath, it makes sense to limit substantive definitions to religion, while reserving the functional for the sacred. Religion is, after all, a category of activity, and the sacred is nothing if not a statement of function. Religious activities do not always have sacred consequences. Expanding the sources of the sacred also enlarges the term for the debate over secularization. Since any cultural activity has potentially sacred functions, secularization needs to be considered as a process that may affect a much larger inventory of any society's cultural stock. By the same token, the countervailing process of sacralization may also involve certain non-religious spheres.

Demarath's approach is an attractive one because he essentially separates functional and substantive definitions of religion in such a way as possibly to suggest the growth of the former and the decline of the latter. While it is clear his understanding of 'religion' may not include a great deal of what is, in essence, spiritual, such as the 'dry' organizational aspects of religiosity, it does imply an orientation towards the other-worldly, supernatural, 'externally' imposed moral systems, and, as explored in Chapter 1, a spiritual awakening and enlightenment that move away from a preoccupation with the self.

By contrast, 'the sacred' is a category of social phenomena which is not religious in conventional terms even though the phenomena may display some aspects of religion. Demerath sees 'invisible', 'folk', 'implicit', 'quasi-' and 'para-' religions for example, as part of the 'sociology of the sacred', conceptions which hitherto had the disadvantage of using a conventional image of religion with unfortunate consequences on several counts. First, using religion as the model tended to narrow the search for the sacred to include only those things which are religious in character. Second, using religion as the model was inclined to imply that organizations, experiences and events that fall short of the model fail in providing sacred consequences. Demerath argues that religion is only one model, and other sources of the sacred can be equally valid despite being far more varied. Third, using religion as a model suggests that, when religion gives way to non-religious alternatives, a secularizing short-changing has occurred.

In terms of secularization, it would seem to follow that it is the 'religious' – that is, reference to the supernatural and its organizational expressions – which is in the decline, but that it is the 'sacred' which endures, indeed is transformed within the contemporary setting. The social phenomena which Demarath identifies as sacred – 'invisible', 'folk', and 'implicit' forms – are, therefore, possible growth areas in everyday life. They are not, however, expressions of religion in a substantive or even traditional sense. Rather, they constitute, for the most part, the 'little transcendences' of earthly life which involve self-realization, self-expression and personal freedoms that are also expressed via several strands of the New Age, and self-spiritualities which are given articulation through client and audience cults – the alleged growth areas identified in a good deal of the revisionist literature.

What are the long-term prospects for these 'sacred' constituencies? Much depends on their pick 'n' mix form of belief and practice, or on expressions of mysticism which may circumvent them altogether. These would be hard to sustain over generations, since personal belief systems would have to be re-invented again and again, and mystical experiences experienced anew. Certainly, the limited value consensus of the New Age reflects the nature of the culture from which its adherents are drawn. However, it fails to give much in terms of guidance as to which new revelations of esoteric knowledge to accept or, in terms of behaviour, how to live by stringent moral and unchanging rules. Such radical individualism also prevents the formation of a powerful and influential movement on the lines of that which informed the great Christian revivals of the past.

Few accounts point to the New Age being a robust and deep form of religiosity. Indeed, over the last twenty years or so, such new expressions of so-called spirituality seem to have been born with a high degree of world accommodation which many of the earlier New Religious Movements had already graduated towards. For some people there may be the felt need to escape from the world into mystical forms of religion exemplified by the New Age. However, the movement now seems a shadow of the counter-culture of the 1960s as it is increasingly sucked into the ubiquitous culture of consumption. Comparable movements may continue to arise, perhaps aiming to blunt some of the more damaging edges of commodity capitalism – bringing a social critique shrouded in a thin veil of mysticism. Yet they will surely remain marginalized forms of spirituality.

The 'sacred', as defined by Demerath, also spawns the ever-growing world of quasi-religions. This should not, however, be seen as a radically new departure. Over thirty years ago Peter Berger wrote his seminal work *A Rumour of Angels*, subtitled *Modern Society and the Rediscovery of the Supernatural* (1970). Berger's phenomenological work was an attempt to show that the 'religious' may be found in the more mundane, taken-for-granted things in our daily lives if they provide meaning and significance – in the modernist faith in order, play, hope, humour, and sense of justice. In the late-/postmodern world, or however it is conceptualized, the taken-for-granted components of everyday life may have changed, but they remain 'sacred' spheres.

There is also a strong link between quasi-religions and self-identity. Lemert (1975), also in an early work, suggested that attributes of religion may be applied to social phenomena when what is held as 'sacred' comes to reify a way of life or culture. This is particularly so when people begin to seek significant meaning and sometimes a moral dimension to their existence and concerns in this world, beyond a mere material aspect. This approach would seem to pre-date postmodernists' accounts of quasi-religions. Hence, lifestyles, especially when tied up with identity constructs, may constitute religions when they are amplified into all-embracing meaning systems. These may now be discernible at a cultural level, for instance in the new 'religion' of consumerism, lifestyle preferences, and life concerns. These are truly the secularized 'sacred' social phenomena which will continuingly fill the gap left by conventional religion.

What of the 'religious' sphere, compared to that of the 'sacred'? The revisionist approaches frequently acknowledge the decline of mainstream Christianity but identify a resurgence in the conservative sector. To be sure, conventional Christianity has suffered a long-term decline. In 2000, at the start of a new Christian millennium, the Archbishop of Canterbury announced in a speech that Britain had become 'an atheist society'. It is significant that the statement came from a leading churchman. In Western countries, millions of people have been lost by the churches. It is unlikely that they will ever be regained. Church activities simply do not feature in the lives of many ordinary people. As many surveys from both sides of the Atlantic indicate, Christian beliefs may remain as a kind of ultimate reference point for a good number of people, but they are beliefs of a pick 'n' mix variety which often substantially depart from Christian orthodoxy. Such syncretic forms only serve to undermine the pillars of faith which once constituted the 'rock of ages'.

Such developments do not mean that resistance is not evident in some sections of Christendom, whether expressed in a reaction of conservative elements to disestablishmental liberalizing tendencies in their churches or moral campaigns conducted by fundamentalist Christians in protest against the permissive attitudes of a secular society. Such cries of resistance have, none the less, become ever more muted. While Christian fundamentalism will have its appeal in the spiritual marketplace in response to a world of risk and uncertainty, those who subscribe remain a small cognitive constituency. At the same time it offers more worldly attractions beyond cognitive certainty – hence the lure of all things therapeutic, of 'strength' but not strictness, and of an increasingly comfortable form of Christianity.

The ethnic religions are also enjoying a high public profile. Given their potential appeal, alongside the media coverage of controversies surrounding them, it might be surmised that they constitute an ever-growing component of religious life. That ethnicity is a resilient area of religious life should not be surprising given its central and traditional role in supporting community solidarity. In this respect ethnic religion will always have some significance even if eaten away by the relentless process of assimilation. The situation none the less needs to be put in perspective and is perhaps best discussed within the context of the USA, which is probably the most ethnically diverse of all Western societies, and where the black–white divide remains an important distinction in the Christian churches.

Recently, change in the non-Judaeo-Christian populations in general has increased, especially the share in the religious market held by Muslims, Buddhists and Hindus. Thus, some commentators such as Eck (2001) write of 'a new multireligious America' in which 'the religious landscape … has changed radically in the past thirty years'. Smith, while accepting that the share of the population following these faiths has increased appreciably in recent times, points out that there is frequently an exaggeration of the figures. For example, the Muslim population is commonly overestimated by a factor of three or four (Smith 2002).

Certainly non-Judaeo-Christian religions make up a small but growing share of America's religious mosaic. According to the 1973–80 General Social Survey they accounted for 0.8 per cent of the adult population. This was up to 2.6 per cent in 1990–2000. Three faiths, Buddhism, Hinduism and Islam, account for about half the number of people following other religions. The remaining non-traditional religions consist of a wide mix of faiths. Smith suggests that these are so small a constituency that detailed delineation is not practical. The leading alternatives amounting to 0.45 per cent of the spiritual market include Jainism, Sikhism and Taoism. Native American religions, pagans and witches, and those with 'personal' religions according to the GSS were merely some 0.1 per cent (Smith 2002: 578). The religions of ethnic minorities, therefore, remain just that – minority religions, while 'personal' religions based on occultism are of minimal significance.

The early chapters of this volume sought to critically appraise the new sociological paradigms in the sociology of religion. Rational choice theory and writings exploring postmodernity rightly recognize the growth of a spiritual marketplace. However, the key question is whether the emergence of such a marketplace has stimulated religion, or at least certain expressions of it. In this discussion sociology has to go beyond the older paradigms for the study of religion. It is thus forced to resituate itself within the contemporary context, whether that is described as modernity or late-postmodernity. While in a good deal of sociological thinking the experience of consumption is said to undermine traditional beliefs and institutions, the processes were already occurring within modernity. It is clear, then, that the privatization of religion antedates the consumer society and essentially marks a response to the withdrawal of institutional religion from many areas of modern social life.

It may also be that those who equate religious growth with the expansion of a spiritual marketplace have missed an essential point. People may choose the religion they wish. Indeed, this is likely to be the case with the decline of the primary associations such as the extended family and the local community which, in the past, enforced religious socialization. Yet, most significantly, people may elect, in a profoundly materialistic world, not to choose a religion at all. It may be argued that this is increasingly the case and that choice is not bringing about, in essence, the religionless society but one where the ever-secularized sacred, rather than religion, will come to enjoy a greater cultural dominance.

BIBLIOGRAPHY

Abdullah, M. (1995) *Muslim Minorities in the West*, London: Grey Seal.

Adams, D. (2002) 'The Defense of Marriage Act and American Exceptionalism: The "Gay Marriage" Panic in the United States', *Journal of the History of Sexuality*, 2 (2): 259–76.

Adler, M. (1986) *Drawing the Moon: Witches, Druids, Goddess-Worshippers and Other Pagans in America Today*, Boston: Beacon Press.

Ammerman, N. (1987) *Bible Believers*, New York: Rutgers University Press.

—— (1997) 'Rational Choice and Religious Vitality', in L. Young (ed.) *Rational Choice Theory and Religion: Summary and Assessment*, London: Routledge.

Ammerman, N. and Roof, W. (1995) 'Old Patterns, New Trends, Fragile Experiments', in N. Ammerman and W. Roof (eds) *Work, Family, and Religion in Contemporary Society*, New York: Routledge.

Anthony, D. and Robbins, A. (1990) 'Civil Religion and Recent American Religious Ferment', in T. Robbins and D. Anthony (eds) *In God's We Trust*, New Brunswick, NJ: Transaction.

Anwar, M. (1981) *Young Muslims in a Multicultural Society*, Leicester: The Islamic Foundation.

Aries, P. (1974) *Western Attitudes Towards Death: From the Middle Ages to the Present*, Baltimore: Johns Hopkins University Press.

Ashford, S. and Timms, N. (1992) 'The Unchurching of Europe?', in S. Ashford and N. Timms (eds) *What Europe Thinks: A Study of Western Europe Values*, Aldershot: Dartmouth.

Atchley, R. (1980) *The Social Forces of Later Life*, Belmont, CA: Wadsworth.

Bailey, E. (1997) *Implicit Religion*, Kampen, The Netherlands: Kok Pharos Publishing House.

Bainbridge, D. (1997) *The Sociology of Social Movements*, New York: Routledge.

Bandura, A. (1977) *Social Learning Theory*, Engelwood Cliffs, NJ: Prentice-Hall.

Barber, B. (1995) *Jihad Versus McWorld*, New York: Times Books.

Barker, E. (1984) *The Making of a Moonie*, Oxford: Blackwell.

—— (1999) 'New Religious Movements: Their Incidence and Significance', in B. Wilson and J. Cresswell (eds) *New Religious Movements: Challenge and Response*, London: Routledge.

Barr, J. (1978) *Fundamentalism*, London: SCM Press.

Barton, J. (1986) 'Religion and Cultural Change in Czech Immigrant Communities, 1850–1920', in R. Miller and T. Marzik (eds) *Immigrants and Religion in Urban America*, Philadelphia: Temple University Press.

Batson, C., Schoenrade, P. and Ventis, K. (1993) *The Religious Experience: A Social-Psychological Perspective*, New York: Oxford University Press.

Baudrillard, J. (1990) *Cool Memories*, London: Verso.

Bauman, M. (1992) *Postmodernity and Its Discontents*, New York: New York University Press.

Beck, C. (1991) *Better Schools*, London: Falmer Press.

Beckford, J. (1975) *The Trumpet of Prophecy: A Sociological Study of Jehovah's Witnesses*, Oxford: Blackwell.

—— (1992) 'Religion, Modernity and Post-Modernity', in B. Wilson (ed.) *Religion: Contemporary Issues*, London: Bellew Publishing.

—— (2001) 'The Construction and Analysis of Religion', *Social Compass*, 48 (3): 439–41.

Bellah, R. (1967) 'Civic Religion in America', *Daedalus*, 96 (1): 30–47.

—— (1976) 'New Religious Consciousness and the Crisis of Modernity', in C. Clock and R. Bellah (eds) *The Consciousness Reformation*, Berkeley, CA: University of California Press.

Berger, P. (1967) *The Sacred Canopy: Elements of a Sociological Theory of Religion*, Garden City, NY: Doubleday.

—— (1970) *A Rumour of Angels: Modern Society and the Rediscovery of the Supernatural*, London: Allen Lane.

—— (ed.) (1999) *The Desacrilization of the World: Resurgent Religion and World Politics*, Grand Rapids, MI: Eerdmans.

Bibby, R. (1978) 'Why Conservative Churches are Really Growing, Kelley Revisited', *Journal for the Scientific Study of Religion*, 17 (2): 127–38.

—— (1987) *Fragmented Gods: The Poverty and Potential of Religion in Canada*, Toronto: Irwin.

—— (1993) *Unknown Gods: The Ongoing Story of Religion in Canada*, Toronto: Stoddart.

Bird, F. (1978) 'The Pursuit of Innocence: New Religious Movements and Moral Accountability', *Sociological Analysis*, 40 (4): 35–46.

Bloul, R. (1996) 'Engendering Muslim Identities: Deterritorialization and the Ethnicization Process in France', in B. Metcalf (ed.) *Making Muslim Space in North America and Europe*, Berkeley, CA: University of California Press.

Bowman, M. (1993) 'Reinventing the Celts', *Religion*, 23: 147–56.

—— (1999) 'Healing in the Spiritual Marketplace: Consumers, Courses, and Credentialism', *Social Compass*, 46 (2): 181–9.

Brannon, R. (1976) 'The Male Sex Role: Our Culture's Blueprint of Manhood, and What It's Done for us Lately', in D. David and R. Brannon (eds) *The Forty-Nine Percent Majority: The Male Sex Role*, Reading, MA: Addison-Wesley.

Breault, K. (1989) 'New Evidence on Religious Pluralism, Urbanism, and Religious Participation', *American Sociological Review*, 54: 1048–53.

Brierley, P. (1991) *Christian England?*, London: MARC Europe.

—— (1993) *Reaching and Keeping Teenagers*, London: Christian Research Association.

—— (1999) *Religious Trends*, London: MARC Europe.

—— (2000) *The Tide is Running Out*, London: Christian Research Association.

Bromley, D. and Shupe, A. (1979) 'The Tnevnoc Cult', *Sociological Analysis*, 40 (4): 361–6.

—— (1981) *Strange Gods: The Great American Cult Scare*, Boston: Beacon Press.

Brown, C. (2001) *The Death of Christian Britain*, London: Routledge.

Bruce, S. (1993) 'Religion and Rational Choice', *Sociology of Religion*, 54 (2): 193–205.

—— (1995) *Religion in Modern Britain*, Oxford: Oxford University Press.

—— (1996) *Religion in the Modern World: Cathedrals to Cults*, Oxford: Oxford University Press.

—— (1997) 'The Pervasive World-View: Religion in Modern Britain', *British Journal of Sociology*, 48 (4): 80.

—— (1999) *Choice and Religion: A Critique of Rational Choice Theory*, Oxford: Oxford University Press.

—— (2001) 'Christianity in Britain, R.I.P.', *Sociology of Religion*, 62: 191–203.

Bryman, A. (1995) 'The Disneyization of Society', *Sociological Review*, 47 (1): 25–47.

Campbell, C. (1999) 'The Easternization of the West', in B. Wilson and J. Cresswell (eds) *New Religious Movements: Challenge and Response*, London: Sage.

Carey, S. (1987) 'The Indianization of the Hare Krishna Movement', in R. Burghart (ed.) *Hinduism in Great Britain*, London: Tavistock.

Casanova, J. (1994) *Public Religions in the Modern World*, Chicago: University of Chicago Press.

Castells, M. (1989) *The Informational City*, Oxford: Blackwell.

—— (1997) *The Power of Identity*, Oxford: Blackwell.

Christiano, K. (1987) 'Church as a Family Surrogate', *Journal for the Scientific Study of Religion*, 25 (3): 339–54.

Chryssides, G. (1996) *Exploring the New Religions*, London: Cassell.

Church of England Board of Education (1996) *Youth A Part*, London: Church House Publishing.

Cipriani, R. (2003) 'Invisible Religion or Diffused Religion in Italy?', *Social Compass*, 50 (3): 11–20.

Coleman, S. (1991) 'Faith Which Conquers the World. Swedish Fundamentalism and the Globalization of Culture', *Ethnos*, 56 (1/2): 6–18.

Cook, G. (2000) *European Values Survey*, London: Gordon Cook Foundation.

Cornwall, M. (1989) 'The Determinants of Religious Behaviour: A Theoretical Model and Empirical Test', *Social Forces*, 68 (2): 572–92.

Coupland, D. (1992) *Generation X: Tales for an Accelerated Culture*, London: Abacus.

Cox, H. (1994) *Fire From Heaven*, Reading, MA: Addison.

Culpepper, E. (1978) 'The Spiritual Movement in Radical Feminist Consciousness', in J. Needleman and G. Baker (eds) *Understanding the New Religions*, New York: Seabury Press.

Cupitt, D. (1998) 'Post-Christianity', in P. Heelas (ed.) *Religion, Modernity and Post-Modernity*, Oxford: Blackwell.

Davie, G. (1994) *Religion in Britain Since 1945: Believing Without Belonging*, Oxford: Blackwell.

Davies, C. (2004) *Death of Respectable Britain*, New Brunswick, NJ: Transaction Books.

Davies, D. (1997) 'Contemporary Belief in Life After Death', in P. Jupp and T. Rogers (eds) *Interpreting Death: Christian Theology and Pastoral Practice*, London: Cassell.

Dawson, L. and Hennebry, J. (1999) 'New Religions and the Internet:

Recruiting in a New Public Space', *Journal of Contemporary Religion*, 14 (1): 17–39.

de Vaus , D. and McAllister, I. (1987) 'Gender Differences in Religion: A Test of the Structure of Location Theory', *Sociological Review*, 51: 472–81.

Delamont, S. (1984) *Appetites and Identities: An Introduction to the Social Anthropology of Western Europe*, London: Routledge.

Demerath, N. (1965) *Social Class in American Protestantism*, Chicago: Rand McNally.

—— (1999) 'The Varieties of Sacred Experience: Finding the Sacred in a Secular Grove', Presidential Address, Society for the Scientific Study of Religion, 6 November, Boston, USA.

—— (2000) *Crossing the Gods: World Religions and World Politics*, New Brunswick, NJ: Rutgers University Press.

Demerath, N. and Williams, R. (1985) 'Civic Religion in an Uncivil Society', *Annals of the American Academy of Political and Social Science*, 480: 154–66.

Dialmy, A. (2001) 'What Does it Mean to Be Religious?', *Social Compass*, 48 (2): 302–13.

Dreitzel, K. (1981) 'The Socialization of Nature: Western Attitudes Towards Body and Emotions', in P. Heelas and A. Lock (eds) *Indigenous Psychologies: The Anthropology of the Self*, New York: Academic Press.

Duff, L. (2003) 'Spiritual Development and Education: A Contemplative View', *International Journal of Children's Spirituality*, 8 (3): 227–37.

Durkheim, E. (1915) *The Elementary Forms of the Religious Life*, London: Allen and Unwin.

Eck, D. (2001) *A New Religious America*, San Francisco: Harper.

Evans, D. (1993) *Spirituality and Human Nature*, New York: SUNY Press.

Evans-Pritchard, E. (1937) *Witchcraft, Oracles and Magic Among the Azande*, Oxford: Clarendon Press.

Featherstone, M. (1982) 'The Body in Consumer Culture', *Theory, Culture and Society*, 1 (2): 18–31.

—— (1995) *Undoing Culture*, London: Sage.

Featherstone, M. and Hepworth, M. (1991) 'The Mask of Ageing and the Postmodern Life Course', in M. Featherstone, M. Hepworth and B. Turner (eds) *The Body Process and Cultural Theory*, London: Sage.

Fenn, R. (1990) 'Pre-Modern Religion in the Postmodern World: A Response to Professor Zylerber', *Social Compass*, 37 (1): 96–105.

Finke, R. (1992) 'An Unsecular America', in S. Bruce (ed.) *Religion and Modernization: Sociologists and Historians Debate the Secularization Thesis*, Oxford: Clarendon Press.

—— (1997) 'The Consequences of Religious Competition: Supply-Side Explanations for Religious Change', in L. Young (ed.) *Rational Choice Theory and Religion: Summary and Assessment*, New York: Routledge.

Finke, R. and Stark, R. (1988) 'Religious Economies and Sacred Canopies: Religious Mobilization in American Cities, 1906', *American Sociological Review*, 53: 41–9.

Finney, J. (1995) *Finding Faith Today: How Does it Happen?*, Swindon: British and Foreign Bible Society.

Francis, L. (1997) 'Psychology of Gender Differences in Religion: A Review of Empirical Research', *Religion*, 27: 81–96.

Gallop, G. and Castelli, J. (1989) *The People's Religion: American Faith in the 1990s*, New York: Macmillan.

Gee, P. (1992) 'The Demise of Liberal Christianity?', in B. Wilson (ed.) *Religion: Contemporary Issues*, London: Bellew Publishing.

Gerard, D. (1985) 'Religious Attitudes and Values', in A. Abrams, D. Gerard and N. Timms (eds) *Values and Social Change in Britain*, Basingstoke: Macmillan.

Gibson, C. (1994) *Dissolving Wedlock*, London: Routledge.

Giddens, A. (1990) *The Consequences of Modernity*, Cambridge: Polity Press.

—— (1991) *Modernity and Self-Identity: Self and Society in the Late Modern Age*, Cambridge: Polity Press.

Gill, R. (2001) 'The Future of Religious Participation and Belief in Britain and Beyond', in R. Fenn (ed.) *The Blackwell Companion to Sociology of Religion*, Oxford: Blackwell.

Glock, C. and Stark, R. (1969) 'Dimensions of Religious Commitment', in R. Robertson (ed.) *Sociology of Religion*, Harmondsworth: Penguin.

Goddijn, W. (1983) 'Some Religious Developments in the Netherlands (1947–1979)', *Social Compass*, XXX (4): 409–24.

Goode, E. (2000) *Paranormal Beliefs: A Sociological Introduction*, Prospect Heights, IL: Waveland Press.

Granovetter, M. (1993) 'Economic Action and Social Structure: The Problem of Embeddedness', *American Journal of Sociology*, 91: 481–510.

Gray, R. and Moberg, D. (1977) *The Church and the Older Person*, Grand Rapids, MI: Eerdmans.

Greeley, A. (1975) *The Sociology of the Paranormal: A Reconnaissance*, Beverly Hills, CA: Sage.

Green, J., Rozell, M. and Wilcox, C. (2001) 'Social Movements and Party Politics: The Case of the Christian Right', *Journal for the Scientific Study of Religion*, 40 (3): 413–26.

Greil, A. (1993) 'Explorations Along the Sacred Frontier: Notes on Para-Religions, Quasi-Religions, and Other Boundary Phenomena', in D. Bromley and J. Hadden (eds) *Religion and the Social Order*, 3, part A, Greenwich, CT: JAI Press.

Greil, A. and Robbins, T. (1994) 'Introduction: Exploring the Boundaries of the Sacred', in A. Greil and T. Robbins (eds) *Religion and the Social Order. Between Sacred and Secular: Research and Theory on Quasi-Religion*, 4, Greenwich, CT: JAI Press.

Greil, A. and Rudy, D. (1984) 'What Have We Learned From Process Models of Conversion? An Examination of Ten Case Studies', *Sociological Focus*, 17 (4): 305–21.

Gusfield, R. (1963) *Symbolic Crusades: Status Politics and the American Temperance Movement*, Urbana, IL: University of Illinois Press.

Gustavsson, G. (1997) *Tro, samford och samhälle. Sociologiska perspective*, Örebro: Bokförlaget Libris.

Hadaway, C. (1990) *What Can We Do About Church Dropouts?*, Nashville: Abingdon Press.

Hadaway, C., Marler, P. and Chaves, M. (1993) 'What the Polls Don't Show', *American Sociological Review*, 58, December: 741–52.

Hadden, J. and Shupe, A. (1987) 'Televangelism in America', *Social Compass*, 34 (1): 61–75.

Hammond, P. (1988) 'Religion and the Persistence of Identity', *Journal for the Scientific Study of Religion*, 27 (1): 1–11.

Hammond, P. and Warner, K. (1995) 'Religion and Ethnicity in Late-Twentieth-Century America', in W. Roof (special editor) *The Annals of the American Academy of Political and Social Sciences* 572, May: 55–66.

Hanegraff, W. (1999) 'New Age Spiritualities as Secular Religion: A Historian's Perspective', *Social Compass*, 46 (2): 145–60.

Harding, S., Phillips. D. and Fogarty, K. (1986) *Contrasting Values in Western Europe*, London: Macmillan.

Hechter, M. and Kanazawa, S. (1997) 'Sociological Rational Choice Theory', *Annual Review of Sociology*, 23: 191–214.

Heelas, P. (1988) 'Western Europe: Self-Religions', in S. Sutherland and P. Clarke (eds) *The World's Religions*, London: Routledge.

—— (1996) *The New Age Movement*, Oxford: Blackwell.

—— (2000) 'Expressive Spirituality and Humanistic Expressivism', in S. Sutcliffe and M. Bowman (eds) *Beyond the New Age*, Edinburgh: Edinburgh University Press.

—— (2002) 'The Spiritual Revolution: From "Religion" to "Spirituality"', in L. Woodhead, P. Fletcher, H. Kawanami and D. Smith (eds) *Religions in the Modern World*, London: Routledge.

Heelas, P. and Woodhead, L. (2004) *The Spiritual Revolution. Why Religion is Giving Way to Spirituality*, Oxford: Blackwell.

Herberg, W. (1956) *Protestant–Catholic–Jew: An Essay in American Religious Sociology*, Garden City, NY: Anchor Doubleday.

Herieu-Leger, D. (1986) *Vers un nouveau christianisme*, Paris: Cerf.

Hertel, B. (1995) 'Recent Trends', in N. Ammerman and W. Roof (eds) *Work, Family, and Religion in Contemporary Society*, New York: Routledge.

Himmelstein, J. (1986) 'The Social Basis of Anti-Feminism: Religious Networks and Culture', *Journal for the Scientific Study of Religion*, 25 (1): 1–15.

Hoge, D., Petrillo, G. and Smith, E. (1982) 'Transmission of Religious and Social Values from Parents to Teenage Children', *Journal of Marriage and the Family*, 44 (3): 569–80.

Hollinger, F. and Smith, T. (2002) 'Religion and Esotericism Among Students: A Cross-Cultural Comparative Study', *Journal of Contemporary Religion*, 17 (2): 229–49.

Hunsberger, B. (1983) 'Apostasy: A Social Learning Perspective', *Review of Religious Research*, 25: 21–38.

Hunt, S. (2002) 'The Lesbian and Gay Movement in Britain: Mobilization and Opposition', *Journal of Religion and Society*, 4: 1–8.

—— (2005) *A Sociology of the Life Course*, Basingstoke: Palgrave.

Hunter, J. (1983) *American Evangelicalism: Conservative Religion and the Quandary of Modernity*, New Brunswick, NJ: Rutgers University Press.

—— (1987) *Evangelicalism: The Coming Generations*, Chicago: University of Chicago Press.

—— (1991) *Culture Wars: The Struggle to Define America*, New York: Basic Books.

—— (1996) *The State of Disunion*, Ivy, VA: In Media Res Educational Foundation.

Ingelhart, R. (1997) *Modernization and Postmodernization*, Princeton, NJ: Princeton University Press.

Iannaccone, L. (1992) 'Religious Markets and the Economics of Religion', *Social Compass*, 39: 123–31.

—— (1994) 'Why Strict Churches Are Strong', *American Journal of Sociology*, 99: 1180–211.

—— (1997) 'Framework for the Scientific Study of Religion', in L. Young (ed.) *Rational Choice Theory and Religion*, New York: Routledge.

Johnson, S. and Tamney, J. (1984) 'Support for the Moral Majority', *Journal for the Scientific Study of Religion*, 23 (2): 183–96.

Johnstone, L. (1996) 'Speaking of Mother Earth: Native American

Spirituality and the New Age Movement', in B. Ouellet and R. Bergeron (eds) *Croyances et Sociétiés*, Montreal: Fides.

Kay, W. and Francis, L. (1996) *Drift From The Churches: Attitude Towards Christianity During Childhood and Adolescence*, Cardiff: University of Wales Press.

Kelley, D. (1972) *Why Conservative Churches Are Growing*, New York: Harper and Row.

—— (1978) 'Why Conservative Churches are Still Growing', *Journal for the Scientific Study of Religion*, 17 (2): 165–72.

Khasala, K. (1986) 'New Religious Movements Turn to Worldly Success', *Journal for the Scientific Study of Religion*, 25 (2): 233–47.

Kirkpatrick, R., Rainey, R. and Rubi, K. (1986) 'An Empirical Study of Wiccan Religion in Postindustrial Society', *Free Inquiry in Creative Sociology*, 14 (1): 33–8.

Kolakowski, L. (1982) *Religion. On God, the Devil, Sin and other Worries of the so-called Philosophy of Religion*, Glasgow: Fontana.

Kosmin, B. and Lachman, S. (1993) *One Nation Under God: Religion in Contemporary American Society*, New York: Harmony Books.

Kosmin, B. and Levy, C. (1983) *Jewish Identity in an Anglo-Jewish Community – The Findings of the 1978 Redbridge Jewish Survey*, London: Research Unit, Board of Deputies of British Jews.

Kubbiak, A. (1999) 'Le Nouvel Age, Conspiration Postmoderne', *Social Compass*, 46 (2): 135–43.

Lambert, Y. (1996) 'Denominational Systems and Religious States in the Countries of Western Europe', *Research in the Social Scientific Study of Religion*, 7: 127–43.

—— (2004) 'A Turning Point in Religious Evolution in Europe', *Journal of Contemporary Religion*, 19 (1): 204–15.

Laythe, B., Finkel, D., Bringle, R. and Kirkpatrick, L. (2002) 'Religious Fundamentalism as a Predictor of Prejudice: A Two-Component Model', *Journal for the Scientific Study of Religion*, 41 (4): 623–35.

Lee, R. and Akerman, S. (2002) *The Challenge of Religion After Modernity. Disenchantment*, Aldershot: Ashgate.

Lemert, C. (1975) 'Defining Non-Church Religion', *Review of Religious Research*, 16 (3), Spring: 186–97.

Lensky, G. (1961) *The Religious Factor*, Garden City, NY: Doubleday.

Levitt, M. (1996) *Nice When They Were Young: Contemporary Christianity in Families and Schools*, Aldershot: Avebury.

—— (2003) 'Where Are the Men and Boys? The Gender Imbalance in the Church of England', *Journal of Contemporary Religion*, 18 (1): 77–94.

Lincoln, C. (1989) 'The Muslim Mission in the Context of American Social

History', in G. Wilmore (ed.) *African American Religious Studies*, Durham, NC: Duke University Press.

Loy, M., McPherson, B. and Kenyon, G. (1978) *Sport and Social Systems*, Reading, MA: Addison-Wesley.

Luckmann, T. (1967) *The Invisible Religion*, New York: Macmillan.

—— (1990) 'Shrinking Transcendence, Expanding Religion', *Sociological Analysis*, 50 (2): 127–38.

—— (2003) 'Transformations of Religion and Morality in Modern Europe', *Social Compass*, 50 (3): 275–85.

Lyon, D. (2000) *Jesus in Disneyland: Religion in Postmodern Times*, Cambridge: Polity Press.

Lyotard, J. (1984) *The Post-Modern Condition*, Manchester: Manchester University Press.

Malinowski, B. (1954) *Magic, Science and Religion*, London: Souvenir Press.

Mandel, R. (1996) 'A Place of Their Own. Contesting Places in Berlin's Migrant Community', in B. Metcalf (ed.) *Making Muslim Space in North America and Europe*, Berkeley, CA: University of California Press.

Marett, R. (1914) *The Threshold of Religion*, London: Methuen.

Marler, P. (1995) 'The Changing Family and the Nostalgic Church', in N. Ammerman and W. Roof (eds) *Work, Family, and Religion in Contemporary Society*, New York: Routledge.

Martin, D. (1991) 'The Secularization Issue: Prospects and Retrospects', *British Journal of Sociology*, 42: 465–74.

Marty, M. (1978) *Fundamentalism*, Boston: Beacon Press.

Marty, M. and Appleby, R. (1992) *The Glory and the Power: The Fundamentalist Challenge to the Modern World*, Boston: Beacon Press.

Marx, J. and Ellison, D. (1975) 'Sensitivity Training and Communes: Contemporary Quests for Community', *Pacific Sociological Review*, 18 (4): 442–62.

Marx, K. and Engels, F. (1957) *On Religion*, Moscow: Progress Publishers.

Mauss, A. and Perrin, R. (1992) 'Saints and Seriousness', *Review of Religious Research*, 34: 176–8.

McBeis, D. (2002) 'Religion and Spirituality', *Social Compass*, 49 (1): 133–8

McCoy, E. (1999) *Astral Projection for Beginners*, Saint Paul, MN: Llewellyn Publications.

McHugh, N. and Swain, G. (1999) *The Mirror*, 7 September: 23–5.

Mellor, P. (2000) 'Rational Choice or Sacred Contagion?: "Rationality", "Non-Rationality" and Religion', *Social Compass*, 47 (2): 273–92.

Melton, G. (1987) 'How New is New? The Flowering of the "New" Religious Consciousness Since 1965', in D. Bromley and P. Hammond (eds) *The Future of the New Religious Movements*, Macon, GA: Mercer University Press.

Milbank, J. (1992) 'Problematizing the Secular: The Post-Modern Agenda', in P. Berry and A. Wernick (eds) *Shadow of the Spirit: Postmodernism and Religion,* London: Routledge.

Miller, A. and Hoffman, J. (1995) 'Risk and Religion: An Explanation of Gender Differences in Religiosity', *Journal for the Scientific Study of Religion*, 34: 63–75.

Miller, D. (1997) *Reinventing American Protestantism*, Berkeley, CA: University of California Press.

Moerland, M. and Van Otterloo, A. (1996) 'New Age: Counter Culture, Paraculture, or Core Culture', *Amsterdams, Sociologisch Tijdschrift*, 23 (4): 682–710.

Moore, R. (1994) *Selling God: American Religion in the Marketplace of Culture*, Oxford: Oxford University Press.

Nelson, G. (1968) 'The Concept of Cult', *Sociological Review*, 16 (3): 351–62.

Nelson, H. (1981) 'Religious Conformity in an Age of Disbelief: Contextual Effects of Time, Denomination, and Family Processes Upon Church Decline and Apostasy', *American Sociological Review*, 46: 632–40.

Nesti, A. (1990) 'Implicit Religion: The Issues and Dynamics of a Phenomenon', *Social Compass*, 37 (4): 423–38.

—— (2002) 'The Mystical Option in a Postmodern Setting: Morphology and Sense', *Social Compass*, 49 (3): 379–92.

Newby, M. (1996) 'Towards a Secular Concept of Spiritual Maturity', in R. Best (ed.) *Education, Spirituality and the Whole Child*, London: Cassell.

Niebuhr, H. (1957) *The Social Sources of Denominationalism*, New York: World Publishing.

O'Connor. T., Hoge, D. and Estrelda, A. (2002) 'The Relative Influence of Youth and Adult Experiences on Personal Spirituality and Church Involvement', *Journal for the Scientific Study of Religion*: 4: 723–32.

Oliveira, R. de (2001) 'Immanent Secularity: A Re-reading of Durkheim's Sociology of Religion', *Social Compass*, 48 (4): 613–19.

Olson, D. (1999) 'Religious Pluralism and U.S. Church Membership: A Reassessment', *Sociology of Religion*, 60: 149–73.

Palmer, S. (1994) *Moon Sisters, Krishna Mothers, Rajneesh Lovers*, Syracuse, NY: Syracuse University Press.

Park, J. and Reimer. S. (2002) 'Revisiting the Social Sources of American

Christianity, 1972–1998', *Journal of the Scientific Study of Religion*, 41 (4): 733–46.

Partridge, C. (2004) *The Re-enchantment of the West*, Volume 1: *Alternative Spiritualities, Sacralization, Popular Culture, and Occulture*, London: T & T Clark/Continuum.

Percy, M. (1995) 'Fundamentalism. A Problem for Phenomenology', *Journal of Contemporary Religion*, 10 (1): 83–91.

Perl, P. and Olson, D. (2000) 'Religious Market Share and Intensity of Church Involvement in Five Denominations', *Journal for the Scientific Study of Religion*, 39 (1): 12–31.

Petersson, T. and Hamberg, E. (1997) 'Denominational Pluralism and Church Membership in Contemporary Sweden: A Longitudal Study of the Period, 1974–1994', *Journal of Empirical Theology*, 10: 61–78.

Phal, R. (1995) *After Success: Fin-de-Siecle Anxiety and Identity*, Cambridge: Polity Press.

Prebish, C. (1984) 'Heavenly Father, Divine Goalie: Sport and Religion', *The Antioch Review*, 42 (3): 306–18.

Putamn, R. (2000) *Bowling Alone: The Collapse and Revival of American Community*, New York: Simon and Schuster.

Puttick, E. (1999) 'Women in New Religious Movements', in B. Wilson and J. Cresswell (eds) *New Religious Movements. Challenge and Response*, London: Routledge.

Redford, H. (1995) *The Celestine Prophecy: An Experiential Guide*, New York: Warner Books.

Reiff, T. (1995) 'Nurturing and Equipping Children in the "Public Church"', in N. Ammerman and W. Roof (eds) *Work, Family, and Religion in Contemporary Society*, New York: Routledge.

Rice, T. (2003) 'Believe It or Not: Religious and Other Paranormal Beliefs in the United States', *Journal for the Scientific Study of Religion*, 42 (1): 95–106.

Richter, P. and Francis, L. (1998) *Gone But Not Forgotten*, London: Darton, Longman and Todd.

Ritchie, K. (1995) *Marketing to Generation X*, New York: Lexington.

Ritzer, G. (1996) *The McDonaldization of Society*, Newbury Park, CA: Pine Forge Press.

Robertson, R. (1995) 'Glocalization: Time–space and Homogeneity and Heterogeneity', in M. Featherstone, S.Lash. and R. Robertson. (eds) *Global Modernities: From Modernism to Hypermodernism and Beyond:* London: Sage.

Rochford, E. (1985) *Hare Krishna*, New Brunswick, NJ: Rutgers University Press.

Roof, W. (1987) *Community and Commitment*, New York: Elsevier.

—— (1994) *A Generation of Seekers: The Spiritual Journeys of the Babyboom Generation*, San Francisco: Harper.

Roof, W. and Gesch, L. (1995) 'Changing Patterns of Work, Family, and Religion', in N. Ammerman and W. Roof (eds) *Work, Family, and Religion in Contemporary Society*, New York: Routledge.

Roof, W. and McKinney, W. (1985) 'Denominational America and the New Religious Pluralism', *Annals*, 480: 24–38.

—— (1987) *American Mainline Religion: Its Changing Shape and Future*, New Brunswick, NJ: Rutgers University Press.

Roof, W., Carroll, J. and Roozen, D. (1995) *The Post-War Generation and Establishment Religion*, Oxford: Westview.

Roozen, D. (1980) 'Church Dropouts: Changing Patterns of Disengagement and Re-entry', *Review of Religious Research*, 21 (4): 247–50.

Rose, S. (2001) 'Is the Term "Spirituality" a Word that Everyone Uses, But Nobody Knows What Anyone Means By It?', *Journal of Contemporary Religion*, 16 (2): 194–207.

Ruether, R. (1994) 'Christianity and Women in the Modern World', in A. Sharma (ed.) *Today's Woman in World Religions*, New York: SUNY Press.

Sandomirsky, S. and Wilson, J. (1990) 'Processes of Disaffiliation: Religious Mobility Among Men and Women', *Social Forces*, 68: 1211–29.

Schoenfeld, E. (1992) 'Militant and Submissive Religions: Class, Religion and Ideology', *British Journal of Sociology*, 43 (1): 111–40.

Sellerberg, M. (1991) 'In Food We Trust: Virtually Necessary Confidence and Unfamiliar Ways of Attaining It', in E. Fursr (ed.) *Palatable Worlds. Sociocultural Food Studies*, Oslo: Solum.

Sherkat, D. and Wilson, J. (1995) 'Preferences, Constraints, and Choices in Religious Markets: An Examination of Religious Switching and Apostasy', *Social Forces*, 73: 993–1026.

Sihvo, J. (1988) 'Religion and Secularization in Finland', *Social Compass*, XXXV (1): 67–90.

Sjodin, U. (2002) 'The Swedes and the Paranormal', *Journal of Contemporary Religion*, 17 (1): 75–85.

Smith, C. (2002) 'Religious Participation and Network Closure Among American Adolescents', *Journal for the Scientific Study of Religion*, 42: 259–67.

Smith, C., Sikkink, D. and Baily, J. (1998) 'Tracking the "Other": Dynamics and Composition of "Other" Religions in the General Social Survey,

1973–1996', *Journal for the Scientific Study of Religion*, 38 (4): 551–60.

Smith, T. (1992) 'Are Conservative Churches Really Growing?', *Review of Religious Research*, 33: 305–59.

—— (2002) 'Religious Diversity in America: The Emergence of Muslims, Buddhists, Hindus and Others', *Journal for the Scientific Study of Religion*, 41 (3): 577–85.

Souza, D. (2003) 'Contemporary Influences on the Spirituality of Young People: Implications for Education', *International Journal of Children's Spirituality*, 8 (3): 268–75.

Stacey, W. and Shupe, A. (1982) 'Correlates of Support for the Electronic Church', *Journal for the Scientific Study of Religion*, 21 (4), 291–303.

Stackhouse, J. (1994) *Canadian Evangelism in the Twentieth Century*, Toronto: University of California Press.

Stark, R. (2001) 'Efforts to Christianize Europe, 400–2000', *Journal of Contemporary Religion*, 16 (1): 640–60.

—— (2002) 'Physiology and Faith: Addressing the "Universal" Gender Differences in Religious Commitment', *Journal for the Scientific Study of Religion*, 41 (3): 495–507.

Stark, R. and Bainbridge, W. (1980) 'Secularization, Revival and Cult Formation', *Annual Review of the Social Sciences of Religion*, 4: 85–119.

—— (1985) *The Future of Religion*, Berkeley, CA: University of California Press.

—— (1987) *A Theory of Religion*, Berkeley, CA: University of California Press.

Stark, R. and Finke, R. (2000) *Acts of Faith: Explaining the Human Side of Religion*, Berkeley, CA: University of California Press.

Stark, R. and Iannaccone, L. (1993) 'Rational Choice Propositions About Religious Movements', in D. Bromley and J. Hadden (eds) *Handbook on Cults and Sects*, Greenwich, CT: JAI Press.

—— (1994) 'A Supply-Side Reinterpretation of the "Secularization" of Europe', *Journal for the Scientific Study of Religion*, 33: 230–52.

Stark, R., Finke, R. and Guest, A. (1996) 'Mobilizing Local Religious Markets: Religious Pluralism in the Empire State, 1855–1865', *Sociological Review*, 61 (2): 203–18.

Steinitz, L.(1980) 'Religiosity, Well-being, and Weltanschauung Among the Elderly', *Journal for the Scientific Study of Religion*, 19 (1): 60–7.

Tamney, J., Johnson, S., McElmurry, K and Saunders, G. (2003) 'Strictness and Congregational Growth in Middletown', *Journal for the Scientific Study of Religion*, 42 (3): 363–75.

Thomas, T. (1993) 'Hindu Dharma in Dispersion', in G. Parsons (ed.) *The*

Growth of Religious Diversity. Britain Since 1945, London: Routledge.

Thompson, E. and Remmes, K. (2002) 'Does Masculinity Thwart Being Religious? An Examination of Older Men's Religion', *Journal of the Scientific Study of Religion*, 41 (3): 521–32.

Thompson, W. (1997) 'Charismatic Politics: The Social and Political Impact of Renewal', in S. Hunt, M. Hamilton and T. Walter (eds) *Charismatic Christianity*, Basingstoke: Macmillan.

Tipton, S. (1982) *Getting Saved From the Sixties*, Berkeley, CA: University of California Press.

Tobacyk, J. and Milford, G. (1983) 'Belief in Paranormal Phenomena: Assessment, Instrument and Implications for Personal Functioning', *Journal of Personality and Social Psychology*, 44: 1029–37.

Tomlinson, D. (1995) *The Post-Evanglical*, London: Triangle.

Turkel, S., quoted in J. Cooper Ramo (1996) 'Finding God on the Web', *Time*, 16 December: 44–50.

Tylor, E. (1903) *Primitive Culture*, London: Mowbray.

Verweij, J., Ester, P. and Nauta, R. (1997) 'Secularization as an Economic and Cultural Phenomenon: A Cross-National Analysis', *Journal for the Scientific Study of Religion*, 36: 309–24.

Walker, A. (1996) *Telling the Story: Gospel Mission and Culture*, SPCK: London.

Wallis, R. (1984) *The Elementary Forms of New Religious Life*, London: Routledge and Kegan Paul.

Walter, T. (1990) 'Why Are Most Church-goers Women?', *Vox Evangelica*, 95: 599–625.

—— (1999) 'Popular Afterlife Beliefs in the Modern West', in P. Badham and C. Becker (eds) *Death and Eternal Life in the World Religions*, London: Paragon.

Walter, T. and Davie, G. (1998) 'The Religiosity of Women in the Modern West', *British Journal of Sociology*, 49 (4): 639–60.

Warner, R. (1993) 'Work in Progress Towards a New Paradigm for the Sociological Study of Religion in the United States', *American Journal of Sociology*, 98 (5): 1044–93.

Warren, M. (1987) *Facing the Problem of Popular Culture, Youth, Gospel, Liberation*, San Francisco: Harper and Row.

Weber, M. (1930) *The Protestant Ethic and the Spirit of Capitalism*, London: Allen and Unwin.

—— (1965) *The Sociology of Religion*, London: Methuen.

—— (1970) 'The Social Psychology of World Religions', in H. Gerth and C.

Mills (eds) *From Max Weber: Essays in Social Theory*, London: Routledge.

—— (1978) *Economy and Society*, in G. Roth and C. Wittich (eds) Berkeley, CA: University of California Press.

Westley, F. (1978) 'The Cult of Man: Durkheim's Predictions and Religious Movements', *Sociological Analysis*, 39: 135–45.

Wilkinson, H. and Mulgan, G. (1995) *Freedom's Children: Work, Relationships and Politics for 14–18 Year Olds in Britain Today*, London: Demos.

Wilson, B. (1966) *Religion in a Secular Society*, London: Weidenfeld and Nicolson.

—— (1970) *Religious Sects*, London: Heinemann.

—— (1976) *Contemporary Transformations of Religion*, London: Oxford University Press.

—— (1982) *Religion in Sociological Perspective*, Oxford: Oxford University Press.

—— (1985) 'Secularization: The Inherited Model', in P. Hammond (ed.) *The Sacred in a Secular Age* , Berkeley, CA: University of California Press.

Wilson, J. and Sherkat, D. (1994) 'Return to the Fold', *Journal for the Scientific Study of Religion*, 60: 84–103.

Wuthnow, R. (1976) *The Consciousness Reformation*, Berkeley, CA: University of California Press.

—— (1993) *Christianity in the Twenty-First Century*, Oxford: Oxford University Press.

—— (1994) *Sharing the Journey: Support Groups and America's New Quest for Community*, New York: Free Press.

York, M. (1995) *The Emerging Network: A Sociology of the New Age and Neo-Pagan Movements*, Lanham, MD: Rowman and Littlefield.

Young, A. (1997) 'Introduction' to A. Young (ed.) *Rational Choice Theory and Religion: Summary and Assessment*, New York: Routledge.

Zinnbauer, B, Pargament, K. and Scott, A. (1999) 'The Emerging Meanings of Religiousness and Spirituality: Problems and Prospects', *Journal of Personality*, 67 (6): 889–919.

Zurcher, L. and Kirkpatrick, R. (1976) *Citizens for Decency: Anti-Pornography Crusades as Status Defense*, Austin: Texas University Press.

INDEX